Deer Hunting
Across
North America

Deer Hunting
Across
North America

edited by

NICK SISLEY

FRESHET PRESS   *Rockville Centre, New York*

ISBN 088395-023-5

Library of Congress catalog card number: 73-79823

Manufactured in the United States of America

To my critic, my confidante,
and my typist—my wife, Mary Ann.

CONTENTS

INTRODUCTION

The concept of *Deer Hunting Across North America* was in my mind many long months before it became a reality. My feeling was that a book on deer hunting of all types—a compilation of writings by acknowledged and recognized experts—was not only necessary at this time, but would be welcome all across the country.

Perhaps no one will learn as much about deer and deer hunting in reading this book as I have; having first edited each chapter, then proofed the final copy several times, and finally checked and rechecked the galley proofs, I've done more than read this book—I've studied it, restudied it, rehashed it, re-everythinged it!

It's been thoroughly enjoyable, though, and I've learned many new things. I am proud of this book, and confident that readers will also learn a great deal, and become better deer hunters.

Please keep in mind that deer hunting is not a science; it's an art, and consequently, there are some inevitable differences of opinion between these covers. But I think that's good. Perhaps most readers won't even notice these little variations; however, I am aware of them because of my deep involvement in the preparation of this book. What I think is more important is the overall agreement that is shown throughout. This is where the great experience of these experts shines through.

I would also like to emphasize that different areas of the country require different hunting methods and techniques if the tyro is to be successful.

Hunting whitetails in the Adirondacks is admittedly different from hunting mule deer in Montana. But hunting whitetails in the Adirondacks is also different from hunting whitetails in the prairies or in Pennsylvania or in Dixie.

Most readers are going to confine their deer hunting to their local area or home state. They will still learn an awful lot from each chapter in this book. Those hunters that branch out and hunt deer in spots other than their home state will benefit even more. If they are traveling from Kentucky to Colorado, they will go armed with the knowledge of how they should hunt and how they can be successful, even if they have never seen the terrain, let alone spent time hunting there.

As enthused as I was about deer hunting previously, the production of *Deer Hunting Across North America* has increased my ardor ten-fold. By the time you've finished this book, I bet you'll feel the same way. I've laid many plans to hunt mule deer, blacktail, and Coues over the next couple of years, plus worked it out so that I'll be able to hunt whitetails in several surrounding states each fall —about the time the first snow blankets the deer coverts, you'll find me in a tree stand in Pennsylvania, still-hunting through the Adirondacks, and trail-watching in West Virginia.

I can't think of a better way to spend the fall months than pitting my outdoor knowledge and skills against the most wily big game animal that walks the face of the earth—the deer of North America. N. S.

Deer Hunting
Across
North America

Roger Latham is a wildlife biologist with a Doctor of Philosophy degree from the Pennsylvania State University. During his twenty-one years with the Pennsylvania Game Commission he headed one white-tailed deer study after another and conducted laboratory and captivity experiments on this game animal.

Roger has hunted big game all over the world and whitetails in many regions of the United States and Canada. As a scientist he has prepared a number of technical papers and bulletins on deer, and he has written many columns on deer hunting and deer management as outdoor editor of the *Pittsburgh Press*.

1

ANATOMY, PHYSIOLOGY AND HABITS

Roger M. Latham

THE DEER IS a remarkable animal, with extraordinary abilities and capabilities. It can run at speeds up to forty miles an hour and can cover long distances without tiring. It is a highly efficient organism (to use a scientific term), which is so constructed and so endowed that it has become one of the most prized game animals in the world. The traits which make it such a great game animal—speed, intelligence and wildness—relate directly to its anatomy, physiology and behavior.

Anatomy

Size of deer. Deer hunters have one bad habit when guessing the height and weight of their deer. Their estimates are usually at least one-third too high. Some guess them at twice their actual size.

The adult whitetail has a shoulder height of thirty-two to forty-one inches, with most measuring well below the maximum. This is the distance from the ground to the top of the back at the shoulder. Even the largest bucks will rarely come to belt-height on a man.

The bottom of the chest, where the heart is located, ranges from seventeen to twenty-three inches above the ground. This is an important point from a safety standpoint, since a person shooting at the heart region of a deer is essentially shooting at a good "down" angle. Rarely should the bullet go more than a few yards beyond the deer before it strikes the ground.

1

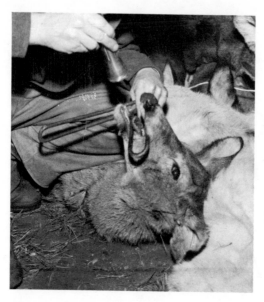

Biologists determine the age of a deer by examining the lower teeth. A more refined method is to extract a tooth, cut a cross-section, and count the growth rings under a microscope.

Deer weights vary considerably. Northern whitetails average much heavier than southern whitetails. Also, deer in overbrowsed range will be considerably lighter in weight than those living where food is abundant.

A hog-dressed, second-fall buck (eighteen months old) in Pennsylvania or Michigan will weigh about 95 to 105 pounds, but some will barely make 80 pounds. In Maine or New Brunswick, a buck of the same age may weigh 120 to 130 pounds when hog dressed.

Whitetails from Maine and New Brunswick will sometimes weigh 350 to 400 pounds, live-weight. In the more southern states, they rarely exceed 200 to 250 pounds.

Mule deer get larger and may weigh as much as 475 live-weight, although this is exceptional. In a California sample of 360 muleys, less than 1 per cent weighed more than 300 pounds when hog dressed.

Fawns vary in weight depending upon sex. At birth, male fawns average about 7.5 pounds, with a minimum of about 4.5 pounds and a maximum of 14.5 pounds. Female fawns average 5.75 pounds, with extremes of 3.25 to 8.25 pounds.

Growth patterns. A fawn will gain about one-third of a pound a day and will double its weight in about his first fifteen days. Under good food conditions, a hog-dressed, six-month-old male whitetail fawn may weigh as much as seventy-five pounds. The mule deer fawns at the same age will usually be larger.

Maximum growth in both height and weight is reached at about five to six years. Fully adult males, under the same food conditions, average about 35 to 40 per cent heavier than females of the same age.

Deer are not unlike trees in their growth habits. They grow rapidly during spring, summer and early fall and then come to a standstill during the colder months. In fact, a deer in its first year will weigh more in early November than it will the following April! But then, growth resumes just as soon as the green vegetation begins to appear in the spring.

Roger M. Latham

WHAT DID MY DEER WEIGH ?

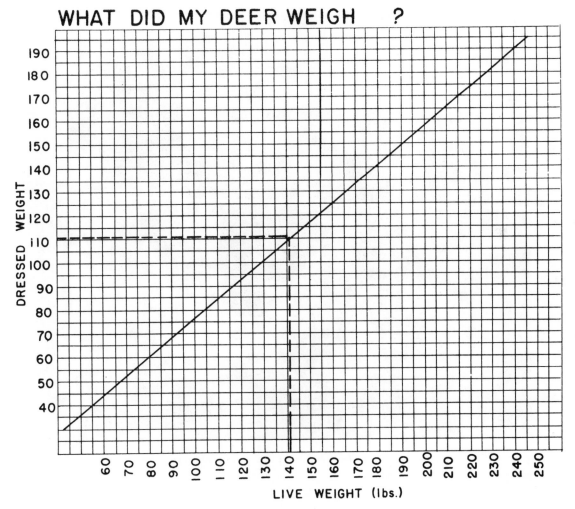

LIVE WEIGHT (lbs.)

Example: Your deer weighs 110 lbs. dressed. (Internal organs including heart, liver, and lungs removed.) Find this point on the left-hand vertical scale. Follow the 110 line across until you hit the slanted line. At this point follow the line down until you hit the horizontal scale. Your deer weighed 140 lbs.

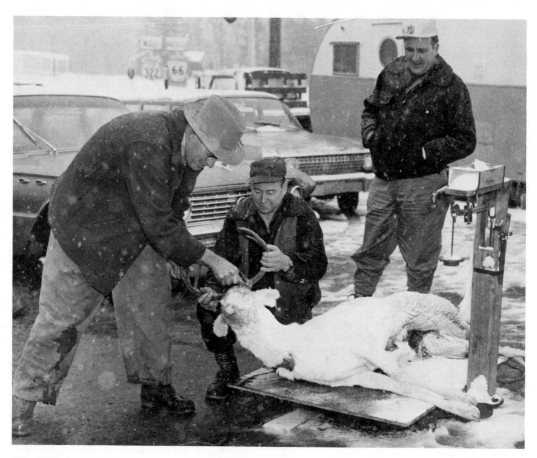

The albino deer is a rarity, but a few are taken by hunters in most states each year. These all white deer often have pink eyes and pink hoofs.

Pelage and Moulting. The deer completely sheds its hair twice a year and replaces the old coat with a new one. This process is gradual, so that there is no period during which the animal has bare spots or is unprotected from sunburn.

The summer coat is made up of thin, solid hairs not dissimilar to those of a cow. These provide little insulation from cold and are truly designed for summer wear. The general color of the deer at this time of year is reddish brown. This summer coat is only worn for about three to four months.

In late summer or early fall—late August to late September—deer replace this coat with the steel-gray or blue-gray coat of winter. Now the hairs are longer, much greater in diameter and hollow. This provides a wonderful, almost waterproof, insulation against cold, rain and snow. The entrapped air, both inside the hair

4

ROGER M. LATHAM

itself and between the hairs, will protect the deer against temperatures well below zero. The insulation is so perfect that deer can lie in a bed of snow for long periods of time without melting it. This coat is remarkably effective against wind, also.

It may come as a surprise to hunters to learn that no two deer are exactly alike in coat color or pattern, or in configuration. Researchers who work with deer in pens can easily identify two or three dozen different deer by name, even though they may all be one age and one sex.

Both melanism (black) and albinism (white) occur in the coat color of deer. True albinos are not extremely rare, and a number of pink-eyed, pink-hoofed, pure-white individuals are bagged annually in most "deer" states. Melanism, the tendency toward a solid-black color, is much rarer. Usually the shade is more of a blue-black.

Spotted, or "pinto," deer are the most common. These partial albinos vary greatly in pattern, some having very little white, while others will be fully three-quarters white.

Often there are "pockets" of albinism, where all-white or spotted deer will appear each year. Evidently, if two albino deer mate, their progeny are likely to be albinos. Thus it is possible to produce an all-white herd by selective breeding in captivity.

Antlers. As every hunter must surely know, a buck deer grows its first set of antlers during its second summer and then drops these and grows a new set each successive summer. Many arguments have developed about this process, especially regarding when and why bucks shed early or late in the fall or winter. There have been even more arguments about the relationship between age and the number of points on the buck's antlers.

Bucks shed their antlers as early as late November to as late as March, April and even May. The time of shedding does not appear to have any relationship to cold temperatures and little relationship to latitude. Instead it appears to be primarily associated with the health and condition of the deer itself. Generally, this is in turn related to the amount and quality of the food available to the individual buck. In other words, if a deer is well fed, fat and healthy, it may retain its antlers into March or April. If, on the contrary, it is living in a "starvation" area, its antlers may loosen and fall even before most deer seasons open in late fall. Presumably ill-health, whether from disease, parasites or injury, could also cause early shedding.

Growth normally begins in April, but it is somewhat dependent upon the length of time the buck has been "bald headed." A deer that has shed in December is likely to begin growth a little earlier than one which has shed in April. However, in almost every case, the healthy deer that retained its antlers the longest will be the first *to complete* growth and "rub out" of the velvet in late summer or very early fall.

During late spring and summer, the buck grows a new set of antlers. These growing appendages have blood vessels and nerves and are covered with a fuzzy skin called "velvet."

At the beginning of growth, the antler is soft, warm, well supplied with blood vessels and nerves and is covered with a brown, fuzzy skin called "velvet." If a fly bites the antler at this time, it may bleed and the deer will feel pain. If the growing tip is injured badly, the antler will be permanently deformed.

Growth proceeds from the head outward, and the ossification of the antler occurs in the same fashion. By the time the new "sprouts" get to be a few inches long, the base next to the head will be hardening. Thus, only the tip of the main beam and the tips of the points will be totally soft and lacking a core of bone. When all growth and ossification are completed, the skin (velvet) loosens and is stripped off by the deer. This is accomplished usually by twisting the antlers into a thorn tree or other brush and pulling backwards. It is not done by rubbing the antlers on the trunk of a sapling, as many hunters believe. "Rubbing" is associated with the rut and is done several weeks after the antlers have hardened and the velvet has been stripped off.

The age of a buck cannot be judged by the number of points on its antlers, even though many hunters still believe that there is a direct relationship. A buck at eighteen months of age, at the time when it carries its first rack, may have from two to twelve or more points. Once again, food is the important thing. A well-fed young buck should have eight, ten or twelve points. A buck of the same age living on some of the country's over populated deer areas is most likely to sport spikes, or at most a scrawny four-point rack. And that's one of many reasons why heavy culling is so desirable.

In the case of deer, it is difficult to have both quantity and quality. There is always a happy medium dictated by the "carrying capacity" of the range. There is one point the hunter should remember, however. Under continued good, or stable, food conditions, a buck's rack should get larger each year until the buck is at

Roger M. Latham

This eighteen-month-old buck lived on an over-crowded range where browse was scarce. Consequently, his first antlers were merely four-inch spikes. Under very poor food conditions, this buck might produce nothing but spikes for the first three or four years of its life.

Buck deer "rub" small saplings during the rutting season. This behavior pattern is associated with the defense of a territory and the buck's willingness to do battle.

DENTAL AGE CHARACTERS OF WHITE-TAILED DEER

(CHEEK SIDE OF LOWER MOLAR TOOTH ROW)

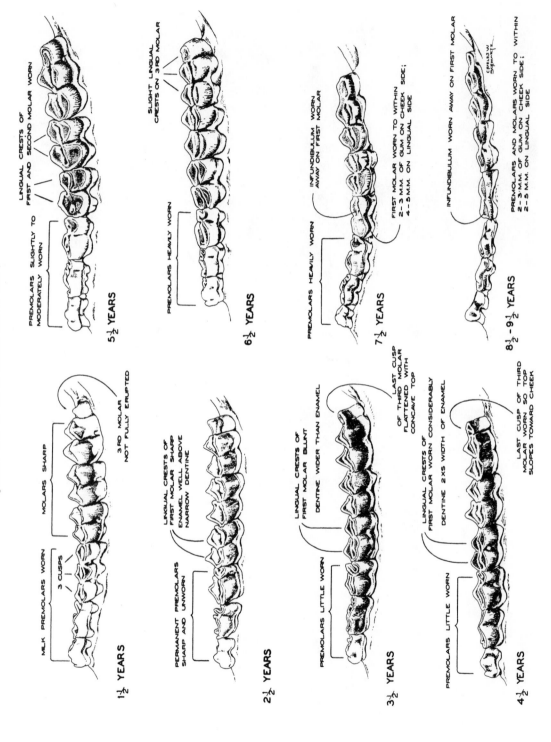

1½ YEARS
- MILK PREMOLARS WORN
- 3 CUSPS
- MOLARS SHARP
- 3 RD MOLAR NOT FULLY ERUPTED

2½ YEARS
- PERMANENT PREMOLARS SHARP AND UNWORN
- LINGUAL CRESTS OF FIRST MOLAR SHARP
- ENAMEL WELL ABOVE NARROW DENTINE

3½ YEARS
- PREMOLARS LITTLE WORN
- LINGUAL CRESTS OF FIRST MOLAR BLUNT
- DENTINE WIDER THAN ENAMEL

4½ YEARS
- PREMOLARS LITTLE WORN
- LINGUAL CRESTS OF FIRST MOLAR WORN CONSIDERABLY
- DENTINE 2 XS WIDTH OF ENAMEL
- LAST CUSP OF THIRD MOLAR WORN SO TOP SLOPES TOWARD CHEEK
- LAST CUSP OF THIRD MOLAR FLATTENED WITH CONCAVE TOP

5½ YEARS
- PREMOLARS SLIGHTLY TO MODERATELY WORN
- LINGUAL CRESTS OF FIRST AND SECOND MOLAR WORN

6½ YEARS
- PREMOLARS HEAVILY WORN
- SLIGHT LINGUAL CRESTS ON 3RD MOLAR

7½ YEARS
- PREMOLARS HEAVILY WORN
- INFUNDIBULUM WORN AWAY ON FIRST MOLAR
- FIRST MOLAR WORN TO WITHIN 2-3 M.M. OF GUM ON CHEEK SIDE; 4-5 M.M. ON LINGUAL SIDE

8½ - 9½ YEARS
- INFUNDIBULUM WORN AWAY ON FIRST MOLAR
- PREMOLARS AND MOLARS WORN TO WITHIN 2-3 M.M. OF GUM ON CHEEK SIDE; 2-5 M.M. ON LINGUAL SIDE;

least five, six or even seven years old. Then, the antlers may begin to deteriorate in size as the buck goes "over the hill."

Teeth. Deer are ruminants and have the typical teeth of browsing-grazing animals. Deer have no teeth in the forepart of the upper jaw. The lower incisors and the gums of the upper jaw are used to break off browse and other forage plants. The tongue is used to direct food into the mouth.

Deer teeth are important to the game manager and the hunter because this is one of the best ways to determine the age of this animal. This is done by examining the teeth of the lower jaw for replacement and wear. Up to 1½ years, the milk teeth, or baby teeth, are still being replaced by the permanent teeth. After 1½ years, age is determined by the amount of wear, particularly on the premolars and molars. The older the deer, the flatter and shallower the teeth become and the more dentine (brown portion of the surface) shows.

An expert can usually tell at a glance what the age of a deer is. An even more exacting method is to extract a tooth and place a cross-section slice under the microscope. The tooth will show growth rings not unlike the annual rings of a tree stump.

Scent Glands. Deer have four sets of these glands: the metatarsals on the outside of the lower hind legs; the tarsals on the inside of the hind legs at the hocks; the interdigitals between the toes of all four feet; and the preorbitals, located at the inner corners of the eyes. All are modified sweat glands.

There seems to be little known about the function of the metatarsals, even though they do secrete an oily substance with a strong odor. Observations in the pens and in the wild have revealed no obvious use for this gland.

The tarsals, on the other hand, are of vital importance. Through these, deer are able to signal danger to each other without any sound. When a deer senses danger, the tufts of hair covering the openings of these glands flare and a strong scent is emitted. Other deer, especially those downwind, will catch this scent almost immediately and be fully alerted.

The interdigitals are responsible for the scent left on the ground. By this means, the doe can locate her strayed fawn or a family group can become relocated following an emergency. This scent is very important in the social life of the deer.

The preorbitals are tear glands, and they lubricate and cleanse the eyes.

Many hunters immediately cut away the tarsal and metatarsal glands after shooting a deer. Most biologists do not believe that this is at all necessary to insure good venison. However, most warn that the gland, or the hair around the gland, should not be permitted to touch the meat. It could cause the portion

When disturbed or frightened, the doe will flare its glands at the hocks of its hind legs and release a scent which warns other deer. Does often stamp a front foot as an additional warning.

touched to have a taste or odor, unless thoroughly washed.

Anatomical Peculiarity. North American deer have no gall bladders. This gland, normally attached to the liver of most mammals, is peculiarly lacking in deer. Many hunters still do not know that this is true, and lively discussions often develop when a deer is field-dressed.

Physiology

The reason that deer are rated as such fine game animals and are recognized as one of the best trophies of the hunt is that they have such highly developed senses.

Probably the sense of smell is the most highly developed of the three and the most useful to the deer throughout its life. Through its nose, it detects friend and foe

10

ROGER M. LATHAM

alike. As every hunter knows, if there is a gentle breeze blowing and a deer approaches from downwind, it has all of the advantages. The older buck which gets a whiff of human scent is likely to melt into the brush and be gone right now. The doe, on the other hand, may whistle, snort and stamp her front feet just to prove to the hunter that she knows he is there.

During the rutting season, the buck stays on the track of the doe through his sense of smell and may follow her for miles without getting in sight of her. In fact, it is through smell that he knows she is "in heat" in the first place.

The doe finds her fawn in the same manner, and a family group, once scattered, reunites through smell.

Obviously, hearing is also acute. This is indicated by the very large ears. Anyone watching a deer in the woods will discover that the ears are almost constantly on the move, testing for sound in almost every direction. Sound is more confusing to deer than smell, however. This animal knows human scent immediately, but it cannot always identify human sounds, such as a hunter walking through the leaves. So hearing is used to direct the eyes more than anything else.

When the animal hears a twig snap or the leaves rustle, it turns its head and looks in that direction. If it sees another deer, a squirrel, a wild turkey or some other non-dangerous forest animal, it will stand its ground and probably go back to whatever it was doing. However, if the sound is being produced by a human, and the deer can see the person making the sound, the reaction will be quite different!

With some regularity, deer will stand their ground until they actually see what is making the noise. This is the reason why a hunter can often walk right up to a deer when he (the hunter) is screened by brush, grape vines or an intervening bit of higher ground.

The eyes of deer are great, too, but they have certain limitations. For example, deer are definitely color blind and do not see the bright reds, oranges and yellows worn by deer hunters everywhere. Also, they do not seem to be able to identify motionless objects very well. There's an old rule of the woods which states that, to the deer, every man is a stump, but to the wild turkey, every stump is a man. This means that if a hunter stands or sits still, he is not likely to be detected until the deer is very close.

However, they don't miss anything that moves. A deer sees every leaf that turns over, every quick move of a hunter's hands or face, and every flash of a gun barrel or shiny gun stock in the sun.

When all three of these senses are functioning at the same time, the deer doesn't really miss very much, and that is why it appears to be so intelligent and wary. That is also why the hunter needs to know how to take advantage of its few weaknesses in order to get close enough for a good shot.

Of course, none of these wonderful safeguards can keep a deer secure when he is outnumbered. When a forest is literally overrun with hunters, the deer has no place to hide. And if they were not endowed with this ability to see, hear and smell danger, none would survive the hunting season in some states!

Reproduction. Deer are polygamous, and one mature buck will normally mate with three to four does—perhaps with as many as six to ten. They are capable of mating .with many more than this number in pens where the females are confined.

The breeding period (called the "rut") varies somewhat from North to South, but generally is confined to October, November and December. As a rule, the season starts and ends earlier in the north.

Bucks reach sexual maturity in their second fall and are capable of mating successfully from September to March. For some strange reason, a very small percentage of does may be bred at the extremes of this long period. Thus, their fawns are born at such odd times as January and September. The normal fawning period is April, May and June, with northern fawns being born later than southern fawns.

The estrus, or "heat," period of the female lasts only about twenty-four hours. If she is not bred at that time, she will reach another estrus period in about twenty-eight days. Normally, she will have no more than three of these periods a year. Gestation is about 205 days, or roughly seven months, for all species of deer.

Doe fawns may breed at an age of

Under ideal food conditions, bucks may boast eight, ten, or even twelve points at eighteen months. The rack should increase in size annually for the first five or six years and then become progressively smaller as the buck approaches old age.

about seven months. Evidently, only those born early in the fawning season are sufficiently mature to breed, because even under good food conditions, only about one-third of all doe fawns become pregnant. Under poor food conditions, only a very tiny percentage will produce a fawn the following June. Almost invariably, these young deer give birth to just one fawn.

Older females should have twins or even triplets, but the number, once again, is related to diet. Does living on

12

overbrowsed range are more likely to produce singles.

Female deer maintain high production through a period of seven to eight years. After that, the number of fawns born annually drops off. However, there appear to be exceptions to this rule. One doe held in captivity had twins at the age of seventeen. During her first fifteen years, she produced thirty-three fawns.

It should be kept in mind that this has little real significance, since under normal hunting conditions few does would ever reach the ripe old age of seven or eight. However, biologists are convinced that the term "old barren doe" is a misnomer.

Diet. Deer are herbivores, meaning that they live exclusively upon a diet composed of plants and plant products. However, it certainly encompasses a multitude of plant species and a tremendous variety of plant products. Deer are both grazers and browsers. Grazing refers to the use of non-woody vegetation: grass, legumes, forbs and other annual or perennial vegetation. Browsing refers to the use of woody species and the eating of the tender twigs or sprouts, the buds and the leaves.

Deer also eat a large amount of forest mast, when available. Mast is a term applied to the "fruit" of forest trees—nuts, seeds and the pulpy fruits. Some of the more important of these are acorns, beechnuts, apples, wild crabapple, pine nuts, etc.

Mushrooms can be an important part of the diet, particularly in late summer and fall. Genera most often used appear to be *Boletus, Russula, Clitocybe* and probably *Tricholoma.*

Deer are resourceful creatures when it comes to food gathering. They eat only preferred species when food is abundant, but can survive on items which are definitely not preferred when under the stress of hunger.

Where deer are permitted to become overabundant and exceed the carrying capacity of their range, they are capable of eliminating preferred browse species. They literally eat the plants to death! In desperation, they invade farm fields (if available), dig roots and make greater and greater use of fallen leaves, even the old brown ones.

During the winter months, deer in the northern states and Canada have a tendency to "yard." They concentrate in sheltered areas, such as cedar swamps or mountain valleys. They usually stay right there during the most difficult part of the winter and compete with each other for the limited supply of browse available.

It is in these yards that most of the starvation occurs, often with a relative abundance of food not a half mile away at a higher elevation or in a more open forest. Because the larger deer can reach so much higher than the fawns for browse when standing upright on their hind legs, the fawns starve first. Not infrequently, some 90 per cent of the dead deer found the following spring are those under a year old.

During a hard winter in northern states, thousands of deer may "starve." These whitetails illustrate the end result when deer are permitted to overbrowse their range. The numbers must not exceed the "carrying capacity" of the range or starvation is lively to occur.

Biologists have discovered that the bone marrow is an excellent indicator of starvation. If the marrow inside a leg bone is cherry pink and jellylike, the deer has exhausted all of its fat reserves and has starved. If the marrow is whitish and still high in fat content, then it can be assumed that the deer died of other causes.

Hunters should know that food is vitally important in deer management. Deer living on good range are large and healthy, produce trophy antlers and reproduce far more successfully. Deer on poor range will be scrawny and small, and are more likely to be "spikes" instead of eight-pointers at eighteen months of age. Under these conditions, one hundred does may produce only about eighty fawns as compared to twice that many for one hundred well-fed does.

This is the basic reason why game departments continually try to balance the herd with its food supply by harvesting the surplus. Often this has to be done by means of an antlerless deer season, because this is the only effective way to reduce deer numbers drastically. Yet, hunters often resist these so-called doe seasons, for they believe that they will ruin their hunting. Actually, it is the only way to save their hunting and the range which produces the deer in the first place.

Diseases and Parasites. Deer are surprisingly healthy animals, with few lethal diseases or parasites of any consequence. However, there is a certain mortality which can be attributed to other things besides automobiles and predators. In this regard, the highway loss in Pennsylvania, for example, annually amounts to about 25,000 to 30,000 deer. This is more than most states harvest during their deer seasons, although other states have highway mortality, too.

Countrywide, the dog is a very potent predator and accounts for tens of thousands of deer, especially during the winter

ROGER M. LATHAM

months when snow is deep. The family pet—yes, good old Rover—can be a killer when he goes for a run in the woods.

Disease seems to be more serious in western deer than in the whitetails of the eastern portion of North America. There have been outbreaks of hoof and mouth disease, hemorrhagic septicemia, hoof rot and others in scattered localities of the South and West. Liver flukes and the nasal bot fly *(Cephenomyia phobifer)* appear to be the most important of the parasites. A serious infestation of either may indirectly cause death, particularly if associated with overcrowding and poor nutrition.

Deer sometimes gets skin tumors of two kinds, papilloma and fibroma. These

Skin tumors sometimes grow very large and actually handicap the deer in its movements.

black growths may be as large as a basketball and can be found on nearly any part of the deer's body. These benign tumors probably cause few deaths but do handicap the animals to such an extent that they may succumb to other causes.

Habits

The whitetail tends to live in a very restricted area, usually no more than one square mile. Western deer living in mountainous regions have a migration to the high elevations in the spring and down to the lower elevations in the fall. Thus, their home range is larger than that of eastern whitetails.

Deer have a remarkable homing instinct. Live-trapped deer, moved many miles from their home grounds, will often return to the exact spot in a few days. A

Chief predator of deer in Eastern United States is the dog. As often as not, the guilty dog is the family pet.

few have returned home from as far as fifty to sixty miles.

Deer are excellent jumpers and can clear an eight-foot fence and jump as far as twenty to twenty-five feet in a single bound. They swim well, attaining speeds of eleven to thirteen miles per hour. In the winter, when they have their coat of hollow hair, they swim very high in the water and float like a cork.

During the rutting season, bucks "stake out" a territory of sorts and mark it by rubbing several pole-size trees with their antlers until the bark is removed. Most of this rubbing is on trees or brush from about three-quarters of an inch in diameter to about three inches in diameter. Evidently, this is his way of venting some of his anger, because he is now ready to fight any other buck which happens to enter his domain. He will also stand and paw the ground, much like a mad bull.

Many fights occur between bucks during the mating season. Most merely result in a few broken antler points, sometimes a broken main beam, and a lot of grunting and shoving. However, they sometimes result in the death of one or both bucks. They are amazingly strong and a simple wrong move may mean points deeply imbedded in the chest or neck of one adversary. Also, two bucks can get their antlers so badly wedged together that they cannot pull apart again. In this case, both may starve, unless found and released by human benefactors.

Deer sometimes use their front feet to maintain a "pecking order" in a family group. Where there is some particularly tasty food, like ripe beechnuts, for example, the older does may thump the smaller deer with their front feet just to drive them away.

Deer are basically nocturnal and do most of their feeding at night. However, they have a tendency to begin to move toward their feeding areas late in the afternoon, especially during that last hour before dark. Hungry deer, living in over-browsed forests, may feed periodically all day long as well. They have to do this to survive.

Deer feed rather daintily on browse. They take a nip here and there as they walk slowly along and seldom stop to "clean" a particularly tasty clump of sprouts. When they are feeding upon fallen mast under an oak tree or beech tree, they may paw in the leaves for many minutes at a time.

Deer are not particularly vocal, but they do make a variety of sounds. Pick up a baby fawn and see how loud it can bleat. Or capture a buck in a live-trap and see if he doesn't bawl loud enough to be heard a mile away when you begin to tie his feet or man-handle him into a carrying crate.

A doe "talks" to her fawn with a sort of "mewing" sound. Bucks following the trail of a doe in heat make little grunting sounds. Bucks also have a rather complicated "victory" snort which is invariably given following an antler-crashing ses-

ROGER M. LATHAM

sion. The winner points his head toward the sky, snorts several times in quick succession, then closes his nostrils tightly and sucks in a full breath while producing a hissing whistle. This sound, properly reproduced, is quite effective in calling bucks during the rutting season. The snort and the shrill whistle of the deer which has sensed danger have been mentioned earlier.

These are only a few of the behavior patterns and characteristics of the deer, but they serve to identify some of this animal's peculiarities and capabilities.

If the hunter wishes to be successful in his outings during the deer season, and to enjoy them to the utmost, he should continue to add to his store of knowledge by reading, by observing and by talking to the experts, whether biologist or experienced hunter. Not until he knows his quarry intimately can he hope to outwit him on his own grounds!

Bob Bell wasn't born with a gun in his hand, but he didn't miss it by much. He got his first, a Daisy air rifle, for his fourth birthday. Two years later his dad gave him a Crosman pellet gun, then a .22 Winchester and a 20-gauge Remington, and when he was twelve years old, he worked all summer to buy a M94 Winchester .32 Special. His high school graduation present was a M71 Winchester .348. Following three years in the Army during World War II, he had his own commercial handloading shop, spent several years working and hunting in the Rocky Mountain States, and wore out a number of high-velocity rifle barrels on varmints and bench shooting. He's hunted from New Jersey to California, with a number of trips to Canada.

Bell began writing for outdoor magazines in the '40s. He majored in creative writing at Penn State, did graduate work at Stanford, has been a newspaperman, associate editor for *Gun Digest* and *Handloader's Digest,* handloading columnist on *GUNsport* Magazine, regional columnist for *Guns & Ammo,* and has contributed to most of the national gun magazines for years. Presently he's editor of *Pennsylvania Game News.* Hunting, shooting and writing about it take up most of his time. It's a tough life—obviously!

2

RIFLE RIGS FOR DEER

Bob Bell

IF *Homo sapiens* were truly a rational creature, the "What-gun-should-I-use-for-deer?" question could be settled very simply. The brush hunter would buy a lever-action .30-30 carbine, the open-country roamer would get a sporter-weight .270 bolt gun wearing a 4x scope, and that would be that. In fact, we could go one step further and add a .375 H & H Magnum and be equipped to handle any wild critter that walks the face of the earth.

There's little doubt that these three calibers would serve at least 99 per cent of the time—and it's possible that minuscule remaining one per cent is responsible for all of the sound and the fury generated when deer hunters get together and the inevitable question arises, for it just might

be true that 99 per cent of our hunters *are* carrying either a .30-30 or a .270, with all the remaining calibers parceled out among that oddball one per cent! At least a jaunt through any deer woods in the nation gives strong indication of such proportions.

The .30-30 has been around for over three-quarters of a century, so there just isn't much to say about it that hasn't been covered by dozens of others. The .270 is about a half-century old and Jack O'Connor has said as much about it as the dozens of others said about the .30-30. If there ever was a "gun that Jack built," the .270 is the gun, and O'Connor is the Jack. Nothing derogatory intended. No better gunwriter than O'Connor ever lived, and as suggested in the beginning of this, no better deer cartridge than the .270 ever went into the mountains.

So where does that leave us? Should we accept the old Maine guide's axiom that "any rifle is a good deer rifle if you're a good deer hunter," or should we look a bit further? Everything considered, I believe we have to look. That old codger doubtless was correct in his own area of operations—the pine thickets and alder swamps where downeast whitetails lurk—but there's more to today's deer hunting than that kind of maneuvering. At the same time that wool-clad oldtimer is bouncing a buck in central Pennsylvania's hardwood slashings, a youngster in Levis and big hat is sprawled over an outcropping of rock in the sage country outside Dixon, Wyoming, following a big-racked mule deer in the scope of his 7mm Magnum. And down on the Sonora border an Arizona rancher is working over a compact Coues buck with his saddle gun, while out California way a red-shirted logger is spending his day off trying to roust a blacktail out of the salal brush and salmonberry that form the understory in much of the redwood country.

Deer hunting is somewhat different in each of these regions, but in the end it boils down to two basic propositions: there is short-range shooting, often at fast-moving animals which are visible for only a few moments or perhaps flicker in and out of sight through the intervening brush and trees, and there is medium- to long-range work, where the hunter usually has more time to do his stuff and, because the country is more open, normally has a clearer view of his target. The first setup requires a fast-handling, natural-pointing rifle capable of quick repeat shots. Extreme accuracy is not necessary, for the distance is short, the vital area large. The second situation calls for a more accurate outfit because the deer's size does not grow with range as competitive paper bulls-eyes do, and for higher velocity cartridges delivering flatter trajectories, as these minimize the problems of range estimation and simplify hitting at a distance. Speed of fire is relatively unimportant, for the animal usually is in sight longer.

I've no data to prove it, but I feel certain that far more deer are killed at less than 150 yards—and probably less than 100 yards—than beyond that distance. This doubtless accounts for the continuing popularity of the "standard American deer cartridge," the .30-30, for at such distances this old load has all it takes to convert a buck on the hoof into pan-fried venison chops. And if the .30-30 will do this, so will other oldtimers such as the .32 Special, and .30 and .32 Remington, for they all use bullets of about the same weight and diameter loaded to about the same velocity. Other oldies that are even more dependable because of their greater power include the .300 Savage, .35 Remington and .348 Winchester. All of these are at their best in the woods, where the

20

Popularity of M94 Winchester .30-30 is indicated by these Lackawanna County, Pa., deer hunters, all of whom are using this model. The reasons are simple; it's light, fast and handy, and it does the job at woods ranges.

fast-working lever and slide action rifles in which they're normally seen are right at home.

When introduced in 1895, the .30-30 was loaded with a 165-gr. bullet at 1970 fps. Compared with the large-bore, low-velocity loads which preceded it, this was really hot stuff. It was a small-bore high-velocity load by the standards of those times. It didn't kill any better in the brush than its predecessors—perhaps not as good as some—but its greatly increased velocity made hitting much easier in the 125 to 250 yard bracket. For example, the

older .45-70 Government load used a 405-gr. bullet at 1300 fps, so the .30-30 offered about 50 per cent more speed. It sacrificed bullet weight and diameter but still was adequate in those categories, and anyone who thinks that velocity increase wasn't significant, should ponder the fact that the jump from the old .30-06 to the highly touted .300 Weatherby Magnum is only 450 fps with a 180-gr. bullet, which figures out to be 16 per cent increase.

Current tables list the following ballistics with some traditional deer cartridges. Chances are they are a bit optimistic in

Cartridge	Bullet	Velocity			Velocity			MRT Inches
		Muzzle	100	200	Muzzle	100	200	200
.30-30 Winchester	170	2220	1890	1630	1860	1350	1000	4.6
.30 Remington	170	2120	1820	1560	1700	1250	920	5.3
.32 Special	170	2280	1920	1630	1960	1390	1000	4.8
.32 Remington	170	2120	1800	1540	1700	1220	895	4.9
.300 Savage	150	2670	2390	2130	2370	1900	1510	3.0
.300 Savage	180	2370	2160	1960	2240	1860	1530	3.7
.35 Remington	200	2100	1710	1390	1950	1300	860	6.0
.348 Winchester	200	2530	2220	1940	2840	2190	1765	3.7

the short barrels commonly used, but at woods ranges they won't be much less efficient than the figures indicate. Generations of observation by countless hunters have indicated it takes approximately one thousand foot-pounds of kinetic energy to reliably kill deer, so it's obvious why this group has been popular wherever ranges are on the short side. Several have more power than is necessary for deer at woods ranges, but except for possibly the .300 Savage, none has the velocity and accuracy required for deer hunting at the longer, open-country distances.

If it's true that most of the deer killed are taken at under 150 yards, it's doubtless similarly true that practically all—say 99.99 per cent—are taken at less than 300 yards. This means that not once in a lifetime will the average deer hunter truly need a Magnum cartridge for his shooting. It's interesting to read about the long-range efficiency of the 7mm Remington and .300 Winchester Magnums,

the big Weatherbys, etc., and if you just can't sleep nights without owning one of these hotshots, just pay your money and take one home. But you don't really need it to kill deer. Where ranges run to 300 yards, the high velocity, medium-size cartridges such as the .243 Winchester, 6mm Remington, .257 Roberts, .25-06, 6.5 Remington Magnum (which isn't a true magnum in my opinion), .270, 7mm Mauser, .280 Remington, .284 Winchester, .308 Winchester, and of course Ol' Faithful—the .30-06—are the answer.

Assuming the correct bullet weight and design are chosen, there just isn't a whole lot of difference in this bunch when it comes to deer killing. Some are better than others, but all will do the job. The .243 and 6mm are not my idea of the greatest deer loads at three hundred yards—or at any other range, so far as that goes—but if the varmint bullets are avoided and broadside shots are offered, as is often the case at long range, their pinpoint accuracy allows precise bullet placement and most users like them. Generally speaking, a 100-gr. spitzer bullet will give the best long-range results on deer when a .243 or 6mm is used, with either the 100-gr. or 117-gr. in the .257 and .26-06, the 120-gr. in 6.5 Remington, the 130-gr. .270, medium weights such as the 139-gr. to 150-gr. in the 7mm's, and 150-gr. to 180-gr. in the .30 calibers. The following table indicates average ballistics with this group up to three hundred yards.

These again are advertised factory ballistics, and the chronographing may well have been done with barrels longer than normally are used for hunting—which is a polite way of saying the hunter doesn't actually get these results in the field. Handloaders can come close in most cases, if they're using strong bolt guns and

know what they're doing. In at least one case, the .257 Roberts, a knowledgeable handloader can surpass the listed velocity easily. Properly loaded, a .257 can give a 100-gr. spitzer bullet over 3000 fps at the muzzle, and at three hundred yards it will surpass the two 6mm's in energy.

Spitzer bullets retain velocity and energy better than blunt designs, and should be chosen when ranges tend to be on the long side. Some experienced hunters feel that blunt-nose bullets are more dependable killers at the shorter distances, claiming that they strike the animal with a greater cross-sectional area of the bullet, thus delivering more of an impact effect. It is sometimes argued that this type of bullet expands more dependably also. A friend who used a .257 to kill several hundred whitetails in a short period of time told me that the 117-gr. RN

										MRT
	Bullet		*Velocity*				*Kinetic Energy*			Inches
Cartridge	Grs.	Muzzle	100	200	300	Muzzle	100	200	300	300
.243 Winchester	100	3070	2790	2540	2320	2090	1730	1430	1190	5.5
6mm Remington	100	3190	2920	2660	2420	2260	1890	1570	1300	5.1
.257 Roberts	100	2900	2540	2210	1920	1870	1430	1080	820	7.0
.25-06 Remington	120	3120	2850	2600	2360	2590	2160	1800	1480	
6.5 Remington	120	3030	2750	2480	2230	2450	2010	1640	1330	5.7
.270 Winchester	130	3140	2880	2630	2400	2850	2390	2000	1660	5.3
7x57 Mauser	139	2710	2440	2190	1960	2280	1850	1490	1190	7.8
.280 Remington	150	2900	2670	2450	2220	2800	2370	2000	1640	6.1
.308 Winchester	150	2860	2570	2300	2050	2730	2200	1760	1400	6.5
.284 Winchester	150	2900	2630	2380	2160	2800	2300	1890	1550	6.3
.30-06	180	2700	2470	2250	2040	2910	2440	2020	1660	7.0

In deer country like this, a high-velocity bolt action rifle with 6x scope is not the best outfit. A good lever or slide action using a large-diameter, heavyweight bullet is far superior.

was definitely a better killer than the 100-gr. spitzer at ranges to two hundred yards or so, but he could not say whether this was due to the bullet's shape or its greater weight. I have a hunch it was the added weight, which gave more consistent penetration.

Blunt-nose bullets may also be a trifle better at brush penetration than pointed styles, though no design can be completely depended upon if it hits anything of noticeable resistance on the way to the target. Even a 48-gr. .220 Swift bullet at 4000+ fps is a good brush bullet if it doesn't hit any brush, and this is often what happens when a shot is taken. It requires only a tiny diameter tunnel

between the gun and the target to let a bullet through unscathed, and many hunters conclude they're shooting good brush bullets when the few shots that provided the data for their opinions never hit any brush. This is the fallacy in most of the so-called testing of brush bullets. Shooting through a screen of twigs or saplings doesn't guarantee that any will be hit, and if they're not, the whole thing is pointless. Furthermore, such tests usually have a target immediately behind the screen; even a bullet which is deflected often hits the target due to its nearness. But in the woods, shooting at a live deer perhaps seventy-five yards away, it's common for the bullet to hit a sapling midway to the animal. Even if deflected at only a shallow angle, by the time it flies on another forty yards or so, it can be well off the target. For example, a bullet which is deflected one inch in reaching a target three feet beyond the sapling will be forty inches off when it's traveled forty yards —and that can be enough to miss a moose, let alone a small whitetail. It's significant that the traditional woods cartridges use bullets of good diameter and weight, with round or flat noses. The 200-gr. round nose in the .35 Remington and the .348 200-gr. and 250-gr. flat-points could well be the best thick-cover deer bullets ever produced.

Despite the current and increasing popularity of bolt-action rifles, most hunters who concentrate on deer in wooded country would be better off with some other type of action. The bolt gun usually

24

gives better accuracy than other repeaters, and its strength permits chambering for the highest intensity cartridges. But nail-driving accuracy is not required to hit deer at ordinary ranges, nor are the hotshot Magnum cartridges reasonable choices for such game. And today's lever, slide and auto-loading rifles are capable of accuracy which will surprise many hunters who for years have been brainwashed by certain gunwriters' propaganda, into believing that bolt guns are the only logical choice. They're not. There's nothing sacred about the turnbolt action; the darn thing wasn't even designed in Heaven. Admittedly, the best bolt guns are great tools, but it takes an expert—a real expert, not a self-styled one—to fully profit from their potential. Anyone who

Group of Pennsylvania hunters moves out to go on stand. Drivers will shove deer toward them— hopefully! In pole timber like this high-velocity loads aren't necessary, can even be a handicap. Good low power scope is useful in picking holes through trees.

wants to get aimed shots off as rapidly with a bolt as with a lever gun is going to spend many long, lonesome hours practicing. He does this because something in his makeup drives him to it; it's a mental thing that perhaps defies rational explanation. The average hunter will find one of the other styles far simpler to use and therefore more efficient.

A woods gun for deer should be short, light, quick-pointing. The lever action carbines such as the legendary M94 Winchester and M336 Marlin have been standard deer guns for decades because they fit these specifications. Browning's newer BLR has some interesting innovations—a detachable clip, rack-and-pinion bolt movement, etc.—but basically it handles like the older lever models. Savage's great M99 comes in various barrel lengths, including the handy twenty-inch model, and is chambered for several hot new calibers, and the comparatively new Winchester M88 can be had with a short barrel also. This length sacrifices a bit of velocity, but that's not as important in the bush as their superior handling qualities. The Browning, Savage, Marlin and Winchester M88 eject to the side, thus will accept a low-mounted scope, something the top-ejecting Winchester models cannot do. And I would not suggest a side-mounted scope. I've tried this, for I'm partial to good glass sights, but found it completely unsatisfying. It's a makeshift arrangement that spoils all the natural handling qualities that make the M94's so agreeable in the first place. Nor would I

Bob Bell's dad, deer hunting in central Pennsylvania in the late 1940's. His favorite woods gun was a .35 Remington M141 with 2½x Lyman Alaskan scope, Redfield Jr. mount, big dot reticle.

advise using a long-eye relief scope that mounts ahead of the action. Its field of view is very small for its magnification (usually about twenty-five feet at one hundred yards with a 2x scope), and esthetically such an arrangement is enough to give a rhinoceros the vapors.

Slide-action fanciers—and anyone who uses a pump shotgun should give serious thought to a similar deer rifle—are more restricted in their choice than those who like the levers. Current American models include the Remington M760 Gamemaster in field and deluxe versions (unless you like purple Cadillac convertibles with zebra skin seat covers, choose the straight model) and Savage's M170, which comes in .30-30 only. The Remingtons are offered in 6mm, .243, .270, .308 and .30-06. For many years Remington also made the M141, its best caliber being the .35 Remington load. If you can find one of these in good condition, grab it. You'll have a great woods outfit for deer. It has a quality look and feel about it, in my opinion, and performs great. This was my dad's favorite deer gun and I shot his often. With a 2½x Lyman Alaskan scope and big dot reticle, it would usually put five shots in about two inches at one hundred yards—a lot of bolt guns won't do better —and when you have five .35-cal. holes in an area about the size of a baseball, it looks like you've used up all the available space. Of course, you'll never have to shoot a deer five times with this load. Once is usually sufficient. It doesn't explode them like the light-bullet, high-velocity jobs; it just puts a big hole through 'em that leaks badly and they die quickly.

I've never been a fan of autoloading rifles for hunting, but quite a few guys like them. I always thought they would gain popularity following World War II, when so many men gained familiarity with this kind of action in the M1 and .30-cal. carbine, as the bolt gun gained followers after use of the Springfield in World War I. But that doesn't seem to have happened. Regardless, in recent years several good models have been marketed, including the Browning High-Power, Remington M742 Woodsmaster, Ruger 44 Autoloader, and the Winchester M100. The Ruger is chambered for the .44 Magnum only—essentially a heavy handgun cartridge, but efficient on deer at short range—while the others come in high-intensity loadings such as the .270 and .308. All can be scope-mounted.

Besides the calibers already mentioned as woods loads, Marlin has recently introduced the M1895 in .45-70, an ancient but deadly load in forested country. Factory loads use a 405-gr. bullet at some 1300 fps, which isn't much velocity but it's an awful lot of deer-killing bullet. Handloaders can improve this performance greatly, as this Marlin will handle hotter pressures than the old "trapdoor" Springfields for which factory loads are geared. Marlin also chambers a lever gun for the .444 Marlin cartridge, which uses a 240-gr. bullet at 2400 fps, and this, too, is more than enough for any deer that walks.

This group of rifles is primarily intended for woods hunting, though in some calibers they will perform well at longer ranges. They are highly portable, quick to get into action, and sufficiently accurate for the job at hand. A fault of some is poor sights. Typical factory open sights have high-rising "ears" that make it hard to see the front bead and even more difficult to maintain proper elevation, especially in shadowy woods. The front sight, usually a half-sphere of indeterminate color, catches the light differently for almost every shot, effectively changing the gun's point of impact by causing the shooter to hold on a different place. It should be replaced by a flat-faced gold bead of 1/16

Bob Bell takes lunch break while on deer stand in Perry County, Pa. Rifle is his favorite .284 Mauser, Weaver V-4.5 scope, large dot reticle.

Eatin' size whitetail from Potter County Pa., killed by Bob Bell with 8mm/06 Mauser, Weaver K2.5, 5″ dot reticle.

inch to not over 3/32 inch diameter. These sizes are large enough to be seen quickly but they do not "overpower" the target and make it appear smaller than it really is, and therefore harder to hit. A sight face angled forward on top to catch the light also works well, so long as the surface is flat. Some hunters prefer a flat top and sides on the front sight, and file their beads to this conformation. There's no doubt that this makes it easier to determine precise elevations for a shot, but I always felt it was more natural to aim with a round front sight than a rectangular one.

Open rear sights should not have ears. The reasoning behind the so-called buck-

horn or semi-buckhorn design escapes me. Open sights are located too far from the eye to serve as substitute aperture styles, so I can't fathom why that extra metal was added. The best open rear sight sits close to the barrel (as low as the front sight will permit with proper zeroing), is flat across the top, and has a tiny notch to accept the front bead. Some experienced hunters like a vertical platinum or white line beneath the notch, but I've never been intrigued with the idea. Others prefer a shallow curve instead of a flat top, and this is all right if the depth is truly shallow. The problem with the big-eared type is that they block much of your view and they shade the notch so fully that it's almost impossible to maintain regular elevations when aiming.

Open sights, if of proper design, are fast in use and entirely adequate for much woods hunting, even in this day of the scope. I won't say they're the best, for I don't believe that, but they'll serve well if you realize their limitations. Incidentally, that much-parroted remark that they're inefficient because the eye must try to focus on three objects simultaneously—the rear sight, front sight and target—is so much nonsense, perhaps the only inaccurate thing the late Col. Townsend Whelen ever wrote. The shooter doesn't even try to focus on the rear sight. He just looks across it in the sense that a person using an aperture sight looks through it, sees the front bead against his target, and shoots. The open sight shooter is no more

Bob Bell

aware of the flat top or the notch than the aperture user is of the rim around the hole. It registers subconsciously, if at all.

Aperture (peep) sights are located nearer the eye, giving a longer sight radius than open sights, which adds a bit to accuracy. They don't block off the bottom part of your view as much as the others, and they usually have accurate adjustments, which greatly simplify sighting in.

The most satisfying aperture sight I ever used on a hunting rifle was the one Winchester used to make as an integral part of the bolt on their Model 71 .348. It was adjustable for windage and elevation and the flat disc which helped to define the front sight for accurate zeroing on paper could be removed, leaving a large thin-rimmed hole, for hunting. It was small, weighed almost nothing, had no projections to distract the eye, and was perfectly positioned for fast, accurate aiming. A few gunwriters objected to its being part of the bolt, claiming that some slight movement of the bolt's position when levered shut would adversely affect accuracy. This was nitpicking of the most ridiculous kind, even if theoretically correct. Any error caused by this would fall well within the normal grouping of the gun and load, which certainly wasn't a varmint outfit to begin with. With either 200-gr. or 250-gr. bullets, my .348 normally grouped in less than three inches at one hundred yards, which is not .222 accuracy by any means, but perfectly adequate for deer and elk. And the

truckload of meat that this combination brought out of the bush for me proved its practicality to an extent that no typewriter-shooter could overcome. Among iron sights currently available, I'd choose the Williams Fool-Proof aperture model

Bob Bell using Super Grade Pre-WWII M70 Winchester, Bushnell 3-9 scope, .220 Swift. A poor deer cartridge under average conditions, but one that works OK when shots are carefully placed. Superbly accurate, so performs well when standing broadside shots are offered, as in some open country hunting field watching.

for all-around suitability It can be zeroed easily on the bench by means of a screwdriver, but has no projecting knobs to interfere with quick aiming or to make it easy for some not-too-bright buddy to twirl.

Iron-sighted brush and woods cartridges should be zeroed in to hit just at the top of the front sight at 100 yards. This will mean they are about three inches above true point of aim, for most hunters naturally use the center of the front bead as their aiming point and it subtends about six inches at 100 yards. Such an adjustment will mean the bullet will hit behind the center of the bead at 160 yards or so and will be only a couple of inches below the center—or still well within the area of the bead—at 200 yards. So zeroed, there's no need to worry about holding high on a deer at any woods range.

All rifles, but most especially deer rifles in the woods, should be reloaded at the shoulder. That is, the butt should never be lowered in order to work the action. Any repeating rifle can easily be worked while keeping the game reasonably well in the sights, yet the majority of hunters I've watched in the woods lower the rifle after firing, work the action, raise the gun and aim again, which takes an awful lot longer than flipping a lever with the gun at the shoulder. This time-lag often gives the animal the chance it needs to escape. Familiarity with the outfit can be gained by dry-firing at home. After making certain the gun is empty, it can be brought

into firing position quickly, the hammer cocked or safety disengaged as it is lifted, aim taken at some small convenient object, "shot," the action worked for another try, and the whole thing repeated. A few minutes a day for a couple of weeks before the hunting season will ingrain the proper habits that make proper procedure easy.

Some firearms, especially some makes of lever-action carbines, have a tendency to slip off the shoulder when the lever is worked hard as it should be. This may be due to improper pitch of the buttplate or the material from which the plate is made. Some are slippery plastic or steel that's not checkered or grooved properly. The simplest remedy is to have a rubber buttplate or recoil pad installed at the proper angle, for this will cling to your jacket. This also gives a chance to alter the length of the stock if it's incorrect.

For many years, rifles of the .30-30 class were standards for deer hunting. They were always popular in the East, and even though it was recognized that their efficiency was severely limited beyond 150 yards or so, they continued to be used in the West too because they were so easy to pack on a horse and so nearly indestructible in a pickup. They're still common anywhere in deer country, but in many places they are relatively inefficient and the trend has been away from them and toward high-velocity loads. This started after World War I, when returning servicemen who had learned to use the bolt action .30-06 Springfield spread over the gamefields. The advent of good hunting

Ultra-long range deer hunters use bench-rest type equipment and the hottest Magnum cartridges for their deer hunting. This photo was made on TrumanRun in Lycoming County, Pa. The "hunting" is easy, but the shooting isn't. These guys are experts.

Good Pennsylvania whitetail buck taken in Centre County by Bob Bell with 7mm, Redfield 4x.

Bob Bell on Pa. deer stand. Pre-1964 M70 Winchester .270, Weaver K4 scope—a great outfit on deer under most conditions, though not ideal in brushy country.

Rifle Rigs for Deer

Bob Clever, of Warren, Pa., with his favorite Kinzua Country deer gun, a M99 Savage .300. This is a great rifle for most deer hunting.

scopes in the 1930's intensified the process, as did the appearance of impressive new cartridges like the .257 Roberts and .270 Winchester. Previously, advanced loads such as the .250-3000 and .300 Savage were used by only the more knowledgeable hunters, and no one but the nuttier guncranks got involved with—or even had heard of—such esoteric items as the .256 Newton or the .275 H & H Magnum, say. There's little point in mentioning these here either, as superior cartridges are now available in any sporting goods store. But back in the days

just preceding World War I, these were truly impressive.

I've already listed (see second table) many of the loads that will be chosen for deer at our longer ranges, such as hill-to-hill shooting in northern Pennsylvania or mule deer hunting in northwestern Colorado. I feel these calibers should be built on good bolt actions, as these permit use of the hottest loadings, generally give better accuracy than a pump or autoloader, and are more practical hunting arms than a single shot—though I do admit a great fondness for Ruger's beautiful Number One. So many bolt guns are available commercially that it would be difficult to list them all, but a few with which I've had good results are the Remington M700, Winchester M70, Ithaca LSA-55, Savage M110 and Ruger M77. For general use with these cartridges in the .243 to .30-06 class, I'd tend toward a 22-inch barrel when available. It sacrifices a bit of velocity compared with a 24-inch, but feels far handier to me. The trigger should be adjusted to about three or four pounds pull—if much lighter it's hard to feel it properly in cold weather—with all creep and backlash removed.

A scope is a necessity for this class of rifles. High magnification isn't necessary. A straight 4x is a good choice—you never need more power on deer—but I prefer a small variable giving a magnification range of 1½-4½. This gives a choice of a comparatively wide field at bottom power, for use in thick cover, and the

BOB BELL

Nice Ontario whitetail taken by Bob Bell, foreground, with .338 Magnum, 275-gr. Speer, 77 gr. 4831—a great example of overkill!—while moose hunting with Ted Davis.

higher magnification for the occasional shot at a deer seen standing on a sidehill or in the sage. The reticle should be highly conspicuous. The Duplex type, which combines four posts with fine crosswires in the center, is as good as anything and better than most. These small variables are built on straight one-inch tubes, for their low and medium magnifications don't need enlarged objective lenses to transmit additional light as the higher powers do. This gives them a neat, "belonging" look on a hunting gun. I currently have four scopes of this type—two Weaver V-4.5's, a Redfield and a Marlin—and I feel they're close to perfect for deer hunting anywhere in the United States.

The mount should hold the scope low and centrally over the gun. Some experienced hunters like quick detachable mounts, which permit use of iron sights during a downpour, a heavy snowstorm, or in the remote possibility of a damaged scope, but I've always preferred solid ones. I started with the Redfield Jr. and have stayed with it for the most part, as I've found it dependable, and having the same kind of mount on most of my guns permits easy swapping of scopes when there's some reason to do that. However, I know from actual use that other mounts such as the Bausch & Lomb Trophy, Buehler, Pachmayr, Conetrol, and S & K also give full satisfaction, so choice becomes a matter of personal preference.

I always zero my rifles three inches high at one hundred yards. Results farther out depend on the exact load combination, but usually cartridges in this longer range group will still be a little high at two hundred yards and only a couple of inches low at three hundred. This means that no thought must be given to holding-over unless a target is so far away that you normally have time to indulge in whatever calculations are necessary to precisely place a bullet. Today's hot loads will cleanly kill deer at three hundred to four

Idaho mule deer taken by Bob Bell on elk hunt. .338 Magnum, 275-gr. Speer, 77 gr. 4831. Weaver V7 scope. Far more power than needed, but toughly built bullet did not cause excessive damage as light, high-velocity loads often do. Neck shot at eighty-five yards.

hundred yards if a standing broadside shot is offered, and if the shooter knows his outfit and can shoot it. It's best to avoid tail-end shots and shots at moving deer at these ranges. At such distances, a solid position is necessary, preferably sitting with a rest for the back of the left hand (not the gun, as many will "shoot away" from a hard object). Target-trained hunters can hold well enough prone with sling, but the average hunter can't and because he rarely zeroes in this way, it's doubtful if he should use the sling, for it often makes a sporter-weight rifle shoot to a different point of impact.

If you insist, you can use a Magnum on deer. If you do much shooting beyond four hundred yards, you should, for at that distance a .300 Magnum is just another .30-30. The .264 Winchester Magnum, 7mm Remington Magnum, .300 Winchester Magnum, the various Weatherbys, the 7x61 Sharpe & Hart, many similar wildcats—all will give somewhat better results at extreme ranges than the loads we've been discussing, if the hunter is truly rifleman enough to take advantage of their ballistics and doesn't mind their recoil. But it's hard to understand why anyone *has* to do much shooting at such distances. Getting within sensible range is part of hunting too. We can't expect the gun to do everything.

Don Lewis is a widely acclaimed and respected firearms expert. He's been around firearms and hunting since he was a youngster. And for the last twenty years, he probably has had as much shooting experience as anyone in the country.

During that time he maintained his own gunsmith shop specializing in scope mounting and sighting-in, although he has done general gunsmithing. He estimates having zeroed in some three thousand rifles—virtually every make and model.

He's also a commercial handloader.

Don maintains his own chronograph range, electrically operated sight-in range, bench rest with adjustable seat, adjustable back and front rests, and does his shooting from indoors. I've been there, and it's an elaborate and impressive setup.

He is currently Firearms Editor for the *Pennsylvania Game News* and has written gun articles for most of the firearms magazines. His special interest is woodchuck shooting and squirrel rifles, but he is widely experienced in hunting whitetail deer.

3

WHITE-TAILED DEER FIREARMS—TAKE THE PSYCHOLOGICAL APPROACH

Don Lewis

Photos by Helen Lewis

I SURVEYED THE landscape with a certain amount of disgust. Several months before, I had picked this high hillside spot for my first watch on opening day of buck season. My intentions had been to get there early in hopes of getting a shot as hunters moved in from roads on three sides of the abandoned strip mine. All through squirrel season I made mental notes on deer signs and came to the conclusion that no better spot existed than the one I had chosen.

My good intentions went down the drain when opening morning found me committed to a gun shop detail I couldn't avoid. It was mid-morning before I left the shop. To my chagrin, at least a dozen other hunters had decided on the same area. I could count that many blaze orange caps within five hundred yards. It was a rotten break, but I had a good vantage point in case a wily buck managed to slip through.

A half hour went by with the silence being broken now and then by distant shots. Nothing that resembled a legal target moved where I was stationed. Almost as if by magic, the hunters disappeared, and I found myself alone. A six-inch snow covered the ground, and any movement stood out like a sore thumb. All was quiet. I felt relieved. I was alone at last.

While daydreaming about my good fortune, I began to ask myself why in the world I had chosen a Model 340 Savage 30-30 when I had several more powerful rifles. It seemed a stupid mistake since I could see three crossings beyond 150 yards. I knew the 30-30 would reach that far, but I also knew my chances would be better with the .270 Winchester. The .270 would whip a 130 grain bullet at over three thousand feet per second with 50 grains of 4895, compared to the 30-30's 2,215 fps from a max load of 34 grains of 4895. Velocity isn't everything, but nearly 1,000 fps has to be considered significant.

I admit it was pure laziness. When I left the shop, the 30-30 was on my workbench with a box of shells, and I simply took the course of least resistance instead of getting the .270 from my gun cabinet.

During my mental chastising, I became aware of a movement in the woods across from me. I didn't need a scope to see it was a deer, and the 6X Weaver showed a small rack. It was no more than one hundred yards across the ravine, but the buck was walking in very dense underbrush. I lost little time in getting into a shooting position, and as I followed him, waiting for a tiny opening, I realized I had accidentally chosen the right cartridge. The 170 grain bullet would stay on course

through the maze of limbs, and I was very thankful I hadn't brought the .270.

It was no pushover, but my third shot made it final. Two bullets had connected, and proof that the 170 grain 30-30 was right became even more evident when tiny bits of wood were found in the fatal slug the next day. Even though I was successful, I can't recommend the lazy method for choosing a rifle for whitetails.

There's a never-ending argument on the merits of certain calibers with regard to their effectiveness on deer, and I suppose the hot stove league sessions will continue as long as two hunters are left. I've been around deer rifles for many years, and have fired literally thousands for testing, sight-ins, and hunting. Strange as it may sound, I am not impressed with the under-gunned or under-powered arguments common among deer hunters.

My concern in the episode I just related was not so much being under-powered as under-ranged. I was apprehensive over the 30-30's ability to reach out, and I still believe my story would have been written with a different ending had the buck been 250 yards away or if I had done my shooting with the .270 Winchester.

I am not trying to take anything away from the famous 30-30. I was attempting to establish that the old reliable caliber was right at home with the short one-hundred-yard shot in heavy brush. There's no question in my mind that more deer have been taken under these

Don Lewis maintains this chronograph setup to check velocities of various calibers and loads.

conditions, and with the 30-30 than with any other two cartridges combined. However, not all shots are one hundred yards or in heavy brush, so, the 30-30 is not the only deer rifle regardless of its past fame.

With all the ado and fuss over calibers and cartridges, it can be confusing to understand what it's all about. From my experiences, I've found that a large segment of hunters with considerable experience really don't understand the maze of statistics and ballistics connected with the big-game rifle. It shouldn't be

like that. In fact, there's no need for all this uproar to be taking place.

Although I can't say my philosophy has received much attention over the years, I'm a firm believer in the psychological approach to choosing the proper whitetail outfit. Also, there's a practical side. I believe some writers make it so complex that the novice or inexperienced hunter is lost. I won't guarantee to come up with all the answers, but I will do my level best to make it a little easier to understand the necessary requisites for choosing the best whitetail outfit.

I lived my early life during the bleakness of the Depression years, when money was not readily available to purchase a new or different deer rifle if a change was wanted or needed. Most of us used what we could buy—for as little money as possible. With a flood of ex-military Krags easily obtainable, the hunter of the Depression years bought one without regard to whether it was right for him or his style of hunting. I remember well seeing dozens of long, uncut Krag's being toted through the woods during the 1930's. There was nothing wrong with the Krag, and it still has the smoothest bolt ever designed. But it was a military rifle first, last, and always!

The more affluent hunters began cutting the Krag down and doing other custom work, and I must admit the old rifle kept getting sharper in appearance although not much could be done with the tool-box-type shell carrier on its side. Still, the old rifle had enough stuff for the shots of that era and was a boon to the hunter who felt the pinch of tight money during those years. I suppose the Krag gained more fame as a hunting rifle than as a military one.

I'm sure today's Krag owners have their hackles up, but I mean no offense. Today in the uncut version, the Krag brings five times what it cost originally, and the nostalgia keeps growing along with the shooting myths connected with the famous 30-40.

When the 30-30, 32 Special, Krag, and 35 Remington were in their heyday, the methods used for whitetail hunting were somewhat different from today. A hunting camp in 1935 came to life at 4:00 A.M., and an hour later the breakfast dishes were washed and preparations were under way for each hunter to be on watch by 6:15 A.M. Legal starting time in Pennsylvania was 7:00 A.M., but any hunter in his right mind was on watch well beforehand.

Not only was an early start required, but the hunter carried his lunch and stayed in the woods all day. The hunter who didn't get a shot carried a fully loaded rifle from daylight till dark.

Today's hunter is mobile. This doesn't mean I am advocating road hunting, by any means. However, the day of leaving camp before daylight and staying deep in the woods until quitting time is disappearing as fast as the butter churn. Mobility is the name of the game now. Hunters still hit the woods early, but sel-

dom stay in one spot more than an hour or two. With all-terrain and four-wheel-drive vehicles, more hunter movement is seen every year. I can't honestly say it's the best style, but it happens to be the modern whitetail hunter's way of doing things.

In the early years, the hunter found his game in the dense woods and heavy mountain laurel growths, and many a fine buck was dropped well under fifty yards. The day had not arrived when miles of rights-of-way would criss-cross mountains and wooded areas making 250-yard shots possible. Also during those years, deer were abundant in the thick mountain brush and were seldom seen on open land.

That was unquestionably a grand era for the whitetail hunter, but how things have changed. Now it's hard to find large sections of land that aren't cut to ribbons by fire roads, rights of way, and thirty-feet-wide gas lines. The modern camp offers all the luxuries of home, and few hunters eat their lunch in the woods. When we come to grips with the matter, it's easy to see why I stress movement as a major factor in today's deer hunting.

The old rifles I just mentioned are fast slipping from the picture, but this is not to be construed that they are obsolete. Similar to the low RPM car engines of yesteryear, time and change are making some rifles antiquated. When I dropped a trotting buck this past season at over 230 yards, I used the long-range 7mm Remington Magnum cartridge in a No. 1 Ruger single shot. As much faith as I had

Don Lewis with his 7mm Magnum Ruger Number One rifle and a fine ten-point buck he took recently.

in the 30-30 170 grain for the 100-yard shot, I would have been over a foot low on the 230-yard shot.

I had the 7mm Magnum zeroed in two inches high at 100 yards which put the 140 grain slug right on the money at 240 yards. This same setting with the 30-30 170 grain bullet would have been roughly ten inches low at that distance. The difference is far more important than most hunters realize. With the 7mm Magnum's cartridge, I didn't lose a second figuring trajectory, nor did I have to

use any Kentucky windage to get the bullet on target. It was a simple matter of getting the best sight picture possible and squeezing off a well-aimed shot.

I relate two episodes only to show that serious thought should be given to the selection of a rifle for deer. Maybe there are those who feel I could wrap the whole affair up by just suggesting one of the more powerful Magnums since distance would never be a factor and killing power would be adequate for all shots. I could suggest this, but I'm not going to. I sin-

Don Lewis records data after each shot at his elaborate shooting range. He shoots from inside.

cerely believe that one of the problems of today's hunters is the power one. Power is uppermost in the modern hunter's mind, and it's doing more harm than good for most whitetail hunters. I don't want to defeat my argument against the 30-30 and its sister calibers, but power is not the only criterion for selecting the proper rifle.

Perhaps I'm one of the few gunwriters who ever talks about the psychological side of this subject. It seems evident most other writers feel every hunter is a he-man and should be capable of withstanding excessive recoil and noise without complaining. My belief is every hunter and his rifle should be compatible, not only in terms of power, but in a psychological sense, too.

I just don't happen to be in complete agreement with those who insist on measuring everything about a deer outfit in terms of cartridge size and super ballistics. For a score of years, I've sighted in rifles for hundreds of hunters from every walk of life. During this time, I have had the opportunity to watch most of these people shoot, and there's no getting around the fact that all of us have an inherent fear of recoil and noise. Dozens of times, men of all sizes have expressed a strong distaste for certain cartridges or rifle models due to recoil or high noise level.

I recall vividly a college halfback who thought nothing of carrying a ball at full gallop against a wall of monstrous linemen, but the new .300 Magnum he had used for three years without success was definitely the wrong cartridge. He freely admitted he was afraid, and I watched with amazement as he tried to fire a five shot group. When I saw him close his eyes before each shot, I knew why the group measured over seven inches at one hundred yards. Less than an hour later, he put five shots in two inches with a .270 Winchester; he left my shop a new hunter.

This is not an isolated case. Although we may not admit it, all of us tend to get set for the recoil of a rifle, and the larger the cartridge, the more we stiffen and brace. In fact, we concentrate so much in preparation for the backward jump of the rifle, we forget to aim and squeeze properly. The end result is poor shooting.

It may come as a genuine surprise for me to reveal that over the years I spent sighting in rifles as a profession, only a small percentage of Magnum owners would fire a group after I finished the initial firing. Some frankly admitted their fear, while others offered lame excuses. It all boiled down to a total dislike for getting belted with heavy recoil. The sad part of it was the new Magnum owner had not enhanced his chances for getting a deer by buying the big cartridge. In reality, the opposite was more likely.

More than once I suggested that a change to a less powerful rifle would be a wise move. To prove my point, I would use a .270 Winchester or a 6mm and have my customer shoot a group. Sometimes it took a few minutes for the shooter to overcome the built-in fear of recoil, but a few tips on how to shoot along with explaining that good shooting was far more important than sheer bullet power, usually did the trick. Most agreed the Magnum had been purchased with the belief it guaranteed instant success.

The shooter and the rifle should be compatible. When a shooter hesitates to practice because of recoil fear, the rifle is wrong, either because of its cartridge size or external design. The hunter going for Cape Buffalo must purchase a rifle to do the job—and is correct in doing so. But whitetail deer are not Cape Buffalo. The deer hunter must keep this in mind.

While we are prone to think in terms of cartridge power, the fact remains—bullet placement is even more important. This must not be construed to mean that I'm suggesting any cartridge is adequate. Not

at all! From my own personal experiences, no .224 bullet, regardless of the cartridge size, is suitable for deer. I have taken three deer with centerfire .224 cartridges. They did not make a believer out of me. Deer aren't the hardest game to bring down, but the bullet used should be sufficient in weight and construction to penetrate and still hang together.

The old belief that lightweight bullets suitable for varmint hunting have much thinner jackets than heavier bullets of the same manufacturer just isn't so. In other words, a 110 grain bullet's jacket is not

Don Lewis inspects an over and under shotgun with a wide variety of rifles shown in the background—his den.

very much thinner than a 180 grain bullet carrying the same company's name. The extra velocity of the lightweight bullet requires a fairly thick jacket to hold it intact.

I mentioned this only to show that good success can be had with bullets normally thought to be varmint types. The worn-out theory that all lightweight bullets explode immediately upon contact also is not true. I have recovered .220 Swift bullets from chucks and foxes on several occasions. These could be considered isolated cases, but it does show that not all lightweight bullets disintegrate upon contact.

It may seem defeating to my recoil argument, but the .224 bullet just doesn't have the stuff it takes to be a deer getter. It surely has the speed, but construction wise, it was never meant for heavy-boned animals. The framework of a deer is vastly different from a fox or woodchuck. The .224 doesn't have enough material and strength to penetrate.

Eliminating once and for all the .224 bullet as a deer slayer, the hunter still has a wide variety to choose from. The hunter should select a cartridge psychologically suitable to him and one that also will meet the needs of the terrain he hunts. Using the short range 30-30 in areas where very long shots are possible is not a step in the right direction. While today's trend is towards power, the Magnum is not always the answer. A cartridge in the category of the .270 or 30-06 is certainly

adequate, and the hunter will not be shooting a powerhouse that he dislikes.

Today there is much talk about an all-around rifle; one that is suitable for either varmints or big game. Winchester's .243 and Remington's 6mm held this questionable position during the last decade. Both are now being challenged by the Weatherby .240 Magnum, and Remington's 25-06. All of these calibers can fill the bill as an all-purpose rifle, but, to lay it right on the line, only the 25-06 comes close to being suited for the dual purpose.

Admirers of the 6mm's may have quit reading by now, and others who have taken deer with the calibers I just mentioned may think I've shot too many rifles. That isn't the case, and I think I can offer a reasonable explanation. The caliber is not the demon; it's the bullet. On larger game, the current run of store-bought 6mm bullets has some of the characteristics associated with the .224 speedsters. Primarily, it's the lack of weight with the 6mm slug. With 105 grains being top weight, the 6mm bullet runs into problems with quartering shots or ones that require deep penetration through heavy bone.

The 25-06 has a mild edge because it offers bullets up to 120 grains in weight—getting very close to the 130-grain .270 Winchester. Too many hunters are impressed with the speed of the 6mm's and 25-06's when they should be concerned with how the bullet will

STANDARD

DELUXE

The Ithaca LSA-55 is an excellent bolt action rifle, offered in several calibers tailor-made for deer hunting. The standard model has no frills, and as you will note in the photo, the deluxe version has several attractive additions.

Remington's Model 788 with scope is an effective deer-getter for those who prefer a bolt action rifle.

The Ithaca Model 51 Deerslayer is an excellent choice for the deer hunter who needs an auto-loading shotgun. It comes from the factory equipped with sights; a telescopic sight can also be added.

Remington's "Woodmaster" is an excellent choice for the hunter who prefers an automatic action.

STANDARD

DELUXE

The Ithaca Model 37 shotgun has long been popular in the various gauges with American scattergunners. But it is also available in the Deerslayer model for the deer hunter. It comes equipped with open sights, but scope mounts and telescopic sights can be added.

The Model 66 Buckbuster is Ithaca's answer when an inexpensive shotgun is necessary for deer hunting. It's a single shot, sports a hammer and rifle sights.

Remington also produces the Model 700 BDL in a left-handed version.

Remington's Model 700 BDL is a top choice among many deer hunters.

For the many hunters who prefer a slide action, Remington's model 760 is a favorite.

react. Naturally, any bullet including the light 45 grain .224 will make instant kills on neck or direct heart shots through the rib cage, and these same results can be expected from the 6mm and 25-06 slug. However, not every hunter has the time or opportunity to make placement shots. To boot, dense brush contributes to the failure of the high-speed, lightweight bullet.

I recall with a degree of disgust the only deer I shot while using the .22 Hornet. My first shot hit the neck of a standing deer less than 150 yards away, but failed to down him. Later, as the deer ran up a hill, I hit it in the hip and rib cage. I was completely unaware any bullet had landed. Since my first shot hit the jugular vein, I finally tracked down the deer, but I promised myself not to expect a medium powered varmint rifle to do a deer rifle's job.

Any of the three shots from a conventional deer rifle would have dropped the buck within a few yards, instead of a half mile. I suspect even the 6mm's or the 25-06 would have given superior results. The deer I took with the .222 and .220 Swift were shot in fatal areas that the lightweight bullets could handle.

I am not trying to be overly critical of the 6mm's, for I am well aware that literally thousands are used successfully every year, and their popularity is not diminishing. My concern is with the bullet. A close friend of mine who took six deer with a .243 Winchester told me not one was an instant kill. He finally changed calibers because he felt the 6mm 105 grain bullet was too light.

I know from past writing on this subject that plenty of hunters will disagree with my feelings, but from penetration tests with the 6mm bullet, I have reached this conclusion: expecting a bullet primarily designed for very small boned animals to be classified a top deer-getter is just asking too much. My critics point to the hundreds of deer taken with the 6mm bullet, but this is not sufficient proof. A bullet primarily designed for deer does not have to have ideal conditions to make a clean kill, and this is not the case with the 6mm.

Although the 6mm and .257 bullets are superior to the .224's, I have always felt the 6.5, .284, and .308 bullets stand head and shoulders above the smaller diameters in the deer-hunting realm. I may be rubbing many hunters the wrong way when I put the .257 bullet in the same class with the .243, but this is not to be construed that I feel the 6mm and .257 bullets won't kill. It's just that I'm convinced they lack the essentials on game the size of a white-tailed deer.

With other writers handling ballistics and technical data, I won't get involved in this. I'll just stick to my theory; the smaller bullet diameters will not compare with the larger ones. No one is more aware how the light recoil of the .243 and 6mm appeals to hundreds of shooters, but after years of helping others learn to shoot, I must advise deer hunters to use calibers and cartridges with enough power for any shooting situation.

Taking a practical look at a deer outfit involves more than just caliber. The type of action many times spells the difference between success and failure. For many years, the southpaw shooter was forced to accept the lever or pump. To show this was not what many of these shooters wanted, bolt actions were used in spite of the fact that the shooter was slowed down considerably. Today, that situation does not exist. Left-hand bolt action rifles are produced by several manufacturers, and the hunter shooting from the south side has the opportunity to have what he wants.

Since I'm pressing hard on the practical and psychological factors in choosing a whitetail outfit, I have to point out it's the little, incidental features that should get more consideration.

During the Depression years, a rifle was used whether it was practical or not, and the psychological side wasn't even considered. This old philosophy is still retained, and many feel a rifle is a rifle. If the cartridge falls in the deer-getter class, use it. This antiquated thinking keeps plenty of hunters from being successful. I know this from first-hand experience in running a gunshop for years. All the persuasive arguments I could muster failed to change some minds. The wife or kid brother was forced to carry an ex-military 8mm or .348 Winchester when a 30-30 would have been a far wiser choice.

I vividly recall a professional man who

Author Don Lewis attaches a drag rope and starts pulling a fine buck from the Pennsylvania deer woods.

brought a .300 H & H Magnum for me to zero in. The rifle was not far off, and a few minor scope adjustments put the bullet in a three-inch bull's eye at one hundred yards, and I complimented the owner for having such a fine rifle. As usual, I offered the customer a chance to check my work, but I got the surprise of my life when this gentleman absolutely refused lock, stock, and barrel. He frankly admitted the .300 H & H cartridge was too much for him, and was in fact, destroying his desire to hunt.

I realized the man was being forced to hunt with the Magnum because he was large in stature, and a smaller caliber probably made him the butt of the camp jokes. As I learned this during our conversation, I pointed out that size had nothing to do with the choice of a rifle—at least not the cartridge. My argument gained ground after he fired a three-inch group with a 30-06. He was elated over his shooting the '06 and asked to fire another group.

This went on for several more groups as I convinced him that the '06 was not a beast, but certainly was more than adequate for all types of deer hunting. The recoil of the .300 Magnum was so ingrained in this man, that it took constant instruction from me to keep him from yanking on the trigger.

During the years I have been sighting in all types of rifles, I have run across similar situations many times. Some I failed to convince, but happily, I got my message home to hundreds that there is a practical and psychological approach to selecting the proper deer outfit. This man was just one of many who listened to sound advice and profited from it.

Deer outfits are usually thought of in terms of rifles, but there are many areas where the long-range rifle is banned and hunting is done with shotgun slugs or buckshot. Most rifle hunters are prone to think the shotgun slug is inaccurate, low in power, and not dependable. I thought the same way until a few years back when I conducted a series of comprehensive tests with both the slug and buckshot.

My beliefs stemmed from the "punkin" ball days when the hunter was lucky to get the round ball out of the barrel, let alone hit a deer seventy-five yards away.

My late brother, Fred, shot at a buck five times at close range with a 16 gauge. Two shots missed, and two penetrated less than three inches. The last shot landed in the neck, bringing down the deer. At forty-five yards, the 16 gauge literally threw the round ball with no semblance of accuracy.

Plenty of deer during the gas light era fell to the old "punkin" ball, but mostly by luck and not good shooting. I won't discredit the hunter of that day, but the "punkin" ball had little to offer. I will say that if everything went according to schedule, the round ounce of lead could be a bugger and hit harder than most regular deer rifles. There were no guarantees, and the hunter never was sure where his next shot would land. Sometimes it was right on the button, but many times the round ball tore up the snow a dozen yards from the shotgun.

The modern rifled slug has changed all this. It's accurate and dependable. I found this out when I fired four hundred rounds through my chronograph screens for velocity tests and on the fifty yard range for accuracy. I used Remington's 870 pump, Ithaca's 900 Semi and Model 37 pump, and Mossberg's 500 ARK pump. All four shotguns were designed for slug shooting with the short, unchoked barrel. The more I shot, the more respect I began to generate for today's slug.

I was impressed with the first five through the chronograph screens that showed the big slug traveling faster than a 22 long rifle bullet. With several brands of factory fodder and some of my handloads with the famous Breneke slug, I topped 1,400 fps at fifteen feet in front of the muzzle. I consider that moving for a big slug. Unfortunately, speed is of little consequence if accuracy is absent, and here again, I was educated.

I drilled and tapped the top of the Remington 870 and mounted a Weaver Classic 2 x 7 Variable scope. All of the shotguns tested come equipped with open sights, but a scope takes the guesswork out of aiming. Being a realist, I was willing to settle for groups at fifty yards averaging under five inches. When the scoped Remington began cutting consistent 3-inch groups and one 2-inch group, I knew the modern shotgun slug was adequate for whitetails.

Even with the open sights, I had little trouble staying under five inches at fifty yards and had some five-shot groups touching the three-inch class. With this accuracy, no hunter should be overly concerned about the shotgun designed to handle slugs. Combining the slug's weight and the potential velocity, there has to be power. My penetration tests on four-inch square blocks of green oak at fifty yards satisfied me that the modern shotgun slug has sufficient killing power. I restricted my shooting to fifty yards, knowing that most shots at game would be near that range, and I suggest keeping all shots under seventy-five.

Before any longtime slug user accuses me of putting a seventy-five-yard limit on the slug's effective killing range, let me explain that I'm more concerned with accuracy than power. I feel that at seventy-five yards the slug is accurate, and I'm dead set against pushing any bullet to its limits just because it retains enough power to kill. With the shotgun, seventy-five yards is a long shot, and to try for longer distances with the slug is unreasonable.

Most of my shooting was done with shotguns designed in barrel length and choke for the slug, but the rounds I fired from conventional shotguns led me to believe that the hunter has a better than average chance up to seventy-five yards with any shotgun. If you are hunting constantly in an area where only slugs are permitted, the regular slug gun should be used. It's more compact and has open sights.

As for the scope, I think it's just as important on a shotgun for deer as on a rifle. Open sights are fine, but no hunter can shoot any better than he can see. Why squint hard through a set of open sights when the scope offers a clear, well-defined picture of the target?

I want to retain my rifle for deer hunting, but if legislation permitted only shotguns, I would not quit hunting. I would always be aware of the slug's limitations, and I would make every effort to get close. But I would never feel undergunned or underpowered.

Buckshot is a different matter. I must be careful with my evaluation since I have never shot any big game with buckshot. Since there are areas where only buckshot is permitted, I ran some tests to satisfy my own curiosity. I can't say my results impressed me, but, as with the shotgun slug, I wouldn't stop chasing whitetails if buckshot was the order of the day. I would be far more cautious with buckshot than the slug, and I would limit any shot to under forty yards!

You don't have a wide selection of buckshot sizes. The smallest is No. 4 (twice the size of a regular No. 5 shot), then comes Nos. 3, 1, 0 and 00. The 00 is ⅓ inch in diameter and weighs about 55 grains. Down South all sizes of buckshot are used for deer, but 0 and 00 are the most popular. The 00 has nine balls in a regular 12-gauge shell, twelve in the 2¾ inch Magnum, and fifteen in the 3 inch Magnum. Buckshot is available in other gauges, but due to the smaller cases the smaller shot sizes are used, so they are much less effective. Personally, I can't recommend them.

I won't get involved with all the results from my buckshot shooting tests, but I learned some of the tales about buckshot are pure myths. I found great inconsistency in the grouping of buckshot. I had read that seven out of nine balls could be counted on to stay in a 40-inch circle at fifty yards with 00, but my shooting indicated this to be more fiction than fact. I did fire one shot at fifty yards that put all twelve balls in a 15-inch circle. If this would have been a deer or the only shot fired, I would probably sing the praises of buckshot for years to come.

Buckshot is just like regular shot; it

Don Lewis and his brother-in-law, C. J. Clawson, talk whitetail outfits in the Lewis livingroom.

Tom Hooks, one of Don Lewis' good friends, shows off a fine whitetail buck that he took recently. Tom is a disabled Koren War veteran who can't walk. But since being discharged, he has bagged sixteen whitetails! Tom loves the outdoors and is a persevering guy.

Don Lewis and compatriot hunter Ray Johns combine forces to drag a whitetail from the woods.

Don's wife, Helen Lewis, is also an experienced and expert shot. She does most of Don's photography, and is shown here sighting in a rifle at Don's inside bench rest.

can't be guided to a given area. I found out that when a load of buckshot of any size is cut loose there is no assurance that even one ball will hit the aiming area. Allowing for the probability that some of the balls will be inside a twelve-inch area at average range is still no guarantee that one or more will strike a vital spot.

Some buckshot users argue that since each 00 buckshot is larger and heavier than a 22 long-rifle bullet, hitting a deer with three or four equals hitting with the same number of 22 long-rifle bullets. Not so. It's true the 00 buckshot ball is larger and heavier, but it can't replace the rifle's precision.

Effective killing range of the 00 buck-shot should be limited to no more than forty yards, and then only under ideal conditions. I've always felt a rifle bullet producing about 1,300 foot-pounds of energy at one hundred yards was ade-quate for deer hunting. A 00 ball pro-duces a mere 145 foot-pounds at fifty, and thus it would take nine hits in a fatal area to meet this requirement. Quite unlikely. Restrict your buckshot range to forty yards.

Getting the right deer-hunting outfit isn't a matter to be taken lightly. From what I've seen over the past thirty years, I know too many hunters have not given proper consideration to this matter. The simple fact that hundreds of hunters come home empty-handed with nothing but excuses is ample proof that something is wrong somewhere. Although most gun-writers keep pounding away on ballistics, bullet trajectory, and kinetic energy plus other ambiguous terms, the truth is that any rifle from the 6mm's up will do the job if the hunter does his.

There's more to a deer outfit than just the size and weight of the bullet. The hunter should choose his rifle with the same degree of concern with which he invests his money in a car or home. Whether it sounds reasonable or not, there is a psychological aspect to the deer-outfit bit, and if more hunters considered this, along with taking advantage of the rifle scope, success would be enjoyed instead of alibis being required.

Total power can be had in the mighty Magnums, but not total success. The hunter and his rifle must be compatible in every respect. The rifle that remains unfired from season to season due to size of cartridge, amount of recoil, or type of action is the wrong one. That particular gun owner should get rid of it in a hurry. In fact, the quicker the better.

Next hunting season will find thousands of hunters with rifles that should have been retired or replaced. Most of these fellows or gals will come home empty-handed, and they have no one to blame but themselves. Applying some common sense, along with a bit of psychology, would have put a new or different rifle in their lives and a different ending to their years of deer hunting frustration. The right rifle with a good scope enhances any hunter's chances. It's really true—there is a psychological approach to choosing whitetail outfits.

George Mattis is one of the few outdoor writers who spends twelve months of the year in the outdoors as a hunter, angler, naturalist, and wildlife photographer. He has studied the whitetail throughout its wide range, and he is in especially close contact with this game animal in the upper Great Lakes area. He is author of the popular outdoor book *Whitetail, Fundamentals and Fine Points For The Hunter,* which reflects some forty years of observing the adaptable whitetail.

Mattis resides in Birchwood, Wisconsin, and is a free-lance outdoor writer. His favorite outdoor subjects are the whitetail and stream angling for trout. Because of his dedication to the outdoors and his love for the unspoiled wilderness, his writings reflect much of the naturalist in him. Searching for and photographing rare orchids in the cold bogs, studying a remote bald eagle aerie, visiting the whitetails' winter quarters, and similar outdoor ventures occupy his time when he is not hunting, fishing, or writing. He studied journalism at the University of Wisconsin.

4

SOLO HUNTING THE WHITETAIL

George Mattis

I KNOW A few whitetail hunters who score with a buck nearly every season. You don't hear much about them, since they are unattached to any hunting group. Consequently, few can proclaim their success. The fact that they go afield alone year after year indicates they are satisfied with their solitary role. You can call these solo hunters loners or even downright antisocials, but you have to admit they have something going for them which they are not anxious to share with the vast army of whitetail hunters.

A successful hunter exposes himself to good deer country under ideal conditions for the longest possible period of time. An inexperienced man might hunt good deer country for the full season, but without the advantage of ideal conditions he may never get seriously involved in the chase.

Restless legs and anxious heart are not the attributes of the good trail watcher or the top still hunter, and very often a man learns this fact only after many years of hunting have slowed him down. He then realizes his best chances come when he waits to be intercepted by the deer rather than when he tries to come upon his unsuspecting quarry.

All any hunter has to do to prove this point is to recall how he came by his deer kills. Chances are he paused near a deer trail to eat a candy bar or a sandwich. Maybe he rested a bit atop a hill after he labored up the long incline, from which point he had a good view of the valley below. Or, if the day was very warm, maybe he sat completely relaxed with his back resting against a tree trunk. Here, from a sunny vantage spot, he drowsily, and perhaps unwittingly, submitted to his most productive hunting hours of the season.

The buck came into view. He was naturally cautious but quite composed, and the relaxed hunter took him easily. The happy redcoat might call this a fluke kill or a fortunate turn of chance. But there is room for argument. I recall many of my buck kills have been made during such idle breaks in my hunt. If all deer were bagged by plan and sheer determination only, the sport of hunting would not attract the horde of followers it does.

Whoever is idle or resting, the hunter or deer, is the one that has full possession of his senses. It is the moving hunter or deer that is readily seen or heard by the other. If the hunter remembers this basic fact, he can expect to see more whitetails, especially bucks, for the good, clean shots that count.

The man on the move necessarily yields some of his time and attention to picking his route of travel. His eyes are not always free to survey the circumference about him. And the lesser noises of forest creatures can be entirely lost because of the walking noises the hunter makes.

Contrast this with the man on a stand overlooking considerable good-looking deer country. He can detect the movement of a fluttering chickadee a great distance off, and his ears can catch the faintest noises of all forest creatures. It is while he is standing that the hunter learns that a buck can loom into view with scarcely an audible sound, while the

Author pauses in his still hunt for good view of valley below.

measured cadence of a moving hunter can be heard and recognized from a great distance.

If the whitetail is elusive, it is because he spends much of his time at complete rest. Even when the animal is afoot and feeding, it cautiously divides its time between mouthing its browse and pausing in utter silence to test the area for trespassers that might invade its seclusion. This is the usual situation that confronts the redcoat trying to outwit his

56

quarry. That's why the odds are not in the whitetail hunter's favor.

There was a time some decades past, when a flushed whitetail evacuated his bailiwick in complete abandon, hastily seeking the security of some more remote area. Now, with more hunters afield and less back country into which deer can escape, these adaptable critters have learned to tolerate the proximity of hunters. No longer do the deer run any great distance, risking the chances of exposing themselves to hunters strung freely along their escape route. The modern whitetail is the progeny of those animals that have learned to accept an environment of hunters on every side.

Since it is his stomach that determines the range of the whitetail, the solo hunter need not spend his time in large tracts of land where deer browse is scarce, however remote they may be. The whitetail belongs to the edge country and is not a creature of heavy timber or even young tree growth if the forest floor is devoid of short shrubbery suitable for food. The once popular clamor to hunt the back country is now largely an echo of the past. Today's redcoat seeks his whitetail on its home grounds, and this is often near or even in populated areas.

Certainly the edge of farm fields, brushy or semi-open country, recently logged-off tracts, abandoned marginal farm lands, and odd wooded pockets, as along streams or rivers, are the home of today's whitetail. The remote back country of heavy timber with little or no undergrowth is at best only a temporary retreat for the hunted animals.

Deer do not travel far when not molested. Even when driven from their home grounds they usually filter back the following night. It is the common experience of many hunters returning from a day afield to see deer slink across the road to enter an area that had been heavily driven earlier in the day. Even a wily and seasoned old stag, however often started, will never completely evacuate his bailiwick, though he might retire for the remainder of the hunting season to some odd pocket nearby where he is bypassed by the regimented hunters with their routine patterns of hunting.

Author skirting edge of tree plantation, always a favorite hideout for whitetails.

When hunters are astir, author prefers to take comfortable seat at edge of woods clearing.

The daily habits of deer are quite routine. Any trails they make are usually between their feeding areas and their bedding grounds. It is these trails that the successful hunter seeks to intercept, not some well defined but presently unused runway, as found in the animals' winter quarters. I have seen many instances of a man watching hopefully over a backwoods deer trail that had not registered fresh sign all season.

There are more deer killed on or at the edge of a thicket, borders of farm hay fields, or woods clearings than are taken in what most redcoats consider ideal whitetail habitat. In fact, many men I know spend much of their efforts throughout the season alternately standing along or footing the wooded or brushy perimeter of a field in which deer have been feeding during the summer and fall.

The whitetail is not adverse to bedding down or resting in the immediate proximity of his feeding grounds, and during the initial morning of the season he can be expected to continue his normal living routine. If the area is not heavily hunted or if there are a few days with a lull in the hunting pressure, the deer are quick to return to their former living pattern. If

GEORGE MATTIS

they have been actively feeding in a field during late fall they might continue doing so, but to a lesser extent as the season progresses. Many times, returning from a hunt at sundown, I've seen deer that had been driven unsuccessfully by several gangs during the day feeding at the far end of an alfalfa field adjacent to brush country.

The point is, the best place for the solo hunter is still the immediate area of the deer's feeding grounds. The animals will continually cling close to the habitat that is the source of their food. Only a fall of heavy snow with accompanying severe weather will cause them to abandon their usual stomping grounds. Then they retire to the protection their normal winter quarters offer.

There's no better place for the lone hunter than a stand watch at some wooded or brushy point that projects into a field. Whitetails have little fear in idling across a large field where they have unobstructed and distant vision to all sides. Often, the only animals seen by some hunters during the entire season are those deer crossing a field to re-enter the home grounds from which they were driven. As the whitetails approach the edge of a large clearing, whether entering it or leaving it, they are likely to follow a projecting point or arm of growth that offers them some scant tree cover while making the sharp transition in the terrain.

Another favorite stand of mine is a high point several hundred yards from the field that overlooks considerable area crossed

Author with buck taken from stand near farm field. (1971)

with trails leading to the feeding grounds. Deer could be bedded down in the environs of the cover here, and there are always those restless hunters afoot to drive for you. Even with no one about to beat the brush, there is the good possibility of deer moving about on their own in a habitat where feeding and bedding sites are in such close proximity.

The very knowledge of this fact bolsters the hunter's confidence in his stand, and confidence in one's stand is a chief ingredient of the trail watcher's success. As soon as one has many small doubts about his choice of stand, he is likely to wander off in search of something better—just over the next hill. He finds nothing better there, and consequently keeps walking aimlessly. Then he becomes a member of that restless army of hunters who continually keep the whitetails on the move for the determined standers.

The very best times for trail-watching in the vicinity of a field are the early mornings and the closing hours of the day. If one approaches his stand with utmost care, any whitetails in the immediate environs soon dismiss what noises are made by the hunter's intrusion. When less cautious men enter the grounds later in the day, the resourceful man, well settled on his stand, has everything going for him.

The waning hours of the day are especially favored because the deer shunted about during the day are likely to return to their home base again. Most hunters leave the woods when trail watching becomes most effective. Whitetails are prone to move on their own when hunters evacuate their sanctuary. Several of my biggest bucks were taken from stands when I was the sole hunter in the area.

There are other places of deer concentration, due to food abundance, where the unattached hunter can fare very well. A recently logged-over timber tract, whether easily accessible or set back, attracts the food-searching whitetail. Tender new shoots springing up after a recent cutting are the natural food for whitetails when fall's grasses are sere or blanketed with snow. In addition to new growth browse, the maze of treetops left in the wake of the loggers provides ideal cover.

The man seeking to get away from the horde of hunters will often find isolation in this jungle of woody debris. Here he will want a well-chosen stand, perhaps on a hillside, one that will give him considerable visual coverage from above. A view from low ground is not usually conducive to good hunting. While still-hunting a logged-over area a man could brush past a large fallen treetop and not see the feeding or bedded deer on the far side. And a whitetail, in making its escape, instinctively keeps this screen between itself and the intruder. Foot the ridges or the higher ground wherever possible.

If the logged country is not under much hunting pressure, the stander can expect to see the whitetails move about and feed on their own in the security of this tangled growth. This is especially so in the mornings and evenings, and even more probable during a slight drizzle or the start of a substantial snowfall.

There is always the hope that some restless hunter will stir about and start a bedded deer. The patient stander has all the odds over the man pushing through the jumbled mixture of young shoots and dead branches. I once took a fine ten-point buck in such a situation, when a hunter hurried through the tangle to join his group that was sounding the car horn to assemble the men at the road. The stray hunter walked noisily, and as he loomed into view over a slight rise to my

Patience on a stand results in easy, clean shot of fine buck taken by author some years back.

concentrated nutrition in acorns and beechnuts. Where this crop is abundant you can be sure that stags will move in on the nut-producing groves. Since the animals seldom feed here in broad daylight and are not likely to bed down on the barren floor of a woods, the hunter will do best by taking a stand nearby, where he can cover a broad area in his surveillance.

Any scraggly growth on a hillside or in some odd pocket could be the bed sites of deer. Novice hunters who roam the woods might pause to study the pawed leaves under the oaks, but they soon move on to hunt the thickets for the animals now retired to rest. The man who can watch over a large expanse of country near the oak grove is playing the big odds.

Any deer stand should give one a good view of as large an area as possible. If one commands a view of under one hundred yards across, it is entirely possible a noiseless, running deer could be out of sight before the hunter is in position to shoot. There is tremendous advantage in being forewarned of any approaching quarry. The hunter can shift to a comfortable stance and bring up his gun in ample time to follow the animal in its progress; if a buck only is his target, he has time to study the animals for antlers, and this is important where only bucks, including spikes, are legal game.

If the hunter is determined to stick to his stand for the entire day, he had best dress on the heavy side, even on the warmer days. When he is even slightly chilled from inactivity, he will move

front, he started the buck and doe that were bedded down some two hundred yards from me.

A very good time to hunt the slashings is after a heavy snowfall has covered grasses and short browse of the fields and edge country. The deer's range is much more limited now, and the knowledgeable hunter has a better chance of bagging his quarry under these circumstances. Where cover and browse are available together, the animals need not roam far to satisfy their needs. Again, it is the patient watcher and not the man pushing through the area that has the advantage.

Big bucks, especially, are fond of the

Whitetails often seek the cover of small, neglected woodlots to escape hunting pressure.

about to regain the warmth afforded by better blood circulation. The far-sighted whitetail can detect movement from a great distance, and the watcher is losing the advantage he seeks to gain.

I recall well the several instances when my movements on a stand caused oncoming whitetails to stop short in their tracks and veer to the side and out of my range. A hunter would be surprised to know how many bucks he never sees, but that are alerted of his presence by simple movements.

When one plans on a long stay at his stand he will want a comfortable seat, perhaps the base of a tree trunk for back support; yet the spot should be such that he has unobstructed views to the sides. For necessary comfort, the feet should be resting at least a few inches below one's seat, otherwise an unnatural and cramped sitting position results in the hunter shifting about to relieve his tiring legs.

It is the sharp outline of the man that catches the eye of the whitetail. Certainly the well defined shape of a hunter standing or sitting against an unbroken background like snow or sky will not go unnoticed by a passing deer. The animal might not always flee in such a case, but it will become so cautious that the redcoat cannot afford to make even the slightest movement.

This problem can be overcome easily if the hunter rests comfortably against a tree or stump, or else has a thicket to his immediate back with a few scattered

George Mattis

shrubs to his front. On some of my poorly chosen stands I have had suspicious whitetails look me over so thoroughly that I could not make the movement to raise my gun without putting the fidgety animals to flight. And again, when I had my back against a fire-charred tree trunk for perfect camouflage, I have had the animals bypass me on either side without giving me more than a casual glance, so completely were they unaware of my presence.

Sometimes, in extremely cold weather, I find it necessary to walk a bit despite my heavy attire. Then, I make the best of the compromise by patrolling between two stands sufficiently far enough apart so that the walk will restore my circulation and warmth. What few hunters are afield on such days will be dressed lighter than I. These cold individuals will be constantly on the move, and they will walk with quick and determined strides, more intent on keeping warm than stalking the whitetail.

Any deer taken on a very cold day is usually bagged by the stander and not by the man stirring around in the crisp, clean air that whets the whitetail's senses of smell, hearing, and vision.

Still-hunting, like-trail watching, belongs to the man who likes to hunt alone. If properly conducted, it retains many advantages of trail-watching. Here the solo hunter moves slowly and noiselessly from vantage point to vantage point, covering a vastly larger area than he could command from a single stand.

Unfortunately, not every day of the deer season is conducive to still-hunting, and there are seasons when only a few days or parts of days lend themselves to this specialty. Too often, a man attempts still-hunting under adverse weather conditions or under other situations that lend themselves best to trail-watching.

The warm, calm day is what the still hunter wants, and the footing should be damp and noiseless. A slight drizzle or a gentle snowfall is most encouraging, for this dulls the senses in the normally alert whitetail. Also, the animals are usually afoot and feeding when they are in this relaxed mood, and the hunter's eyes can readily catch their movements. The animals, busy with their browsing, can be approached much more easily than the bedded or resting deer.

Another consideration for the still hunter is the amount of other hunters stirring about the area he plans to cover. The still hunter prefers to have the grounds to himself, for the deer are then least edgy, and they might even be disposed to feeding during midday. It is the composed animal in its normal routine of daily living that the hunter hopes to surprise.

The occasion for a still hunt can arise most any time during the day if weather conditions take a sudden favorable turn. I never fail to take advantage of the situation, for the ideal prospects for slowly and silently footing the ridges comes all too infrequently.

The good still-hunter can pride himself

The ideal hunting grounds for the solo hunter. Whitetails have been feeding in the slashings, and they are still confined to the area.

in being able to approach his quarry at close range for a standing, clean kill. There is no great achievement or virtue in hitting a running deer by firing a barrage of quick shots at a fleeing animal. Such over-anxious shooting too often results in needless wounding and consequent loss of our big game animals.

The solo hunter, because he is not attached to any group, can be extremely versatile in his hunting. He is free to enter the small nooks that are naturally bypassed by gang hunters, and he is at liberty to change his hunting methods and grounds whenever conditions warrant.

Whitetails, if shunted from their sanc-tuary often enough, will retire to odd pockets where they might remain for several days. This is especially true of a seasoned, old sire that has experienced a few tight squeezes evading redcoats. The lone hunter will find it most fruitful to probe these lesser spots, for he can be sure the animals have evacuated the big, heavily hunted country to find refuge in the immediate fringe areas. Fortified with this heartening knowledge, the hunter willingly puts careful and determined effort into these short probes.

When one still-hunts, he is pitting his senses against those of his quarry. If he is to succeed, he will have to make use of

64

every advantage available to him in order to overcome the superior senses in his game.

If one moves slowly with studied step and brief pause, his movements are not easily detected by the farsighted whitetail. The quick movement of any body part is what catches the eye of the deer. Any pause of duration should be made against an available tree trunk to help break up the body's outline.

The man plans his hunt so that he moves into the wind whenever possible. It is the odor of the energetic man's perspiration that registers strongly on the whitetail's keen and sensitive nostrils. This is another reason for moving at a pace so slow that it does not bring on even a hint of perspiration. Another good point to remember is that clean clothing is most important to the still hunter. Old clothes saturated with human odor are a great handicap to the man hoping to outwit the keen-nosed whitetail.

It is the man's eyes that do most of the hunting. He walks the higher terrain, studying the grounds to all sides for the slightest movement or shape that could suggest the presence of his game.

The alert solo hunter, being resourceful, is quick to appraise a situation and make the best of it. If he finds deer sign scarce along his route, he will naturally move a bit faster. But when he is confronted with fresh sign, either in snow or soft soil, he will put full effort into his stalk. If the deer slots indicate his game is

idling about feeding, the hunter pauses after each step, probing the area. The animals could be afoot, in which case a moving twig in the thicket could reveal their presence.

This is the time to take advantage of any slight elevation in order to survey the environs. Even a deer in its bed can be spotted by moving ears or the straight line formed by its back. Many times I have surprised a resting whitetail at such close range that the animal chose to remain in its bed, hoping to get by undetected rather than risk an attempted escape.

The hunter who walks through these

The crisp outline of a buck is easily discerned in the whiteness of freshly fallen snow.

grounds rather hastily might flush deer without seeing anything more than a flickering flag in the distance. And, unfortunately, the deer leaves the better country to enter grounds that might be less worthy of the hunter's time. The lone redcoat must remember to concentrate his best efforts in those spots and instances where he is reasonably sure the animals are present.

Big bucks are not easily taken in drives because they have long learned to escape the squeeze play. Nor do they take to reckless flight for any great distance. Experience has taught them that deliberate evasion is better than fleeing in total abandon. The mature sires live because they do not expose themselves to the numerous hunters afield. Often these stags live in a very limited area, and here is where the patient still-hunter comes into his own.

Buck rubs and scrapings or pawings can indicate the size of the animals that made them. A large and well rubbed shrub or tree of two inches or more in diameter is made by a male carrying a respectable rack. Any dirt scrapings or pawings show imprints of the animal's hoofs. Remember, these could be of the buck that made the pawing or a doe that visited the spot later.

Certainly the man who hunts alone can go all out in an attempt to bag a specific animal when he finds evidence his quarry is a fine buck carrying a trophy rack. Usually, if the rut is still on, the buck is

within several hundred yards of a concentration of rubs and scrapes.

The still hunter can do no better than loiter in the established bailiwick of a big buck, covering it conscientiously so that he gets some picture of the animal's daily habits. He might locate the stag's bedding area and his browsing grounds. The animal will likely be somewhere in between the two points, bedded down during much of the day and browsing both mornings and evenings.

During any gently falling rain or snow, whitetails could be astir and busily feeding. At times like this they can be quite composed, and, in fact, spiritless to the point where they might show more curiosity than fear at the intrusion of a hunter on their grounds. The determined man will dress comfortably for the occasion and put in his best efforts—when they count most.

Another good situation for the still hunter is the morning after a snowfall which has ceased sometime during the very early hours. If the snow is soft and several inches in depth and there is little or no wind, the whitetails will probably be browsing during the early daylight hours.

Nothing gladdens the heart of a hunter more than finding fresh deer tracks weaving through a thicket. The animals are either still browsing or else bedded down in the vicinity. Usually, while feeding, they move generally into the wind so the stalker's scent becomes no problem. Also, a browsing deer does not hear as well when it is nibbling twigs as when it is at complete rest. And certainly a soft layer of damp snow does much to muffle the measured walking sounds of the stalker.

The hunter now has only the whitetail's sense of sight to lick, and this he can cope with by reducing his pace to slow steps, followed by long pauses. His attention should be mostly on locating his quarry; only an occasional glance at the deer tracks is necessary to assure him he has not strayed off the course of the animals.

The dark, smooth coat of a deer with its sharp outline makes a bold contrast against the pure white of freshly fallen snow. With little experience the hunter learns to spot his game though it might be half screened by brush. Even the mere head or the dark back of a deer bedded in deep snow stands out in crisp detail. It is a fact that whitetails are not overly fearful of a man if they see him without smelling or hearing him. This is the case when one sees a deer standing far out in a field or when it pauses out of shooting range while making a road crossing.

The hunter must respond to all possibilities that are to his advantage. If, for instance, while he is footing a ridge that commands a good view of a valley, he sees another man in the distance entering this lowland thicket, he should avail himself of this unwitting driver and pause at a strategic stand.

When a lone man walks quietly through deer country, any animals he starts will normally retire slowly from his route of travel. They are not as alarmed now as when they are forced into flight by a gang of noisy drivers. Consequently, the whitetail moving aside to let a lone red-coat by makes an easy target for the still hunter who intercepts the animal at a stand.

The same can be said when one hears considerable shooting a mile or less to one's side or front, indicating other hunters are moving game. By the time any deer reach the still hunter, they are alternately walking and pausing, perhaps glancing over their shoulders in the direction of the country from which they have just been driven.

Though many men might pause at a vantage point in such a situation, few wait long enough to have the deer intercept them. The startled animals might leave in full flight, but they soon slow down to a trot, then a walk, and finally reach the point where they regain their composure and settle down to idling about and perhaps partaking of browse.

One of my favorite hunting grounds after the deer season is in full swing is any semi-wooded pasture land devoid of cattle. As the hunting season progresses and the deer have been harassed for some time, the big bucks, especially, like to retreat to such neglected refuges, at least for the day, where they are seldom bothered. If the pasture land is hilly, this makes the ideal sanctuary for a big sire who likes to

An innocent whitetail fawn that has not yet learned to fear man.

bed down on a hillside to survey the semi-open country below him.

Once resting here the whitetails seem far less edgy than they would be in the adjacent deer country from which they have just been driven. In several instances, as I drove down roads that separated fenced-in pasture lands from wilderness deer country, I've seen whitetails bedded down on hillsides far back in the pasture.

The couchant stags, watching me from a safe distance, invariably stayed put as long as I remained at the roadside and posed no threat to their safety. Any buck I might have seen in a similar situation across the road from the cattle grazing land would have left his bed and fled over the ridge as soon as I spotted him.

It is surprising how closely one can approach a whitetail on grounds where the animals are seldom molested. I have stalked deer in their beds to within shooting range if I made an indirect approach to them as though I were merely passing through the area. One can walk almost noiselessly on the short cropped grass of a pasture, and this is most helpful in the stalk.

When whitetails are not flighty, as in this case, one can appraise a situation and plan a stalk, knowing that the game will remain as long as one does not frighten it with a direct and threatening approach.

GEORGE MATTIS

Some of my easiest buck kills were made through well planned and careful stalks of deer I saw bedded down in full view on a hillside. Such animals, feeling at ease in their accepted security, watch hunters in the distance with no more than passive interest.

These deer can be approached from the back side quite easily as long as the hunter knows their exact positions. This is in considerable contrast to the hunter hoping to walk within good shooting range of a deer by mere chance. One always stalks best when he knows the exact location of his game, for he can move with a screen of protective shrubbery between him and his quarry.

There are other possibilities that challenge the patience and resourcefulness of the solo hunter. The environs of an old apple orchard or the wild, overgrown abandoned farmstead will often harbor deer. Odd woodlots and small wasteland acreages are normally overlooked by most redcoats. No deer habitat is too small for the lone hunter's consideration. He hunts where his chances are best, and they are not necessarily best in the big country.

The science of still-hunting is being somewhat neglected today because of the trend of sociability in all our outdoor recreations. But the camaraderie of gang hunting is often maintained at the cost of the success of the individual; and the hunting pattern of the group becomes something of a standard ritual from which no single member must depart. Consequently the routine hunt goes on day after day with little regard to weather conditions or any other situations that might suggest a needed change in hunting plans.

In contrast is the flexibility of the solo hunter who plans his hunt from day to day and even from hour to hour to take advantage of weather change, deer movement, or hunter concentration on his hunting grounds.

If the solo hunter scores better, it is because he hunts better.

Dick Dietz began his writing career at the age of fifteen as sports editor of a weekly newspaper. He bagged his first buck the same year and has been hunting and writing both as a hobby and profession ever since. For the past seven years he has been a member of the Remington Arms Company public relations staff, and his pieces on wildlife and hunting in the *Remington News Letter* have made him one of the most widely read writers on these topics in the United States. In addition, he is a free-lance contributor to a wide variety of outdoor publications.

His wildlife background comes from a lifetime spent outdoors and almost daily contact with game department officials and outdoorsmen throughout the country. "New England is my special hobby, though," he admits, "and I'm interested in any part of it that isn't under a roof or covered with concrete."

When Dick isn't hunched over a typewriter, you can generally find him poking around outdoors somewhere in the vicinity of southern Connecticut to northern Maine.

5

NEW ENGLAND WHITETAIL HUNTING

Dick Dietz

DEER HUNTING CAN range from poor to excellent in New England. The average lies somewhere in between. The quality of deer hunting at any given time depends on where you hunt and what has happened to the deer herd in that location in the recent past.

On a long-term basis, say from five to twenty-five years, the status of the deer herd in a single state, or within specific parts of a state, will be the result of management practices, harvest controls and land-use trends. All can alter the area's ability to support reasonable and well-balanced population densities. On a short-term basis, New England deer populations are affected by the severity of recent winters, particularly in the northernmost states of Maine, New Hampshire and Vermont.

The sum of this is a variable and varied pattern for the numbers and locations of New England deer. Some of the heavily settled regions, for example, are quite low in deer numbers and there is little chance in increasing the herd. Then there are areas where deer have been on the increase, and still others where declines have been occurring. But, with the exception of the cities and heavily settled suburbs, the wily whitetail ranges the length and breadth of Yankee Land. He is still to be seen within commuting distance of New York City, bounding across the blacktop roads that thread the mini-estates in Connecticut's southwestern panhandle—just as he will be seen ghosting through the unbroken forests of northern Maine, fifty miles from the nearest paved road.

No one knows for sure just how long the whitetail deer has been a New England resident. Almost certainly he was here long before the two-footed creature we call man first drifted into the neighborhood. He was around, of course, long before the Pilgrims landed and well before any intrepid Norsemen may have navigated the perilous waters of the North Atlantic to these shores.

The whitetail was here when the earliest Indians of whom we have record were present. More than that, it is apparent that he played an important and integral part in their lives. Among the unearthed kitchen middens of New England's oldest, pre-historic human inhabitants, deer bones were the most prevalent animal remains recovered. And in ancient Indian burial grounds, numerous artifacts fashioned of deer bones and antlers indicate that deer were an important element in their daily lives.

That close relationship, though altered significantly by what we call civilization, remains in effect today. In ancient times it appears that man depended heavily on the deer as a source of food, clothing and small tools—but that man had a minimal effect on the numbers and destiny of the deer.

Today the situation is reversed. Man no longer depends on the deer in a comparable way. But the destiny of the whitetail now rests most dependently on the whims and activities of man. Nowhere in the United States is this more evident than in New England.

Patient waiting along dirt roads in back country areas often produces venison. Buck above "freezes" at sound of camera.

The influence of human activities since the time of the Pilgrims has made a graph of New England's historic deer populations look something like a roller coaster. The peaks and valleys are a direct result of both land use and harvest activities.

In earliest New England pioneering days, reports by the first settlers to broach the wilderness, indicate that whitetail

72

Dick Dietz

deer were scarce or non-existent in the mature, virgin forests of the hinterland. Based on our knowledge of deer today, it's not hard to understand why. The dense, overhead canopies of the primeval New England forest shut out the sunlight below and left a barren forest floor—too barren for the browsing whitetail to find sufficient food. The deer that were present existed in the more open, lowland areas nearer the seacoast, or where forest sections had been opened to new growth by such natural causes as forest fires.

In the beginning, the clearing of the land for farming provided an increase in "edge" growth that is so attractive to deer. The immediate by-product was an increase in deer numbers around the perimeters of the first farms. But then, continued leveling of the nearby woodlands and heavy harvesting of the deer themselves turned the situation around and deer again went into a decline.

A different population pattern occurred a few years later, in the deep forests. Lumbering operations were opening up, permitting new growth on the forest floor. A whitetail supermarket resulted. At that time, however, another factor entered the picture—predation. When the forests were opened and the deer moved in, they were quickly followed by the gray wolf. But the reign of Lobo in New England was a short one. As far as the settlers and lumbermen were concerned, he was persona non grata. Wolves were shot on sight and eventually a bounty was placed on their heads. Once the wolf was gone,

the door was opened for a dramatic increase in deer numbers.

From that point on, the numbers of forest deer fluctuated wildly at times. Rapid population increases followed by severe winters were one cause of the cyclic patterns. Heavy kills during the market hunting days were another.

Then, back among the farms, another phenomenon began that was to institute New England's greatest whitetail population explosion. Not all the land cleared in the early rush of settlement was well suited to farming. Much of it was too steep, too rocky, too poor in mineral content, or a combination of all three. Reports of better land to the west began to draw early Yankee farmers away from their hardscrabble hillsides. The movement accelerated after the Civil War, and New England farms were abandoned in a continuing trend that lasted into the early part of this century. The early stages of brush growth on thousands of these abandoned farms provided New England deer with more food than had ever existed before. Wherever this feast of abundant browse occurred, it was matched by a rapid build-up in deer numbers.

Ultimately, in some areas, the inevitable occurred—overpopulation. While harvests were frequently high, they weren't always high enough to keep the expanded deer herds in balance with the range. As the quality of the range declined, the size and vigor of the deer declined as well, and there were heavy die-offs during particularly severe winters.

This is often the clearest sight of a buck hunters get in New England cover. Can you spot the shape of the doe in the background?

Today, if you compare New England deer hunting to that of other sections of the country, it will rank not at the very top, but close to it. Specific figures on deer populations can be misleading. Such figures vary too much from year to year as a result of hunter harvest, winter losses and management practices. But if you take New England as a territorial entity, and compare it to the large states with high deer populations, it would rank eighth in the size of its resident deer herd. Remember that all of New England is still smaller than the states of California, Minnesota, Texas, Oregon, or Washington. Even more revealing is New England's ranking by density of deer per square mile. On this point it ranks fifth,

behind only Pennsylvania, Wisconsin, Michigan, and Texas.

However, deer populations vary considerably from state to state in New England. In size of their average herds, New England states rank, from top to bottom in this order: Maine, Vermont, New Hampshire, Massachusetts, Connecticut, and Rhode Island. In deer density per square mile, Vermont surpasses Maine, while the others remain in the same order.

New England whitetails, like all our deer, require a dual type of habitat, one that provides both food and protective cover. Wherever you find minimum amounts of each, you'll find deer. This can range from a fifty-acre patch on the outskirts of town, through the rural farm areas, and on into the beginnings of the continuous forests.

While deer do inhabit the patches of woodland around suburban and other heavily populated areas, their numbers are understandably limited in such locations. The majority of New England deer live in the forests and rural farmlands. Where the individual chooses to hunt them is largely a matter of convenience and personal preference.

There's no question that much of the mixed farmland areas provide optimum conditions for deer. The woodland patches remain open enough to permit plenty of browse growth. And along the edges where woodlands meet cultivated fields and pastures, browse is always ample inside the tree line where the sun can penetrate from the outside. Deer in these

DICK DIETZ

sections also adapt to pasture grasses and will often utilize them heavily during nocturnal feeding where darkness gives them the sense of security they'd normally lack in the open.

Throughout New England these mixed farmland areas traditionally account for the highest percentage of deer hunting success. It's not difficult to see why. Often these sections are hunted by the actual landowners who know them as well as they do their own living rooms. Further, on working farms, the owners are on location twelve months of the year and have repeated opportunities during the summer and early fall to observe deer movement, feeding habits and daytime bedding locations. On opening day, they know not only if there are deer present, but pretty much where they're likely to be.

One of the best examples of successful farmland hunting I've ever seen, occurred on opening day of the 1963 season in the town of Benson in western Vermont. It was typical mixed farmland with a generous amount of reverted woodlands dotting the countryside. Taking a stand near the edge of a wooded bluff that enabled me to watch several deer trails below me as well as the interior of the woods, I was lucky enough to bag a fine, fat buck about mid-morning. Since others in the party were continuing to hunt, I used my remaining time to drift around the surrounding farms observing. The take was amazing. There was scarcely a farm that did not have at least one buck hanging in

the barn by nightfall of the first day. Most of the hunting was performed in organized drives of from ten to twenty persons. It was, in truth, more of a harvest than a hunt. But venison was part of the winter food supply for these farm folk, and they looked upon the deer as another crop produced by their land. The buck I collected, incidentally, was in prime condition and one of the best that ever honored our table.

The Vermont deer herd was near its peak that year and already too big for the available winter food supply. Subsequent years were to witness severe over-browsing of the range, heavy winter losses and a steady decline in the annual harvest.

At the opposite extreme in New England is the big woods hunting found in the forested sections of northern and central New Hampshire and Vermont and northern Maine. Hunting this type of terrain is more challenging and more difficult. The deer are more widely scattered, more spooky since they are less accustomed to the presence of man, and have more escape room to roam when pressured. However, these are also the areas that offer the rewards of big bucks and big racks for the hunter who has the skill, woods lore, and the time and patience to pursue them successfully.

Lumber operations can play a significant role in deer concentrations and potential hunter success amidst New England's forests. In areas where no cutting has occurred for a number of years, deer numbers may be rather sparse and well spread out. In sections where cutting operations have been prevalent in recent years, deer numbers tend to build up. There's a saying that Maine loggers have discovered a fool-proof deer call. It's called a chain saw. The procedure is to run a chain saw for about five minutes, shut it off, pick up your rifle, and wait for the deer to come drifting in looking for the toppings.

I've seen it happen almost that way. In 1964, I hunted with a party of eleven out of a Great Northern Paper Company logging camp in the Baker Lake area of northwest Maine. Active logging operations had been going on in the surrounding area and were still under way in several nearby locations. For obvious reasons we stayed out of those areas where cutting was still being conducted. But we were able to work many other locations that were strewn with fresh toppings. Before the week was out, all eleven of the party had scored—with eight bucks and three does. And those bucks were big, with three going over two hundred pounds, and one immense old graybeard actually making the three hundred-pound mark. The surrounding area was alive with deer. I have no doubt that the cutting operations brought them in.

Yet, I've hunted other sections of northern Maine, again with veteran hunting companions, and seen the entire party go home empty-handed after six full days of hard hunting. No matter how experienced and skillful you are, it is al-ways possible to be blanked in the big north woods.

Skill in pursuing the whitetail requires knowledge and experience, just as does any other type of skill. If one hunted deer for thirty years, but always alone, never having discussed the subject with anyone else, nor listened to or read the advice of other practiced hunters, he should still become a skillful hunter himself from the sum of personal experience.

But that's the long, hard, slow way. There are short cuts. You can often learn more from one week's hunt with a wise, old veteran than you can from five years of learning by yourself. He can point out things to you in one day that may have taken him twenty years to learn. It pays for beginners to hunt with an old pro whenever possible. It also pays to read all you can about the experiences of other deer hunters and to learn as much as you can about deer themselves and their habits. Last, but equally important, work at becoming a knowledgeable woodsman and naturalist so you can read the forest.

It is one thing, for example, to be able to recognize deer tracks, but much more if those tracks are able to tell you something. Are they new or old? How old? Were they made by two does or a buck and a doe? Were they hurrying or just drifting along? Again, it's one thing to know what kinds of food are preferred by deer, another thing to be able to recognize such plants when you see them. The more of a naturalist and woodsman you be-

DICK DIETZ

Game warden checks hunter's license and also his healthy Maine buck.

come, the better a deer hunter you will be.

Priorities are a personal thing. For some hunters, the major goal is simply to be able to bring home venison. For others, the hunting experience in a particular location is more important. On the average, I've always had more success hunting New England's farmland areas. The overall harvest percentage is definitely greater in such sections. But one must remember that, because these areas are the most accessible and the easiest to hunt, they also attract the heaviest hunting pressure. Consequently, I'm not sure the success ratio per hunter is always better among the farmlands than up on the high ridges or in the deep woods. My preference for the latter is based on the reward

of being farther from the sights and sounds of civilization.

No matter where one hunts deer in New England, advance familiarity with the area is critical to chances of success. For those who hunt their own property or areas only a few hours' drive from home, this presents no problem. But for those seeking new hunting locations in distant parts of their state or in another state, prior knowledge of the area is essential to prevent a disappointing situation where there is poor hunting or even no hunting.

Most game departments either publish or will provide reports of the previous year's harvest on a county-by-county or

In an intensive study area, Maine wildlife biologists prepare to weigh a buck taken by a northern Maine hunter.

even town-by-town basis. This, by itself, can give you an indication of where to look. The same source can also give you leads on the amount of public and private land in an area.

For likely looking locations, you should know in advance if private land is posted or if permission to hunt is implied or obtainable. On public lands, you may wish to learn how heavily they are hunted. If you require lodging, you'll need to know if there are any restrictions on where you might set up or park.

As a general rule, you can assume that anywhere paved roads pass through good deer habitat in New England, sections off these roads will be hunted heavily. To some degree this also applies to dirt roads in good condition passing through densely wooded areas.

This doesn't have to be a serious problem. You will find that very few hunters venture more than a mile into the woods off the road. Those who have the skill and confidence to move in deeper will usually find they have to share the cover only with the deer that have been pushed deeper in by the heavy activity along the roads.

Some of New England's best potential deer hunting can be found along the back roads of hilly, abandoned farm country. A topographical map showing elevations of an area can indicate where to look. But you'll have to scout for the roads because the ones you'll want to follow won't appear on most road maps. This is where a four-wheel-drive vehicle can be most use-

Two important tools for those who ply New England forests—topographic map and compass.

ful—not so much for the back roads, but for the old farm wagon paths that lead you into second-growth cover.

In the forests of northern New England, there's another useful way to penetrate deep into the woods where there are no roads and consequently few or no other hunters. One can find plenty of practically virgin hunting territory by car-topping a canoe and traveling up the streams or chains of lakes. First, this will get you into sections where hunting pressure is light. Second, deer have a habit of frequenting waterways in rough country. Third, the waterway provides you with a way of getting your buck back out if you are successful. One warning about this procedure, however—watch the temperature. If it drops below freezing and stays there, you'd better start back before you get iced in.

The better equipped the experienced New England deer hunter is to reach poorly accessible areas, the better are his chances to find a potentially productive and uncrowded place to hunt. Remember that high harvest figures for a given spot can result from a combination of two factors—easy accessibility and heavy hunting pressure. There may well be other spots of lower recorded success simply because they are hard to reach and therefore lightly hunted.

The hunter who opts to hunt his own township or county, or to stay in a motel, takes his chances on the kind of hunting he happens to find—good or poor. On the other hand, the hunter who has a rough-country vehicle, is willing to set up his own camp and sleep in a tent, and who can travel the waterways as well, has many more options at his disposal. At worst, if he finds the hunting poor in a given area, he is not locked into it and can seek another spot. At best, he may stumble into a truly productive area and, even better, have it all to himself or his party.

The major New England deer hunting states are the northern trio of Maine, New

Author's portable deer camp. When canoe replaces van, pop tent replaces trailer.

Hampshire and Vermont. Reasons for this can be found by comparing the topography, land use and population densities of these states to those of Massachusetts, Connecticut and Rhode Island. The northern trio is three-and-a-half times as large as the southern group but has less than a quarter as many residents. Further, large portions of the upper three states are either mountainous, forested or a combination of both.

Starting from the top, Maine has the largest deer herd and is second to Vermont in deer density. Being the most northern of the New England states and near the upper limits of North American whitetail range, the severity of its winters tends to have the greatest effect on fluctuations in the Maine deer herd. Nevertheless, Maine deer have remained in relatively sound shape, in good balance with their habitat as a result of sensible and, at times, courageous management by the state game department. Much of the credit for this must go to Maine's either-sex law which permits the hunter to take one deer per season, either buck or doe.

Estimated size of the Maine deer herd has run around 300,000 in recent years and the annual harvest has fluctuated in the neighborhood of 30,000, about 10 per cent of the herd. In 1971 the take dropped to 18,903 as a result of a shortened season. This was declared after the season had already begun, a move that took some courage by the Commissioner of the Department of Inland Fisheries and Game at the time, George Bucknam. The decision was based on evidence of higher than normal losses from the severe winter of 1970-71. Yet the following year, 1972, the harvest returned to almost 29,000.

Where you hunt deer in Maine is a matter of preference and availability. Most resident hunters tend to hunt in their own counties. Non-residents go to areas where they may own property, have prior familiarity or have a hunting camp connection of some sort.

Maine's southern, mixed farmland section accounts for three-quarters of its annual harvest. Leading counties on the basis of kill per square mile have been Waldo, York, Lincoln, Knox, Sagadahoc, Kennebec and Cumberland—all in the southern part of the state. Lowest kill ratios per square mile come from the northern, heavily forested counties of Aroostook, Piscataquis, and Somerset. The individual takes his choice. But Maine deer hunting has been generally good and promises to remain good in the future.

Vermont, with the greatest density of deer in the United States, has had one of the highest harvest ratios as well. But the Vermont deer herd encountered serious problems in the late 1960's. The state had just grown too many deer for the carrying capacity of the range. Severe overbrowsing and habitat deterioration were already evident. The result was inevitable. From a peak harvest of 17,834 bucks in 1966, the take plummeted to 7,760 legal bucks in 1971. This increased somewhat

A check of the deer's teeth by a Maine wildlife biologist gives a good idea of its age. Removal of an incisor tooth for laboratory examination is often done to get a more precise determination.

to 8,980 in 1972 but habitat problems still exist. The harvest percentage is too small in relation to the herd, and the herd itself is still probably too large. Until Vermont's deer range is given a chance to recover through greater reduction of both sexes, the future of the state's deer hunting and the quality of its herd will remain cloudy.

Vermont deer seem to be more numerous in the state's central and southern regions of gentler topography. But, as in Maine, the biggest bucks and racks usually come from the northern regions and the rugged back country. Some of the most productive areas on a kill-per-square-mile basis have been townships in

Bennington, Windham, Windsor and Orange counties. The lowest kill densities occur in the northern lake counties of Caledonia, Essex, Orleans, Franklin and Chittenden. Again, the individual hunter's own priorities and opportunities will dictate where he goes.

New Hampshire is another New England state with an either-sex harvest law. And, as in Maine, the practice seems to have been a sound one. The ruggedness of winters in terms of snow and temperature is apparently the major cause of fluctuations in deer numbers from year to year. If New Hampshire has a particularly tough winter that seems to have had a measurably adverse effect on deer numbers, the Commissioner of Fish and Game can work toward rebuilding the herd by shortening the subsequent season. This was done during the years of 1969 through 1972—reducing the total take to seven thousand animals in 1972 after the peak of fourteen thousand in the mid-60's.

Yet the future of New Hampshire deer remains promising. All evidence indicates that the herd is in good balance with its range and that there is no serious habitat deterioration.

Harvest densities in New Hampshire have been heaviest in the middle part of the state, occupied by Grafton and Cornwall counties. They tend to be lowest in the southern counties of Cheshire, Hillsborough, Rockingham, and Stafford, and the northernmost county of Coos. But county-wide figures can be

Author and six-pointer taken minutes earlier.

misleading. Individual towns in almost any county become "hot spots" at times, while others may drop off in productivity.

Three localized areas that have been highly productive in recent years are the towns in the southern half of Carroll county, those along the Connecticut River in the northern half of Grafton county and the towns along the western border of Merrimack county.

Of the remaining three New England states, a truly promising picture comes from Massachusetts. The Bay State is almost as large as Vermont and New Hampshire but has had a much smaller deer herd, estimated between 11,000 and 13,000 in 1969. But in recent years a combination of relatively mild winters and an enlightened deer management program has more than doubled the Massachusetts herd. It had grown to over 22,000 by 1972.

In building up its deer population, Massachusetts has been holding a comparatively short season each year. In addition, it has followed a limited-permit system for antlerless deer that has maintained a harvest ratio of about two to one of bucks over does. This has apparently proven to be a good ratio when the goal is to increase the size of the herd—something Massachusetts can afford. The 1972 harvest was 2,215, or about 10 per cent of the herd, a percentage similar to those of Maine and New Hampshire.

Massachusetts is a shotgun-only state, permitting either slugs or buckshot. Since the state has virtually no wilderness areas and most deer habitat exists on private property, permission to hunt should be obtained well in advance of the season.

The best Massachusetts deer hunting will be found west of the Connecticut River. Two of the most productive locations are Berkshire and Franklin counties along the New York and Vermont borders respectively. Under current wildlife management and harvest practices, the odds are good that the Massachusetts deer situation will continue to improve in the future.

Deer hunting regulations vary considerably throughout the United States. But the strangest set of laws governing the whitetail exist in my home state of Connecticut.

The unique situation results from the

82

fact that, in Connecticut, deer are classed as an agricultural pest rather than as a game animal. All regulations pertaining to them come from the state legislature instead of game department professionals.

Deer may be hunted by longbow only on designated state lands or private lands with permit from the owner during the months of November and December.

On private lands used for "agricultural purposes," deer may be hunted during the month of December by obtaining a permit from the owner that is also approved by the game department. Landowners can make no more than five such applications and an individual can obtain no more than three such permits. He is still limited to one deer.

The property owner himself, however, or an immediate member of his family, may take deer on his own property at any time of the year, with any weapon of his choice. In other words, if you own land in Connecticut that is also deer habitat, you have a twelve-month, open deer season.

You may wonder what kind of a deer herd such unusual laws have created. The answer is, a surprisingly sound and healthy one. Despite the year-around option for property holders, a certain percentage of illegal kills, and a fairly high rate of losses from auto kills and dog harassment, the Connecticut deer herd has been growing at a rate of about 8 per cent a year. It is not being over-harvested and, in fact, shows some evidence of being under-harvested.

Where is the best place to hunt deer in Connecticut? The northwest corner bordering New York and Massachusetts is probably a good location. But deer are scattered around the state. If you own property, you can hunt deer whenever they happen to drift onto your land. Otherwise, you had best make friends with some cooperative landowners, or become a bowhunter.

Rhode Island, geographically, is an extension of eastern Connecticut. It is the smallest state in the Union and has a correspondingly small number of deer. Actually, for 311 years there was no legal deer season in Rhode Island. But in 1957, a twenty-day bow season was permitted on state-owned land. And in 1967, the first shotgun deer season was opened.

The annual take is quite light—no more than a hundred deer of either sex. Shotgunners are about three to four times as successful as bowhunters, and the annual loss from autos usually exceeds the number taken by bow.

Not a significant deer hunting state by any stretch of the imagination, Rhode Island still offers a chance for venison to those who are willing to try. The hunter's best bet, based on past figures, is Washington county in the southern part of the state.

That's it—New England—one of the country's most popular areas to hunt whitetails. It's been a top spot for a long while, and it's getting better!

A sportsman with wide interests in the great outdoors, Hans C. Paller has extensively hunted big game across the United States and Canadian provinces. His favorite game animal is the whitetailed deer, and he has successfully harvested many fine trophies from the Adirondacks. He is a licensed New York guide with a thorough knowledge of his subject. Well known for his efforts in behalf of the environment, the author was selected for inclusion in the 1973 edition of *Who's Who in Ecology.* He is currently President of the New York State Outdoor Writers Association and a member of the Board of Directors of the Outdoor Writers Association of America. Hans Paller is the outdoor columnist for newspapers owned by the Northern New York Publishing Company and a freelance journalist. A native of New York, he lives with his wife and children on the shores of the St. Lawrence River.

6

ADIRONDACK DEER HUNTING

Hans Paller

THE FIRST WHITE man to gaze upon the Adirondack Mountains of northern New York was the French explorer Jacques Cartier, in the year 1536. From the site of a small Indian village that later grew in size to become the city of Montreal, Cartier pondered over that unbroken region to the south that contained a myriad of lakes and mountains.

It was not until July of 1609 that Samuel de Champlain penetrated the edges of that wilderness as he ventured south to enter a large lake that he named after himself. A few months later Henry Hudson sailed up the Hudson River to view the Adirondack Mountains from their southeastern boundaries. During the next 170 years the country on the eastern side of the Adirondacks became the scene of bloody French and Indian wars. First the French and British and later the British and American forces fought terrible battles for control of the lake routes through Lake George and Lake Champlain.

Although a few white men settled on the fringes of the Adirondacks, the interior of the mountain region was not explored until 1830. Early western settlers actually reached the Pacific before Mount Marcy, the highest of the Adirondack peaks, was scaled by the first intrepid climber. But when this beautiful wilderness was "discovered" it didn't take long for rapid development of summer tourist facilities and establishment of major lumbering operations.

Today, the Adirondacks have become a playground for millions of people on the eastern seaboard. Easy access on the Adirondack Northway (Interstate 87)

The Adirondack Park, a wilderness area of approximately 2,260,000 acres of state-owned lands beckons sportsmen each fall. COURTESY N.Y.S. DEPT. OF ENVIRONMENTAL CONSERVATION

places the area within a six-hour drive of New York City and major population centers. The Adirondack Park contains six million acres of land, of which 60 per cent is in private ownership. The remaining portion is owned by the State of New York and managed as a Forest Preserve. It is the largest state or national park in the contiguous United States.

Deer hunting in the central Adirondacks is much more than an overnight trip to "bag a buck." It is an unforgettable rejuvenating experience amidst the beauty of untrammeled wilderness. A deer camp in the heart of this primitive area is a hypnotic communion of sportsmen with nature. The act of deer hunting itself becomes almost secondary as one enjoys the tranquil beauty of the changing seasons in the north country.

What are your chances of harvesting a trophy deer from the Adirondacks? Approximately 500,000 deer hunters take to the woods each fall in New York State, but a very small percentage hunt in what is known as the central Adirondacks. There are many sections of public land in the interior where it is possible to hunt for weeks without seeing another sportsman.

Established records indicate that statewide approximately one hunter in twelve is successful in harvesting an antlered buck. During antlerless seasons of the past, the success ratio has climbed to a

HANS PALLER

point where one hunter in eight is successful. The chances of bagging a deer in the wilderness areas away from the highway are even more favorable.

Although our main subject is deer hunting, the prospects of bagging a black bear is worthy of attention, since it is a bonus game animal in the north country. Populations are at a high level, and special pre-season hunts are allowed since there have been many nuisance complaints from marauding bears. The annual bear take in the state averages 550 per year and approximately 400 are taken in the Adirondacks.

At some hunting clubs, there are just as many bear taken during the opening week of the season as there are deer. The first real cold wave and snowstorm will send the majority of bears into their winter quarters, but there is always a very good chance that the early season hunter will score on a magnificent trophy. The leading counties in bear take are Hamilton, Essex, Herkimer, St. Lawrence, and Franklin, in descending order.

Sprinkled throughout the Adirondacks are thirty-seven state parks and campsites that are ideal jump-off points for the big-game hunter. With modern truck campers, tent trailers and other recreational vehicles, the sportsman is not tied to a motel room. An Outdoor Recreational Map of New York and a campsite circular can be obtained from the Department of Environmental Conservation, 50 Wolf Road, Albany, New York 12226. It lists all the public campgrounds in the Adirondack Park.

At some campsites, the water systems are shut down in the fall to prevent freeze-up, but this should not present any great difficulty for the hunter-sportsman. The Recreational Map also lists thousands of acres of prime hunting areas on private lands where controlled hunting is

The famous "Luckey Head" is a fine example of the trophy bucks that are produced in the Adirondacks. It was the world record up until 1960 and scored 198⅜ under Boone & Crockett Club measurement. COURTESY N.Y.S. DEPT. OF ENVIRONMENTAL CONSERVATION

Hunting by canoe is an excellent method of penetrating wilderness areas to establish your deer camp. COURTESY N.Y.S. DEPT. OF ENVIRONMENTAL CONSERVATION

in real comfort at beautiful lakeside settings.

With today's lightweight backpacking equipment, it is a relatively easy matter to escape from the crowded hunting corridors along the highways. Open camps or "Adirondack Lean-to" type of shelters in the interior of the forest regions provide excellent base camps for the deer hunter in the fall. Without any problem from insects after the first frost, these structures provide shelter and comfortable sleeping

Typical deer cover in the Adirondacks in early fall. Most shots at game will be less than seventy-five yards. CREDIT- N.Y.S. DEPT. OF ENVIRONMENTAL CONSERVATION

permitted. Generally these lands are owned by lumber companies that allow hunting under the Fish and Wildlife Management Act. For the most part, the lands are under active forest management that produces ideal deer range.

Many deer hunters prefer to stay at motels and hotels. There are excellent accommodations at such Adirondack communities as Cranberry Lake, Saranac Lake, Tupper Lake, Long Lake, Racquette Lake, and Old Forge that cater to visiting sportsmen in the fall. A number of these resorts offer guiding services and all are located a short distance from good hunting territory. Obviously, it is not the same as hunting from a deer camp, but many hunters have spent enjoyable trips

HANS PALLER

without the need for erecting a tent. Each camp is equipped with a fireplace and simple pit privy. There are 268 open camps, and most of them are located in prime hunting territory. Many fine bucks have been shot within close proximity to an "Adirondack Lean-to."

Perhaps one of the best methods to quickly reach good hunting grounds with a minimum of effort is by canoe. The Cranberry Lake area, as an example, is one of the largest wilderness areas in the state. If you own a canoe or car-top boat, I would put this location at the top of the list for hunting territory that should be explored. The perimeter of the lake itself offers fine hunting with over forty miles of well maintained trails and seven open camps. The Oswegatchie River, inlet to the lake, provides an easy canoe trip by motor over twenty miles of waterways into the heart of unbroken forests that stretch south to the Beaver River country. This area provides deer hunting with a true wilderness flavor and is certain to be a memorable trip.

Another fine canoe route is from Old Forge to Paul Smith, a total of 125 miles. This network of beautiful lakes and ponds are so closely connected that trips can be planned by canoe with only short "carries" or portages. The sportsman-hunter has but to pick his hunting territory and chances are it will be accessible by water. Nowhere in the East coast may be found such a combination of wild, great scenery, and easy travel, lying in the

Old style wall tents are still traditional in the Adirondacks but require far more work to set up than the newer models. COURTESY N.Y.S. DEPT. OF ENVIRONMENTAL CONSERVATION

heart of big game country. A complete list of Adirondack canoe routes may be obtained from the Department of Environmental Conservation.

For the first Adirondack visit, any group of sportsmen would do well to consider the Moose River Recreation Area in the western part of Hamilton County. A tract of land approximately fifty thousand acres in size, it provides excellent trout fishing and deer hunting in a remote region. Access is good with two entrances from the east and west. The main entrance at the west end is at Lime-kiln Lake and is reached by a feeder road from Route 28 near the Village of Inlet. The east entrance is at Cedar River Flow, on Route 28, a short distance from Indian Lake Village.

An abundance of access roads and trails will lead the hunter into every reach of the Moose River Recreation Area, but all persons must register with the caretaker in charge. Tent camping is only allowed on designated sites, and permits are required for periods exceeding three nights. U.S.G.S. Quadrangle maps for the region are the Old Forge and West Canada Lakes sheets.

The Moose River Plains has been the scene of intensive deer studies by wildlife biologists for over forty years. Year after year, it has been conclusively established that not enough deer are being harvested from the area. During the past severe winters, as many as twenty to thirty dead deer per square mile have been counted in the deer yards. The deer increase at a far greater rate than they are killed by hunters. It is only starvation that ultimately brings down the population. For most of the hunting season, the deer are well scattered in the region and hunting pressure is too light. A post-season hunt during December has been recommended by wildlife biologists to harvest deer that are simply being wasted as a valuable resource. Any late season hunt would concentrate deer for the hunters and permit a higher success ratio. The situation is typical of other forest areas that receive low hunting pressures from one year to the next.

It is impossible to discuss deer hunting in the Adirondacks without reference to deer management. The Adirondack Mountains are a mature mountain range. Tall white pine and spruce were once the predominant trees in the virgin forest, but these great giants were lumbered off in the early 1800's, and the white pine blister rust finished off the white pine as an important species.

Actually, the selective cutting of pine and spruce for timber was extremely beneficial to the whitetail deer and the populations began to explode. The deer herds reached their peak in the late 1890's. Then came disaster. Cutting for pulpwood became profitable in the 1900's, and the severe cutting of softwoods destroyed thousands of acres of winter cover in deer yarding areas. Severe competition for winter browse almost completely destroyed the more valuable deer foods such as American yew, witchopple and white cedar.

In the Adirondacks, by provision of a constitutional amendment written in 1894, the Forest Preserve must be forever kept as wild forest lands. The timber therein cannot be sold, removed or destroyed, and this prevents any possibility of habitat improvement on public land. As the trees reach maturity in the Forest Preserve, the overhead crown closes and little sunlight reaches the ground. New growth is inhibited and the food supply dwindles rapidly.

This group of deer is in good condition early in the year but a high percentage will die during a severe winter. Sensible deer management should include an antlerless season. COURTESY N.Y.S. DEPT. OF ENVIRONMENTAL CONSERVATION

The only feasible method of game management on state lands within the Adirondacks is by regulation of the deer population to a level that is consistent with the ability of the winter range to support the deer herd. Buck hunting in the central Adirondacks has no effect on the rate of increase in the deer population and will only remove a small fraction of deer that would eventually die of starvation. An antlerless deer season is the only method that will effect a reduction of a herd to within manageable levels.

For ten years, from 1960 to 1970, slightly over 64,000 antlerless deer were harvested by hunters along with record buck kills. The deer take was still not high enough to keep the herd in check, and the bubble burst during the winters of 1969-70 and 1970-71. Severe starvation quickly reduced the Adirondack herd to its lowest level, and old-time north country hunters screamed for an end to the doe seasons. Sensible wildlife management gave way to emotion and long-entrenched beliefs in buck-only regulations.

Supervising Wildlife Biologist C. W. Severinghaus, in the Division of Fish and Wildlife, has developed an excellent deer management program for the Adirondacks, but his hands have been shackled because politics prevent antlerless deer harvests. Deer hunters must now contend with a boom-or-bust deer kill that is totally dependent upon the severity of each winter.

Now let's get down to hunting! The big game season for deer and bear in the Adirondacks is very liberal and extends from October 25 to December 5. Bag limits are one deer and bear per license year and license fees are $4.25 for resident and $18 for non-resident. A special bow-hunting stamp of $3.25 in addition to the big game license will allow the archery enthusiast to do his thing for fourteen days prior to the regular season. Antler size must be at least three inches in length.

Minors must be sixteen years to hunt big game and accompanied by a parent, guardian, or person over twenty-one years of age. This is an unfortunate regulation, and hopefully the age limit will be lowered in future years. Other states allow big game hunting at twelve or fourteen years of age, and New York is losing many potential sportsmen as well as an important and substantial source of revenue. With the hunter-safety training courses required today, there is little danger of accidental shooting when responsible teenagers are accompanied by adults in the woods. Youngsters should be introduced to the hunting experience before they lose interest in this form of outdoor recreation.

The hunting season coincides with the mating season for the whitetail deer. Bucks will begin following does in October, but few does will breed until November. Breeding reaches its peak in mid-November and most does are bred by the end of the month. "Buck rubs" are common throughout the forest as the lord and master polishes his antlers on saplings. It is the wise hunter who looks for a buck-rub because it is evident that a trophy is not far away.

There are many methods of hunting the whitetail and the "drive" has consistently produced deer at hunting clubs. It is highly effective throughout the entire season, although the author does not particularly enjoy this type of hunting. Usually four to eight men will participate in the drive with watchers and drivers being split somewhat equally, depending upon the terrain. In a narrow section of cover with natural boundaries such as a stream, woods road, or lakeshore, it is possible to use fewer drivers and station additional watchers along the edges of the drive.

A whitetail deer cannot be driven like a mule. He will choose his own escape route which may be toward the watchers, to either side of the drive, or he may double back between the drivers. The yearling buck may panic and run with the does, but the old trophy buck is unpredictable. He will skulk his way through every available bit of cover and may even choose to let the driver pass within a few feet of his bed.

A drive should not be of any great duration and certainly no longer than a thousand yards in heavily wooded terrain. Any greater distance will result in spending most of the day looking for lost hunters, and a deer will simply not be driven this far in a straight line. It is strongly recommended that blaze orange clothing be used by every hunter participating in this method of hunting. It is essential that drivers and watchers be aware of each other's presence and absolutely no one wearing blaze orange fabric mistaken for game. A deer drive can be compared to Russian roulette if the game is played by careless hunters.

There is no real advantage for the drivers to whoop, holler, and bay at the moon during a drive. Excessive noise will only serve to pinpoint all the drivers for the deer and permit easier escape. Two-way radios are convenient tools in con-

HANS PALLER

ducting a drive and are used more extensively each year. Principal advantages are to signal the beginning and completion of the drive, and they are very useful during searches for lost hunters. The range of these units can be very limited, however, in dense areas of the forest.

Still-hunting, in my judgement, is far more rewarding than hunting with a group. A deer has the advantage, while the hunter must use his skills and knowledge of the deer's habitat. Early in the season, when a hunter may have to contend with dry leaves and a noisy forest floor, it is next to impossible to outwit a deer. Under these conditions the lone hunter can only select a good watch in productive cover. In every type of deer habitat, there will be resting and bedding grounds. The experienced hunter will seek out well-traveled routes at the edges of swamps or dense cover. Buck rubs are a good indication that you are visiting the promised land. The hunter should place himself in front of a tree or brush to soften his silhouette and screen his movements. Wind direction must be considered and should be moving from the cover being watched toward the waiting hunter. The first hour of daybreak is most productive as deer slowly return from the feeding grounds to their protective cover. At dusk the hungry and thirsty whitetail will reverse the routine.

Trail-watching is really a deadly way to fill out a buck license. The secret is in picking out trails that show the most activity and if possible, a crossing where se-

A whitetail fawn on legs that are still a little uncertain, but mother isn't too far away. COURTESY N.Y.S. DEPT. OF ENVIRONMENTAL CONSERVATION

veral trails intersect. Far too often, a hunter will pick a commanding view of a hardwood forest and sit watching an empty landscape all day long. The area may be all torn up by deer that have been pawing for beechnuts, but few hunters realize that an old buck will only use these open areas in the safety of twilight or darkness.

A hunter must think like a deer. Would you take a stroll through an open hardwood forest knowing that a sharpshooter is lying in wait with a scoped rifle?—Not on your tintype! And a buck isn't all that stupid, even though he does lose a great deal of caution during the rutting season. Concentrate your trail-watching along the edges of swamps, at natural crossings where blocks of cover neck together. It is difficult for most people to sit for any great length of time. As a youngster, I could only manage about an hour's wait at any particular spot. But those were also the years that I didn't hang a deer on the back porch with any regularity. Patience is the name of the game.

Under heavy hunting pressure, a wise old buck simply will not voluntarily move from cover until it is dark. In the wilderness areas, a deer will travel and feed during longer periods of daylight. This is one of the advantages in hunting the interior forests where deer have had infrequent contact with human predators.

My favorite kind of hunting begins on the heels of the first snowstorm. As the snow blankets the earth, conditions are near perfect for the still hunter. The recent movements of deer lie before him as a picture puzzle in the snow. The hunter's movements are muffled and he has a slight advantage over the keen hearing of his quarry.

It is sometimes difficult to make out the difference between a buck or doe track in freshly fallen snow. An old doe may leave a very large imprint. But the slightly rounded track and drag-marks in the snow are a good indication that it is indeed a buck. A doe will usually pick her feet clear of a light snowfall and leave a clear hoof track. Evidence of a drag mark in the snow is the only reliable indication that you are following a buck.

Like a hound dog on a fresh rabbit trail, I take off on the tracks of the buck, knowing that a trophy deer lies at the end of the stalk. It is a fascinating method of hunting that has provided me with a great deal of insight into the private world of the whitetail. The stalk begins with a keen sense of suspense and excitement. A fresh track means that a buck is not far away, since he rarely covers more than a half mile in an evening of travel. If you are lucky, it will be a short stalk with a buck bedded down within a few hundred yards of where you first cut his track. At times, you may have to follow the trail for several hours as he seeks out the company of a doe in heat.

The stalk must be carried out with extreme care even though the hunter's footsteps are muffled. A buck always watches his back trail and it is a natural trait that is perhaps a throw-back to the days when wolves followed the scent. The wolves of yesteryear have today been replaced by domestic dogs who travel in packs and are just as efficient in killing members of the deer family.

The stalker must proceed very cautiously, a few steps at a time, pausing frequently to observe the terrain on both sides of the track. Be alert for the slightest movement and look for that telltale splash of brown at ground level. On two occasions I have shot deer as they lay in their beds, and a third time I downed a buck as it rose to its foreknees before gaining its feet. Frequently the hunter will approach the buck as it is feeding ahead of him or the deer may even be

Those tracks in the snow can lead you to a fine buck with a little patience and basic skills. COURTESY PHOTO OF KENNEDY WILSON

A new snow! This successful young sportsman has tracked down his trophy under ideal hunting conditions. COURTESY PHOTO OF KENNEDY WILSON

doubling back on his trail. There is usually plenty of time for the hunter to pick his shot for a clean kill.

If the hunter surprises his quarry without getting a shot or misses his target, the chase becomes difficult. It is best not to continue on the trail for at least a half hour unless you are hunting with a partner. When a deer is frightened, he will burst headlong at top speed from danger. But his flight will only be across a swamp, hill or ridge that puts him out of sight. The tracks of a fleeing deer show that he will stop and pause frequently to watch his back trail. If pursuit continues, the buck will lead you on a merry chase through heavy cover and terrain that he knows so well. But don't be surprised if you find yourself walking over your own footsteps within a short time. A deer will circle a large swamp just like a snowshoe hare chased by hounds. A buck is reluctant to leave familiar territory and may even seek the apparent safety of crossing a river or pond before abandoning his old stamping grounds.

The whitetail's habit of watching his back trail can lead him to trouble when two or three hunters are working together. With one hunter dogging the track, the other hunters can make half-circle loops ahead of the trail. Frequently the buck will make a mistake and stumble right into range of the waiting rifleman. A moving deer against a white background is not difficult to pick up, and the deer has lost his advantage when he is forced to travel.

As the deer season moves into its final two weeks, the Adirondacks are usually blanketed by several good snowfalls. Travel in the woods becomes more difficult, but deer hunting is increasingly more productive. The woods are not crowded, as the less dedicated hunters have laid aside their rifles for the year. The large bucks begin to descend from the higher elevations toward the low-lying swamps along the brooks and shorelines of the ponds. The does begin to herd up and bucks are still looking for romance. Cold weather combined with deep snow, forces deer to search for food during daylight hours, and the hunter will see far more deer on the move than he did during the opening week of the season.

There are also definite disadvantages to cold weather hunting. Tent camping becomes uncomfortable since outside temperatures are well below freezing. Camp stoves or other sources of heat are a must for personal comfort. Unless you are in top physical condition and equipped with good tenting gear, it may be prudent to operate from a recreational vehicle or convenient motel. Warm clothing is essential and proper footgear a necessity.

A word of caution to those sportsmen who are planning a trip to the central Adirondacks for the first time. It is not farm-country hunting, and the novice can become turned around or lost in a matter of minutes without a compass. Confine your hunting to a small section until you become familiar with the area. Re-

The "Adirondack Lean-to" is a popular home away from home for the deer hunter. Most of these open shelters are located in good hunting areas. COURTESY N.Y.S. DEPT. OF ENVIRONMENTAL CONSERVATION

member that the interior of a cedar swamp will look identical from end to end, and one ridge is similar to the next. There are very few distinguishing landmarks and visibility is often limited to short distances.

The sportsman should carry a good reliable compass and a topographical map of the area he is hunting. Learn how to use a compass! In addition, it would be wise to carry a flashlight with spare batteries. If you stay too long on watch, it will provide enough light to get you out of trouble and back to camp. Should you become

lost, the flashlight will also be of great help in gathering firewood. Dry matches, a candle stub or a cigarette lighter are indispensible items for starting a fire.

In the event you become lost after dark, stay in one place and do not panic. Chances are you will be less than a mile from camp, and your companions will find you once they discover you are missing. If there is no response to your signals, build a fire and make yourself as comfortable as possible. By daylight, it will be possible to reach a road or truck trail in less than a day's travel. Daniel Boone was known to have said that he never got lost in the forest, but often had been "bewildered for a few days." With compass and maps, the modern hunter should never be "lost" for any extended length of time.

If the reader is looking for a permanent camp which will provide top-notch deer hunting, he should inquire locally about membership in a private club. Many large lumbering industries such as Newton Falls Paper Company, Diamond International, etc., lease their lands for deer hunting to private hunting clubs. Often these clubs have vacancies for new members that conduct themselves as responsible sportsmen. Annual membership fees range from fifty to two hundred dollars per year, depending on the size of the lease and type of facilities.

The larger clubs usually have year-round caretakers, complete dining facilities, and bunk-house type sleeping quarters. A hunter has but to drive into camp with his rifle and bed-roll to begin

Hunting lodge at a private club on leased land. The day's hunt is over and it is time for conversation and perhaps a friendly poker game. COURTESY PHOTO OF KENNEDY WILSON

his hunting trip. Hunting is generally excellent, since most of the leased land is under active lumber management with continuous cutting and new browse generated each year.

The north country produces big deer and big racks. It is not due to a better food supply, but simply because the deer live a longer span of life. A whitetail doe attains maturity at 3½ years, while the male deer doesn't reach full skeletal size until he is 5½ years of age. In the interior forest, about one-fourth of the bucks taken are 4½ years or older, while in the southern

farm belt, only about 2 per cent of the deer reach this age.

It is rare that a buck deer will ever attain full maturity in the southern zone, while large numbers of deer die of old age in the Adirondacks or finally succumb to the rigors of a severe winter. The last two deer taken by the author were aged at deer checking stations and found to be 10½ years of age or older. These deer were ready for an old age pension. Both bucks carried nice eight-point antlers and would have supported even larger racks if shot at the peak of their physical condition. The

HANS PALLER

odds are much greater in shooting a large trophy deer in the Adirondacks than anywhere else in the state.

On a weight basis, the Adirondack buck will be larger only because it attains a ripe old age. When comparing deer of the same age groups, it will be found that the southern and western deer will average 20 pounds heavier than Adirondack deer. Overbrowsing and deterioration of winter range in the north country is the primary reason for this weight differential, since all deer have the same average weight at birth—7 pounds, 7 ounces for males, and 5 pounds 11½ ounces for the females. But because of longevity, the odds are 50-50 that the northern hunter will harvest a buck that will be at least 145 pounds, while the odds are only one in four that you will ever take a deer of this size in the southern zone. The southern deer never live long enough to make it out of kindergarten!

Under normal conditions, a deer herd can double in size every few years, but it will take a little longer in the Adirondacks. Excessive browsing of forage plants has reduced their vigor, and it will be some time before the plants respond to abundant growth.

But the deer are making a rapid comeback and there are some great trophy bucks in the Boone and Crockett class available to hunters. The key to continued fine big-game hunting is a return to either-sex seasons in the Adirondacks. A sustained harvest of does will not only insure a higher rate of fawn production and winter survival, but will provide a greater economic return for those Adirondack communities that rely on deer hunting for a substantial source of revenue.

A well-planned wilderness camping trip combined with deer hunting is one of the great opportunities still available. It is trophy buck hunting at budget prices for the sportsman that wants something special for his deer hunting vacation.

The visitor to the Adirondacks is invited to experience a different kind of outdoor adventure. A hunting trip in one of the few quiet places left in the East.

Dave Drakula made his first trip to a northcentral Pennsylvania deer camp at the age of nine. He went as an observer, and three years later became a participant. Since that time, Dave has never missed a Pennsylvania buck season and has killed a buck in every one of his seventeen hunting seasons. In 1967, Dave was awarded the Pennsylvania Game Commission's coveted Triple Trophy for killing a wild turkey, black bear, and whitetail buck in the same hunting season.

Today, Dave lives in Cameron County, the center of big-game hunting in northcentral Pennsylvania. He is literally surrounded by mountains and whitetails. "The whitetail is an important part of my everyday life," he says. "I see them all, the first fawns and autumn's bucks. There is no greater game animal."

7

DEER HUNTING IN NORTHCENTRAL PENNSYLVANIA— THE PAST, PRESENT AND FUTURE

Dave Drakula

The past: the golden days. Northcentral Pennsylvania is the last remaining extensive forest area in the Keystone State. Composed basically of Cameron, Elk, McKean, and Potter Counties, the area totals some 3,294 square miles. It is crossed by numerous streams, and its steep mountains are covered with hardwoods. Much of the area is part of the Allegheny Plateau, a great flat region that has had its face scarred and twisted by the forces of man and nature. It is a remote area where the modern traveler familiar with super highways must content himself with narrow blacktop or meandering woods roads.

When the white man first came into this country, he found it dark and forbidding. Most of the region was covered with huge stands of white pine and hemlock. It was virgin timber, except for areas that had been burned over by Indians or where lightning had caused fires. A man might walk for miles in a park-like atmosphere. Fish were plentiful. Bear, wild turkeys, panthers, and bobcats roamed the forest.

Although pictures of buckskin-clad pioneers making their way home with a whitetail slung over their shoulder lead us to believe that vension was easy to come by, that was not the case. In some areas deer were plentiful, but many huge tracts were devoid of whitetails. Early settlers moved into the area and began to clear the forest land. This improved the situation for deer to a small degree. However, it took the navies of the world to create the fabulous era of deer hunting.

The end of the Civil War marked a beginning for northcentral Pennsylvania. The steam engine was just starting to make its mark on the transportation industry, but world travel, trade, and exploration still depended on the breezes. Good, strong straight masts were required to hoist the sails and carry the rigging of the world's navies. And it was those masts that northcentral Pennsylvania had in abundance.

The great white pines that clothed the mountain sides and rendered much of the forest floor lifeless now became the object of an influx of a new kind of "mountain man"—the logger. While his earlier counterpart had been interested solely in game, fur, and fish, the new resident looked with delight upon the timber. The logging era began.

At the same time the logger was making inroads into the Pennsylvania mountains, the hunters of the day were fast

eliminating the white-tailed deer from his home grounds. Hunting in those days was much different from what we know today. Shooting over a "lick" was regarded as one of the best methods to secure venison. A "lick" was a boggy area where mineral water, primarily salt, bubbled or seeped to the surface. The deer came to these locations with regularity. The hunter simply constructed a blind near the lick and waited until a deer made his appearance.

The waiting period was not always serene. Numerous accounts of hunters being attacked by panthers fill the pages of historical documents recorded during this period.

Deer were also hunted with dogs, and a dog's value as a deer hunter was often based on the number of whitetails he had run down and killed for his human companion.

Despite the fact that using dogs to hunt deer was barred in Pennsylvania in 1873, the practice continued until the beginning of the 20th century. Today, some old-timers can still recall the days when they let the dogs loose and waited until they "brought a deer to water," that is, ran the deer until it became exhausted in a stream or creek bottom.

Deer killed during these years became an important part of the family larder. Lumber camps frequently augmented their meat supply with fresh venison. However, it was the hotel, the saloon, and the neighborhood market that combined to spur on the killing of whitetails. For some 35 years northcentral Pennsylvania provided venison and other game for free-lunch counters in the better saloons of Philadelphia and Pittsburgh.

Near the turn of the century the white-tailed deer was practically eliminated in northcentral Pennsylvania. The combined forces of unrestricted hunting and complete clearing of the forest left the whitetail in a precarious position.

In 1887, Andrew Kaul and J. K. P. Hall of Elk County established Trout Run Park, a 600-acre area located between St. Marys and Bennezette in the heart of the wilderness. The area was completely enclosed by an eight to ten foot fence and stocked with twelve deer. Sometime later, the Williamsport *Republican* of Williamsport, Pennsylvania, reported, "There are not less than one hundred and fifty deer within the park." A historian of the period commented on the Park, "While the unthinking hunter has for years industriously engaged in killing the deer, it is a relief to think that two citizens at least, have succeeded in saving a number of them."

With the great stands of white pine eliminated, the loggers turned their attention to the hemlock. At first, only the bark was taken, to be used in tanning. In time, however, mills were established to produce lumber. In their day they were regarded as giants. The mill at Austin, Pennsylvania, in Potter County could produce 100,000 feet of lumber per day, a marvel of the times.

By the year 1900, most of the white pine and hemlock had been cut from the mountains. Great barrens stretched for miles. Masses of impenetrable slashings lay upon the mountain sides. Forest fires ran rampant, denuding the hills even more and completing what appeared to be a scene of utter destruction.

But it was far from total destruction. Even before the woodsman's ax had ceased to ring, nature had begun to heal her wounds. Vast regions sprang to life with blackberry thickets and fire cherry. Second-growth hemlock and denied hardwoods found the sun and turned the mountain sides into a jungle. Out of the ashes of destruction, the embers of life began to burn.

During these years, deer became increasingly rare. Hunters who sighted an animal or even a track talked about the occasion for many nights. Plans were carefully laid, supplies were accumulated, and snow was awaited. When it came, the hunters packed their belongings and the hunt began. Often it was several days before the hunters "picked up" a deer track. Once a track was found, the hunters remained on the trail until the deer was killed. This often required several nights in the woods. These nights around the campfire produced numerous hunting stories, and were often garnished with the contents of a stone jug. All in all, it was regarded as an inevitable part of the hunt.

Shotguns loaded with buckshot were the order of the day. Rifles were sometimes used, but they just didn't handle fast enough. In thick cover, where the object of a four-day hunt could disappear in one jump, pattern and brush-busting ability were the attributes most desired in a "deer gun."

Perhaps it is a sad commentary on human beings to say that we often fail to give a matter attention until it reaches a state of seriousness and is termed critical. As sad as the commentary may be, it is certainly true with regard to the mountains and the deer herd of north-central Pennsylvania.

With the deer herd on the verge of extinction and the mountains struggling to reforest themselves, the state government began to move. During the years 1898 to 1913, almost a million acres of land were acquired by the then Department of Forests and Waters. By the year 1949, the land acquisitions had reached 1,723,764 acres.

Great tracts of this land were labeled "worthless" and were subsequently acquired for unpaid taxes. Trees do not grow to marketable proportions overnight, and these were lean years for the Department of Forests and Waters. As late as 1939, "Pennsylvania had dropped to twenty-third place in lumber output and the actual cutting of saw lumber was less than one-twelfth of what it had been in its greatest productive year."

One of the greatest benefits resulting from the acquisition of land by the state was protection accorded the forest from fire. This was the era of the fire wardens, a heirarchy of men headed by the chief

warden and extending downward to the special warden. Their constant battle with the "red horse" brought security and stability to the mountains.

Organized as the Board of Game Commissioners in 1895, the Pennsylvania Game Commission began to play its part in bringing the deer back from the edge of the cliff. In rapid succession, a series of laws was passed offering great protection for the whitetail. Killing deer over salt licks and hunting deer with hounds were forbidden. Buckshot was banned for deer hunting. The first Game Refuge Law was made a reality in 1905. In 1906, fifty deer were imported from Michigan and stocking began in northcentral Pennsylvania.

After years of unrestricted hunting, residents did not take kindly to the new laws and the men who were sent to enforce them. This was the time when game protectors became legends. Cecil Marsh, who served as game protector for Cameron County, reportedly "sent the fear of the Lord into every would-be violator."

Marsh was kindly compensated with threats, and brawls, and was occasionally the target of off-season shooting practice. Climbing into his car one day, he noticed a thin wire leading under the seat. Investigating, he discovered a bundle of dynamite wired to explode when he started the engine. No, sir, game protectors just weren't appreciated by everyone.

In 1907, the Pennsylvania Legislature passed the first of two pieces of legislation that would affect northcentral Pennsyl-

DAVE DRAKULA

Outstanding food, excellent habitat equals bucks like these. This picture taken in the late 1920's shows why hunters referred to these years as " The Golden Days of Deer Hunting." Many of these bucks weighed close to two hundred pounds and their racks were heavy and well developed.

vania deer hunting for all time. It was known as the Buck Law, and under it antlerless deer were given complete protection.

If proof is desired of the oft-quoted statement, "Nature abhors a vacuum," then northcentral Pennsylvania can offer the evidence. With the lands coming back into brush-stage timber, fire protection doing its job, game refuges established, game laws being enforced, and the importation of deer for stocking, the whitetail began its climb back.

At first the climb was slow, but gradually the herd picked up size until the deer population literally exploded in the 1920s and 1930s.

For many hunters, this will always remain the "Golden Age" of deer hunting in Pennsylvania. Medix Run, once a bustling lumber town in southeastern Elk County, became the center of operations for the deer hunter. During deer season, its population skyrocketed as hunters came for their two weeks in the "north woods."

There were no paved roads in this section, so hunters came by train, some appropriately named "Hunters' Specials." Local people with horses and wagons hired out to act as chauffeurs. The wagons were loaded with supplies, and the occupants began the last leg of their trip to camp. It was a festive occasion.

If there wasn't a deer behind every bush, there must have been one behind

This was the way the fellows went to camp in the "good ol' days." Camp was a canvas tent set up by local guides before the hunters arrived on the Hunter Special, a special train for anxious gunners. The horse and wagon brought hunters and supplies to camp and carried venison back to the railroad siding. In the background, the brush stage timber is beginning to take hold.

every other stand of foliage. Jim Ross, veteran hunter and outdoor writer from DuBois, Pennsylvania, recalls that on one occasion he watched a herd of 85 deer go past him.

"At the end of the string, there were three bucks," Jim says, "and I killed one. If you missed a buck, it was nothing to get excited about. Just wait around and another one would come by in a little while."

With good food and cover, the deer were heavy and the bucks well supplied with antlers. Pictures taken at the time show many trophy bucks weighing well over 150 pounds. Today, many camps, restaurants, and taverns have the mounted head of a trophy buck that was killed during those "Golden Years."

Although still-hunting was practiced by many hunters, the organized drive with tree stands was a real venison getter. More and more camps were springing up in this area, and 25 hunters was not an unusual number to have bunked out for the deer season. Each evening the captain

106

DAVE DRAKULA

of the camp would call a get-together and the strategy would be laid for the next day's hunt. Regular turns were taken at driving and watching. Drives were named for some outstanding feature of the landscape—the Big Pine Drive, the Round Mountain Drive, and the Crow's Nest Drive, the last being associated with a tree stand.

In 1923, the period of the "sacred doe" came to an end when the Pennsylvania Game Commission was given the power to declare an antlerless deer season. Although for some years the Game Commission only declared "doe season" in specific counties, the problems of an expanding northcentral Pennsylvania deer herd would soon look to the doe season as a savior.

As time passed, there were ominous signs that the days of plenty were about to end.

Winters were terribly hard on the deer herd. Game Commission employees often spent days bringing in dead and starving deer. In the spring, trout fishermen were often kept from fishing certain streams because of the stench of rotting deer carcasses.

The quality of the deer range was rapidly deteriorating. Areas that once held fantastic numbers of deer and even more fantastic supplies of grouse and rabbits were simply "eaten out" by their larger four-footed neighbors. The "Golden Days" of deer hunting were over.

The Present: stability in the mountains. To a deer, the forest is home. Today, much of northcentral Pennsylvania is not a hospitable abode for the whitetail. Bushy hillsides where deer disappeared in a single bound, where man struggled to penetrate

In the "Big Woods" country of north-central Pennsylvania, deer have tough going during long, severe winters. This young deer shows the effects of a hard winter in an area where browse is scarce. Timber cutting operations produce food supplies, promise better hunting, healthier whitetail specimens. PHOTO COURTESY OF POTTER ENTERPRISE.

Don Wills, forester for the Hammermill Paper Company, examines a young pine that clearly indicates the effects of heavy deer browsing. In some areas, natural reforestation is made impossible because of deer that concentrate on lands that have timbered. Keeping the herd in balance with available food supplies is a major goal of the Pennsylvania Game Commission.

the dense undergrowth, have disappeared. They have been replaced by big timber, timber that effectively shades out light and renders the forest floor almost lifeless.

From its high point in the 1920s and 1930s, the deer herd has declined, seeking a level commensurate with the land's ability to provide. Where a hunter once saw one hundred deer in a day, today he is more apt to see 10 or 15.

Despite the obvious drop in overall numbers, the mountain herd has remained relatively stable over the past fifteen years. An analysis of the deer kill figures for the area shows an average harvest of approximately 8,000 bucks and 7,500 does. Potter County has long been recognized as one of the top deer-producing counties in the Commonwealth. Over the years it has averaged a total deer kill of between five and six thousand animals per year.

Variations do occur, of course. Weather is an important factor in an area where the deer range is in poor condition. The long, bitter winter of 1969–1970 dealt a severe blow to the herd in many localities. Nevertheless, milder winters followed the next two years, and these same areas once again provided good deer hunting.

Many hunters reminisce about the

DAVE DRAKULA

"rocking chair racks" that once adorned every buck that crossed their watch. At present, a real trophy buck from the northcentral mountains is an exception. In some years almost 75% of the deer killed are spike bucks.

Food supply is certainly one factor involved in antler growth. However, the age of northcentral Pennsylvania deer also plays an important part. Let me illustrate with a story.

The opening of the 1966 buck season was one of the most uncomfortable, most frustrating days I have ever spent in the woods. At 7:00 a.m., it was misting and foggy. By 10:00 a.m., rain was coming down in torrents. At 3:00 p.m., there was four inches of heavy wet snow on everything. Tree branches were bent to the ground, making the woods a wall of white. Visibility was absolutely zero. The snow continued on through the night, and deer hunting slid to a stop.

It is the custom of many visiting hunters to make a three-day trip to northcentral Pennslyvania. After their time has elapsed, they pack up and go home. In 1966, many hunters gathered their gear and left after the first day.

The result of the bad opening-day weather was an equally poor opening-day buck kill. Bucks that normally would have fallen victim to the hunter were spared. After a cold and snowy first week,

Like many other game species, winter range is the most important factor in determining how many deer will be available come next hunting season. The fawn in the foreground is already beginning to show some signs that point to starvation. Sunken eyes, protruding hip bones and a fuzzy appearance of the hair about the head indicate the animal's poor physical condition.

the weather turned mild and a buck bonanza was set for 1967.

Bonanza is about the best word to describe the situation. Along with the high carry over of deer, the mountains were blessed with a tremendous mast crop. Trees were literally bending under loads of acorns, beechnuts, and wild cherries.

Big bucks were everywhere. That year our deer camp played host to twelve hunters. After the first day, ten bucks graced the hemlock in front of camp. Only one of the ten was a spike. The largest was a monster of a nine-pointer.

We were the rule, not the exception, in 1967. After the season I investigated a number of camp rosters and found that many were even more successful than ours. I recall one camp in the Four Mile section of Cameron County that had fourteen bucks for fifteen hunters. All were taken on the first two days and only three were spikes.

The year 1967 was abnormal and is probably as close as we shall ever come to the good old "Golden Days."

Although the major area of northcentral Pennsylvania is made up of forestland, there are some sections that boast forest intermixed with farms. Northern Potter County and the area around Smethport and Port Allegheny in McKean County are two such places. The Potter County Big Buck Contest provides proof that in areas with good feed, big bucks do exist. Still, the 180-pound trophy buck is a rarity. Most bucks killed are yearlings and average close to one

The farm country of Potter County and other agricultural areas of north-central Pennsylvania still produce trophy racks like this one. In the past few years, more and more hunters are beginning to concentrate their efforts in areas like these. PHOTO COURTESY OF POTTER ENTERPRISE

hundred pounds hog dressed. Does will average eighty to ninety pounds.

Aside from the obvious changes in the forest and the deer herd, perhaps the most significant differences between the past and the present rest with the hunter himself. To begin with, there are more hunters today than at any time in the past. Undoubtedly, part of this is due to population increase. But an important part of the increase has also been made possible by the present-day hunter's mobility. Northcentral Pennsylvania lies within easy reach of most of the large

DAVE DRAKULA

metropolitan areas of the East. With the opening of new highways such as Interstate 80, hunters from surrounding states and Pennsylvania's largest cities have little difficulty reaching their hunting grounds in a matter of a few short hours.

A great part of our hunting tradition is still going "north" to camp. However, an increasing number of hunters carry their camps with them. The advent of the truck camper has revolutionized deer hunting in this area. If a hunting party is not particularly successful in one area, they simply load up their gear and strike out for new country, taking everything including the kitchen sink with them. Convenience, comfort, and mobility have never been closer together.

The impact of the deer hunter in a tent, mobile home, or truck camper has been enormous. Whereas state parks used to close their gates after Labor Day, now they prepare for the onslaught of hunters. Private camp grounds have also multiplied in an effort to take some of the pressure off the state facilities and to "cash in" on the visiting hunters. From comfortable motel rooms to well-selected tenting sites, the present-day hunter has a choice that will fit his pocketbook and his comfort. Like the "Golden Days" of deer hunting, the evenings around a campfire far back on a mountain ridge are gone.

There are other differences in today's Nimrod that mirror the changes that have come over deer hunting. The 30/30, 32 Special, and 35 Remington are rarely seen in the northcentral mountains. Ask today's aspiring young hunter what gun he uses for deer hunting and he'll probably answer, a 243, or 308, or a 6.5 mm. Chances are, his father is already shooting that kind of gun.

Scopes, once rare and regarded as unnecessary gadgets, are present on just about every rifle used for deer hunting. Today's hunter is likely to see deer at ranges that weren't even discussed in the "Golden Days." Trying to pick out four spikes on a moving deer 150 yards away isn't easy, and most hunters don't trust the human eye to perform that task.

Weather is an important consideration for the deer hunter. Several years ago, opening-day bear hunters basked in 60- and 70-degree temperatures. Overnight the temperature plunged and twenty inches of snow blanketed the mountains. Being prepared is a good standing rule.

Years ago, a hunter learned the country by spending time in it, memorizing the ridges and etching a map of all the area's peculiarities in his mind. Today, many sporting goods shops, hardware stores and restaurant in the "big woods country" carry complete lines of topographic maps. Although they may be outdated in respect to trails and buildings, the maps give the weekend deer hunter an excellent idea of the lay of the land.

Perhaps every deer hunter imagines or looks forward to the day when he jumps a buck, takes up the trail, and without interference stalks the animal until he bags his trophy. That "dream" can still be a reality in northcentral Pennsylvania.

However, it will have to happen after the first two or three days of the season.

During the first few days of deer season, the human population of the northcentral counties doubles, even triples in size. With so many hunters in the woods, the deer are kept moving. The best idea is to find a good place to sit and wait it out. That's the way most bucks are bagged.

In a final look at deer hunting today in northcentral Pennsylvania, the greatest attraction for the hunter is the opportunity to pursue this fine game animal without numerous land restrictions. Taken together, Cameron, Elk, McKean, and Potter Counties have over one half million acres of Game Lands and State Forest Lands. Add to this the nearly one and a half million acres of private land that is open to public hunting, and it is obvious that here is a place where hunters seldom have to worry about posted ground and finding a place to stretch their legs.

I think my father once summed it up best when he said, "Well, maybe there aren't as many deer as there used to be and maybe they aren't as big as they once were. But the greatest satisfaction I get out of these mountains is just being here where the air is fresh, the water is clean, and it's quiet for a while."

Maybe these are "Golden Days" of a different type?

The Future: a change in priorities. The future looks bright for deer hunting in northcentral Pennsylvania. After interviewing experts, talking to hunters, and personally watching the situation for a dozen years, that is the consensus of opinion.

There will, of course, be changes. The huge deer herds and unlimited trophy racks are gone. They will never reappear. But the deer herd will continue to exist, experiencing periodic ups and downs.

As always, the condition of a deer herd depends directly on the condition of its winter range. But there is reason for optimism. The Bureau of Forestry, Department of Environmental Resources, and large private lumber companies have formulated ambitious plans for the management of their large land holdings. An important part of these plans calls for the improvement of wildlife habitat.

Clear-cutting, criticized in many areas of the country, will be an important tool in many land-management programs. However, unlike some areas of the country where clear cuts have been carried out with little pre-planning, the proposed clear-cut sites on these forest lands will be studied carefully beforehand. The studies range from soil samples, to evaluations of slopes, to aesthetic considerations.

Clear-cutting has already been carried out on some sections of northcentral Pennsylvania forest land. The effects on the deer population have been immediate and beneficial. An instant abundance of food from the cuttings plus a sustained production of browse from new growth are drawing cards for whitetails. In fact, some clear cuts have attracted too many

DAVE DRAKULA

Successful hunters at an early deer camp. Clothes, guns and accommodations have changed, along with the rise and fall of whitetail populations. Despite ups and downs in deer numbers, the present population continues to hold its own and promises good hunting for the future.

deer, and the desired forest reproduction has not been successful. The Department of Environmental Resources and private companies urge and request hunters to concentrate on these areas.

In sections where clear-cutting is not deemed practical, timber-stand improvement cuts will be made. Though they do not provide as much browse as the clear cuts, they are still beneficial to the deer herd.

In the mid-1960s a serious insect pest struck much of the northcentral Pennsylvania deer range. This insect, the oak leaf roller, stripped extensive stands of oak of their foliage. Mortality among the oaks was high. Many hunters predicted the end of the oaks as a mast producer and the beginning of the end of the deer herd. They compared it to the loss of the American chestnut.

Just when the oak leaf roller looked like it was dealing a final blow to the oak, the insect began a downward trend. An interesting development followed. Large areas once shaded from the sun were suddenly basking in light. The forest began to come alive with fireweed, fire cherry, maple sprouts, mountain laurel and luxuriant growths of weeds and grass. Deer were frequently observed in these areas. In many respects, it began to take on the appearance of a forest in 1900.

In addition, the Department of Environmental Resources launched extensive cutting operations designed to salvage as much of the oak as possible for timber.

The two factors combined have produced several areas of excellent deer hunting.

As an example, the Quehanna area of Cameron County has generally been regarded as being on the downhill slide in regard to deer habitat. However, the 1972 buck season dispelled many of those ideas. Researchers from Penn State University checked bucks taken from this area that had fine racks and weighed more than 35 pounds above the average weight of northcentral Pennsylvania bucks.

According to the researchers, the reasons for this growth and size were twofold. First, an increased food supply through cutting and the production of a good mast crop. Second, the lack of hunting pressure, which permitted the deer to reach an older age.

It is difficult to predict what will happen to the northcentral forests in the future. Just as the market for spars and masts dictated the cutting of timber in the late 19th and early 20th centuries, today's wood markets will determine just how much and what type of timber will be cut in the future. Recycling technology could drastically cut the demand for pulpwood. And the development of building substitutes for lumber could seriously affect the demand for saw timber. The American consumer could well determine the future of northcentral Pennsylvania's deer herd.

If predicting the future of the forests is somewhat clouded, there is one area that receives a positive prediction. In the years ahead, more hunters will come to northcentral Pennsylvania to seek their venison. The reasons are numerous. Urban sprawl alone renders upwards of 43,000 acres of Commonwealth land incompatible with hunting each year. Posting and leasing of land by private hunting clubs removes thousands of other acres. As this land is lost to the hunter, he will concentrate his efforts on areas that have considerable public and private land open to public hunting.

From the standpoint of deer management, antlerless-deer seasons will continue to be the important element in the control of the region's deer herd. When winters are mild and the size of the herd is able to grow, antlerless license allocations will have to be increased to prevent over-browsing and starvation.

History is a great teacher. Pennslyvanians have seen what can happen when a deer herd is unprotected or when it is permitted to grow beyond what the habitat can support. They recognize the value of this animal as a game species and as an addition to life in the mountains. The tradition of deer hunting in this part of Pennsylvania is deeply ingrained. Nevertheless, it will undergo changes. Even today, there are hunters who indicate these changes. I asked a hunter recently why he left a good deer-hunting area to come to northcentral Pennsylvania. He mused for a while and then replied, "I probably could have killed a buck back home, but it's too crowded. I just want to come up to the big woods for a couple of days."

In an unstated way, this man realized that the quality of the hunting experience is becoming more important. In the future, the memories a deer hunter carries from the mountains will be more important than the game in his freezer. From all indications, the "big woods" white-tailed deer will continue to inspire those memories.

John O. Cartier shot his first Michigan whitetail buck in 1942 when he was fifteen years old. Since then he has hunted deer every fall except for a few seasons during his college and military years. He served in the Army Air Force during World War II, attended Notre Dame and Michigan State Universities, and received his degree in Industrial Engineering. He began free-lance outdoor writing twenty-three years ago as a hobby, and in 1964 he gave up his executive position as plant manager of a Michigan manufacturing corporation to accept an appointment as Midwest Field Editor of *Outdoor Life*. His duties for the magazine have included hunting and fishing trips ranging from the north slope of Alaska to southern Mexico. He has scored on many trophy whitetail bucks, and he has hunted deer across North America. The author of nearly two hundred magazine stories, plus two books, Cartier resides with his wife and family in Ludington, Michigan.

Portions of this chapter are adapted from *Outdoor Life* magazine; *Watch the Buck Runways* © 1968; *Foray for Deer* © 1968; *Hotspot for Trophy Whitetails* © 1970; Popular Science Publishing Company, Inc.

8

OUTWITTING MICHIGAN WHITETAILS

John O. Cartier

THE BIGGEST WHITETAIL buck I ever saw in Michigan offered me one of the finest shooting opportunities I've had in thirty years of chasing venison. I blew that long-ago opportunity. The reason I failed to score is the same reason many of today's hunters head home without a buck.

The place was the edge of a dirt road near the far western end of Michigan's Upper Peninsula. Our group numbered ten experienced deer hunters. We had driven two pickup trucks down a little-used road, and parked where the sandy ruts turned sharply along the edge of 120 acres of farmland thickets. We were about to put on a drive. Our host, who owned the property on which we were hunting, explained the logistics of his strategy.

"It's a half mile through these thickets," Bob told me. "On the other side a big

pasture field borders another road. The field runs to a creek bottom edged with swamp and thick timber. If the drivers spook any deer out of here, they'll likely run across that field and head for the woods. I'll put you on a stand where you'll have a clear shot across the whole field."

"You fellows know the lay of the land," Bob said to the rest of the group. "Spread out along this road, and head straight north. Give us ten minutes to get in position, then start your drive."

Moments later we'd driven around to the north side of the thickets, and I'd stepped out of the pickup near a roadside clump of willows. Ahead of us, the pasture field stretched four hundred yards to the east and six hundred yards to the north. "Stand right here," Bob instructed me. "Usually, the deer will run the field, but sometimes they'll bolt across that little clearing behind you. I'll go down the road a half mile, then cut in south."

I watched the pickup move away while I pushed cartridges into my rifle. To the south, fifty yards away, the 120-acre thicket ended in a red-tinged border of willows. The willows came closest to the road near the small clearing to the west. I heard the drivers then, distant yells marked the beginning of the march. "I would guess," I muttered to myself, "that no buck in his right mind would run an open field when he can cut across a smaller clearing."

With that conviction in mind, I faced west and concentrated on the edge of the willows. If a buck bolted out of there, he'd be anywhere from 50 to 200 yards away. My rifle was sighted for 250 yards, so I'd have to hold a bit low. "On the other hand," I thought, "I wonder how far it is to the middle of that open field. Maybe I better check that distance too." I slowly turned to the east.

The buck was running like a race horse, broadside and straight out at full throttle. There had been no sound, no forewarning of any kind. He was simply there, already halfway across the dull brown pasture. I saw the antlers as soon as I saw the deer, and I don't think I'll ever see another whitetail rack like it. The thick tines appeared ivory-colored, and they rode above the buck's head and neck like a massive crown. There wasn't a twig between us.

I put the crosshairs of the scope on his

chest and touched the trigger. I fully expected him to crumple, but he never missed a step. I bolted in the second cartridge and fired again. The buck never wavered, and never changed direction. Still, I knew I'd get him.

I increased my lead, held a foot high, then crashed away the third bullet. The monster buck veered into a dip in the field, and when I touched off the fourth cartridge my scope showed only his head and neck. My breath was coming in gasps, and the range was over four hundred yards. The incredible was happening, I was about to lose that magnificent trophy.

My fifth and last cartridge was in the chamber when the buck reappeared in full view. He was going straight away now, and he was only a few yards from the safety of the woods. Through the scope, I noted his wide-beamed antlers extending far out beyond the sides of his body. "My gosh," I thought, "what a rack. I've just got to hit him!"

The crosshairs of the scope wavered, then steadied a couple of feet above the buck's head. I held my breath, and the 100 grain slug was on its way. The deer was at the edge of the woods when the rifle jolted. When I regained my view through the scope I saw a blur of white and brown disappearing into distant trees. Did he go down, or was he bounding to final safety? In my heart, I knew I'd missed again.

Numbly, I walked to the middle of the field, picked up the buck's tracks, and followed them far into the woods. There was no blood, no hair, no anything. I had simply goofed the greatest deer hunting opportunity I'd ever had. I'd missed a record-book buck. I'd missed him five times, and I'd missed him in an open field.

The moral of that story involves two major points concerning whitetail strategy. First, Bob was a veteran deer hunter and he lived on the property he hunted. He knew the habits of whitetails in the area. He knew where the deer would likely be bedded, he knew their probable escape routes, and he knew which direction they would run when driven with a special technique. Sportsmen who kill Michigan bucks year after year almost always have intimate knowledge of the ways of whitetails. More on that later.

The all important reason why I didn't nail that enormous buck was because I didn't know enough about shooting my rifle to put my bullets where I wanted them to go. At that time I was a young man and my main interest in deer hunting was meat on the table. As far as shooting interest was concerned I was a shotgun nut. I used my shotguns all fall for waterfowl and upland birds, and during the off-seasons for crows, barnyard pigeons, skeet and trap. I could shoot with the best of wingshots, but my deer rifle stayed in my gun cabinet year around except during whitetail season.

I was so disgusted with myself for missing the big whitetail that I vowed it would never happen again. The following winter I purchased a Winchester Model 70 in

Hunting in farm lands often offers wide-open shooting opportunities.

.243 caliber, and I used it for fox and crow hunting. During the summer I shot at targets at a local sportsman's club. I used the rifle practically year round for shooting at moving and still targets, plus varmints.

As the years passed I became very interested in hunting for trophy bucks over much of North America. The payoff came one year in Saskatchewan when that Upper Michigan scene was almost exactly duplicated.

A drive was involved again. I was on a stand, and again an enormous whitetail buck was driven across a wide-open field in front of me. But this time I was well aware that a whitetail running broadside at full steam, and at long range, can very easily be missed if you don't lead him by an amount that would seem ridiculous to

Most Michigan bucks with large racks head for remote areas when deer season opens.
Hunters with the physical stamina to go "back in" after them often score on trophies.

the unknowing rifleman. I put the cross-hairs of my scope more than a deer-length in front of the animal's chest and touched off. He never faltered, but I heard the unmistakable "thump" of my slug hitting flesh and bone. I shot again with the same lead, heard the same result, and watched that fine trophy pitch forward on his face. The eleven-pointer was dead when he hit the ground.

The point is that a deer hunter who doesn't know how to use his rifle with efficiency is going to miss out on harvesting a lot of venison. All the knowledge of stalking, trail-watching, driving or whatever, goes down the drain if you can't capitalize on a shooting opportunity when it's presented. When you become as familiar with handling your rifle as you

are with handling your car or a much-used camera, then you'll be a proficient rifleman. If you hunt in a shotgun-only area you have to know what your shotgun can do when loaded with slugs. It all comes down to practice with your firearm. I can say no more on the subject than, if you don't know how to shoot accurately, you're bound to be a disappointed whitetail hunter.

How to get a good shooting opportunity at a fine whitetail buck has been the subject of hundreds of magazine articles and dozens of books. The picture in Michigan has changed in recent years. Let's consider what we're up against.

As recently as 1966, Michigan deer hunters harvested an estimated 112,000 whitetails. That's a whale of a lot of deer,

120

JOHN O. CARTIER

and it's the reason why the state enjoys its reputation of offering great deer hunting. But the harvest figure is misleading. Up to 500,000 hunters go after Michigan deer, so the hunter-success ratio seldom tops 25 per cent. That's not very impressive when it's stacked against hunter-success ratios averaging better than 50 per cent in several western and prairie states.

Add to that fact that Michigan venison chasers, overall, have racked up ever lower success ratios in recent years because the state's whitetail herd is declining due to decreasing habitat. However, there's another side to the picture. In 1972, one of the state's hunters received some publicity concerning the fact that he had harvested twenty-six whitetails during his twenty-six years of deer hunting in the Wolverine State. That's unusual in itself, but it was astonishing to learn the hunter had achieved the feat with bow and arrows.

A friend of mine who never missed getting his buck for many years, gave up hunting with a rifle because, as he says, "Killing a deer with a firearm is too easy; I've switched to archery gear. I get lots of shooting opportunities every fall."

In 1973, one of the state's popular TV outdoor shows presented a most enlightening program. It was a panel discussion between three masked and shadowed deer poachers and a team of deer experts from the state's Department of Natural Resources (DNR). The amazing thing that came out of the talk session was that all three poachers freely admitted they could

kill deer anytime they wanted venison, and that they never resorted to jacklighting or night hunting because they didn't want to get caught violating.

Such examples of fantastic deer-hunting success are too frequent to mention. But ask the super hunters for the secrets of their success and you'll invariably get the same answer—"Go where the deer are and know how to hunt them."

As this was being written, in 1973, the best places to hunt deer in Michigan were the northcentral and southern counties of the lower peninsula. Twenty years earlier there were hardly any deer in the southern farmlands. At that time the upper peninsula was noted for its trophy bucks and its huge herds of whitetails. By the early 1970's the long famous deer harvests of the U.P. had hit the skids in drastic fashion. The herds declined because the habitat declined. Second-growth browse, which had covered the land, matured to the point where it no longer offered food for deer.

That picture may change. In 1972 the state's DNR began a massive program to rebuild prime whitetail habitat throughout northern counties. The program involves great expenditures of money for management techniques including specialized bulldozing, controlled burning, and planting of shrubs and trees. The Department's announced goal is to build the state's whitetail herd to one million animals by 1980. That's almost twice as many deer as Michigan has ever had.

Whitetails have an astonishing ability

to explode their populations when offered top habitat, so the DNR's plan may meet with great success. The point is that there's no sense in my telling you where the best deer hunting will be in Michigan during the next several years because the picture may change dramatically. Your best bet is to get current information on deer concentration areas from game officials, DNR publications, or other media reports.

That takes care of the problem of where to go. I'll devote the rest of this chapter to discussing the tricks to be used for outsmarting your buck.

It's my opinion that still-hunting is almost a total waste of time in Michigan. Too many odds favor the deer. They have senses of hearing and smell far superior to ours. And their eyesight isn't nearly as bad as claimed by some so-called experts. This has been proven to me many times in the western states where you can see for great distances.

One time my guide and I tried stalking a big whitetail buck which was browsing on the side of a canyon. When we first spotted the animal he was fifteen hundred yards away and unaware of us. We made our approach from behind a ridge that completely screened our movements. The wind was in our favor, and the ground was soft enough to muffle the sounds of our footsteps. We had traveled less than half the distance to the buck when my guide risked a peek over the ridge.

"Damn whitetails," he said. "That old boy is looking right at us, and he's alerted.

If that was a mule deer he wouldn't be so smart. Something tipped that buck off. About the only way you can kill a smart whitetail is to make him come to you. They're almost impossible to stalk."

Many are the times I've set up a spotting scope and tried to locate big bucks bedded under rims of ridges and knolls. I've spotted a lot of them, and almost invariably they were staring straight at me, well aware of my presence and ready to bolt at any second.

I couldn't begin to count the times I've seen Michigan whitetails move into pockets of cover and not come out. I knew the deer had bedded down, and I thought I had perfect opportunities to make a stalk. Sometimes I got close enough to see bouncing white flags flash through the brush ahead of me as the alerted animals made their escape. Often I'd spot the critters crossing knolls or ridges so far ahead I thought it was impossible they had become warned of my approach at such great distances. Those many experiences taught me long ago that there is almost no way for a single man to outsmart a whitetail at his own game on his own grounds. When you come to the realization that the best way to score on whitetails is through some system of trail-watching or driving you're on your way to success.

This is as good a place as any to mention other examples pointing out why the odds are stacked so highly against the still-hunter or stalker.

A few years ago a rancher in a southern

Fine whitetails on farm-country buck pole.

state decided that his spread was becoming overrun with whitetails. During previous years he had allowed hunters on his land. The annual harvest averaged eight to ten deer. During the year in question he decided to permit hunters to use dogs for the first time. Though the use of dogs was legal in that state, the landowner had not allowed their use previously, nor had he allowed hunters to use the driving technique.

But this time, because he wanted a lot of deer killed, he placed hunters on strategic stands. He got his wish when gunners harvested nearly one hundred whitetails. The reason for the tremendous increase in kill was that the dogs kept deer moving past gunners hidden on stands. The lesson? Running whitetails are far less cautious than deer that aren't being chased.

A Michigan story proves the same point in reverse fashion. The Cusino wildlife experiment station held an experiment that involved "sight-hunting." Six veteran hunters and thirty-nine deer (seven bucks) were pitted against each other in one square mile surrounded by deer-proof fencing. It took four days before one buck was seen! During the next four years, with the herd growing in numbers, the best sighting record by experienced stalkers was fourteen hours to get within shooting range of any deer, and fifty-one hours to locate one buck!

In South Dakota, a radio transmitter was attached to a buck along with long orange streamers through its ear tags. Hunters sent into the area saw no trace of the buck for seven days! During this period, many hunters passed within forty yards of him. Finally, using the radio receiver, a bush-by-bush search was conducted all morning and afternoon. No deer! Then, just when they were going to quit, the animal was found by a searcher who almost stepped on the buck curled up under a bush.

Similar tests in Wisconsin and other states have produced the same results. They all conclude that a crafty whitetail buck is almost impossible to stalk.

For my money, one of the greatest myths in whitetail hunting is the so-called advantage of "tracking snow." In reality, the big advantage is offered to the trail-watcher, not the tracker. Let's look at the reasons.

Most hunters do what comes naturally

on new snow, they pick a big set of fresh deer tracks and start tracking. When a lot of hunters do this it keeps the deer moving, and it keeps them traveling throughout the day. The more that deer move, and the longer they move, the better the chances a trail watcher has of seeing a buck. Also, new "tracking snow" has a magic appeal to most deer hunters. When such a snow comes, a lot of hunters will drop everything to get out in the woods and go tracking. Simple logic tells us that the more hunters there are in the woods, the better the chances of a trail watcher seeing deer. Also, when given a white background, a hunter on a stand can spot an approaching deer from a greater distance and get a better view of the animal.

I guess I've said enough to prove that your odds of downing a whitetail buck are far greater if you participate in drives or take a stand along a trail. The preference of many hunters is to participate in drives because they don't have the patience to sit long hours on stands. Driving techniques are simpler too, so let's discuss them first.

The basic drive is made by as few as two hunters. One makes the drive while the other positions himself on strategically located stands. The key to success of the system is knowledge of local conditions. Two of my friends have the technique down pat, as evidenced by the fact that they eat a lot of venison.

They do a good deal of pre-season scouting. Let me emphasize that pre-season scouting is the smartest thing a whitetail hunter can do. You have to know where your deer are, and you have to be aware of their travel routes to and from feeding and bedding areas. It's reasonably easy to discover these things for several reasons.

First and foremost is the fact that whitetail deer have the ability to thrive and prosper in close proximity to civilization and human development. They are found in herds on farmlands and woodlands which other species of wildlife may not be able to tolerate or cope with. So if you live in whitetail country you have deer relatively close to home. In addition, because these deer have learned to cope with civilization, they're very much aware of when they're being hunted and when gunning seasons are closed. When they're not hunted they roam relatively free. Spotting whitetails in fields, crossing roads, or traveling cross-country are common sights in deer country. Such off-season viewings give a clue to what areas harbor herds.

My two friends pick such an area, they talk with landowners about more specific locations frequented by deer, and they ask for permission not only to hunt but to engage in pre-season scouting. If they get that permission they begin scouting a month before the gun season opens. They do a lot of walking to find runways, feeding and bedding areas. They discover routes the animals use, and they select likely locations for stands. They go through the same act on public hunting lands except they don't have to bother with the permission bit.

JOHN O. CARTIER

Well organized group-type "drives" produce many Michigan bucks. These gun-wary whitetails proved no match for veteran hunters using a drive technique.

All the knowledge of deer-hunting methods won't pay off unless you can handle your firearm well enough to capitalize on a shooting opportunity when it's presented.

Since only two men are involved—one driver and one stander—their stand sites are chosen in places where deer runways route through narrow areas of cover. Narrow creek bottoms, gullies, fingers of woodland or brush are the places to look for. When driven deer funnel through such places, the man on stand is much more likely to see them than if they were driven through large woodlands. These fellows have several areas they know intimately, and they're able to make up to half a dozen drives each day. With their knowledge and technique they're bound to see lots of deer.

Successful gang-type drives are just as precisely organized. The technique works best when positions of drivers and the directions of travel are closely coordinated. Each driver must keep in voice or sight contact with his adjacent companions, and everybody moves on a compass bearing. Such procedure keeps the line straight and tight enough so that most deer prefer running ahead of it, instead of trying to sneak back through it. The system won't work, especially in large forests, unless you have a large group of at least eight to ten drivers. All drives should be map-coordinated so everybody knows where everybody else is going to be, where the drive will start and where it will end.

Such drives, executed with military precision, move a whale of a lot of deer. They're fun too, for the hunter who likes companionship. Gang drives can be carried out almost anywhere in whitetail country. They're most successful in semi-

Successful gang-type drives should be map-coordinated and executed with military precision.

open areas harboring islands of woodlands which vary in size from forty acres to several hundred acres. When you drive such isolated woodlands, you're almost bound to move any deer that might be present. Those deer would likely never be seen by still hunters working the same areas. Whitetail bucks are geniuses at outsmarting single hunters. They live in their home woods 365 days a year. They know every foot of their territory like you know the floor plan of your house. But they can't sneak around in front of a line of organized drivers. They take their chances on moving out, and that's when a lot of venison gets harvested.

If you want to get your buck on your own, if you want the challenge of outwitting crafty whitetails, and if you have the patience to sit still for hours, then trail-watching should be your game. The method works great in all types of deer

126

country, but it demands some definite skills in woodmanship, plus a large dose of self-discipline. There is no companionship, no smoking, no fires to keep warm by, no moving around. There is nothing except absolute quiet and attention to specific details.

The secret to successful trail-watching is that you must do your hunting from precisely located stands. The most important principles are to use an absolutely natural blind, and to locate so that all deer can freely use the nearby runway without the slightest suspicion of your presence. The latter factor is a must since does normally travel ahead of bucks. If a passing doe is alerted by an unnatural blind or other man-produced alarms you'll never see the buck that is following her.

Stands should be located near bedding areas. Why? Because whitetails leave their beds and move toward a feeding area sometime within the last hour before dusk. Conversely, they leave feeding areas on a schedule enabling them to reach bedding locations shortly after dawn. Stormy weather, of course, prolongs normal daylight movement of deer. In any event, a stand near a bedding area offers much more shooting-light potential than does a stand near a feeding area.

Veteran trail-watchers, those few experts who always score on big bucks, share a common secret. They know there's a difference between runways. They're aware that there are normal runways, and that they differ from buck runways. A

buck with a rack is a loner, and he uses his own route of travel. He stays away from well-traveled trails.

A buck runway is a narrow, well-packed depression showing few fresh tracks. It will be used by only one or two deer, but it will be used frequently. Lone does have their runways too, but a doe runway lacks an all-important distinction. It has no antler rub-marks on adjacent trees.

The key to discovering a buck runway is finding fresh rub-marks on sturdy trees near fall feeding areas. By October, whitetails begin feeding on beechnuts and acorns along hardwood ridges. Abandoned apple orchards offer choice dinner tables. So do winter wheat fields, farm-crop fields, and areas supporting

Big buck taken in thick cover by hunter who knows tricks of trail-watching.

clover or browse. When you find fresh deer sign in any of these terrain types you're close to a hotspot.

The trick is to scout around a feeding area till you find runways leading to bedding areas. Don't pay much attention to the heavily traveled routes. Look for the well-packed, narrow, but recently used trail. You may have to follow quite a few trails before you find one with fresh rubmarks on nearby trees. When you find that sign, you've found a buck runway.

At this point, continue scouting along the runway until you find a bedding area. Then backtrack till you find a crossing runway. Somewhere in the immediate vicinity you should select a stand site, the location of which will depend on prevailing winds. Incidentally, I like to locate near crossing runways because I double my chance of seeing deer. Also, trail use varies with wind changes, and a crossing area allows you to pick the one best stand among numerous possibilities.

Your first decision must be to determine from which way your buck is most likely to come (feed area in the morning, bed area in the evening), then select a downwind location. The next problem is selecting adequate concealment. I believe in getting low to the ground. The lower you are, the less concealment you need. Windfalls, stumps, small cedars and big rocks will conceal your body when you're sitting on the ground behind them. Now the trick is to screen your face. You have to be able to see without being seen.

Nothing serves the purpose better than a few conifer branches jabbed into the soil.

The third thing I consider is light density. I try to locate in a shadowed area so any movements I make are less noticeable. The edge of a clump of pines produces heavy shadows. So do the ground-hugging limbs of a hemlock or the upturned roots of a windfall. It's all-important to camouflage and minimize your movements. A buck will often materialize out of nearby thickets and be in plain sight before you suspect he's anywhere near you. I'll never forget the sage advice I received from an old-timer many years ago: "Hunt as if you're the hunted," he'd said. "Be so well hidden that slight movements won't betray you."

Don't give up proper concealment for a better view. Most stand hunters tend to "farm" too much territory. The object of the game isn't to see a lot of deer, it's to see one buck and get a good shot at him. I like to locate about fifty yards from a runway. I may not be able to see much of the surrounding terrain, but the area near the runway is where my buck is going to be and that's all I care about.

For many years I assumed that horizontal wind drift was my most important ally or enemy, then I discovered a flaw in this reasoning. Where should your stand be when there is very little breeze or none at all? There's an answer, and it ties in with the understanding of thermal currents. These currents are vertical air drifts. They develop with temperature

JOHN O. CARTIER

Some farm-country bucks grow to enormous size.

changes, and they carry your scent in the same way as an obvious breeze.

Cold air falls because it is heavy. Lighter, or warmer air tends to rise. At dawn, temperatures normally begin to climb. The air begins to warm, and therefore it begins to rise. If you're in a dawn stand in the lowlands, your scent will flow up the hillsides with the rising thermal currents. On the other hand, if you locate just below a ridge top, the rising thermal drifts dissipate your scent into the sky.

An opposite condition occurs during afternoons. As evening approaches, the day becomes cooler, and the thermal currents begin falling. A hillside stand would now be an unwise selection since thermal drifts will be carrying your scent into the lowlands below you. I have a simple rule I always follow on quiet days; dawn stands should be up on hillsides, evening stands should be in lowlands.

One of the most important principles of hunting from a stand is careful housekeeping. When I select a site I scrape away all dry leaves and twigs in the area where I'll be sitting. Then I shoulder my rifle

Author approaches his best-ever whitetail buck.

and swing it through a circle. If it brushes any branches, I cut those obstructions away so I can pivot freely and soundlessly.

Keep in mind that bucks often use the same runways year after year. When you kill one, another will likely inherit the trail by the next hunting season. Remember also that a big mistake made by many stand hunters is arriving at their site too late and leaving too early. You should be positioned well before dawn because whitetails begin moving with the first hint of daybreak. If you wait till it's light enough to walk to your stand without a flashlight you'll miss seeing a lot of deer. And don't leave your stand in the evening till you can no longer see details of terrain.

I would be remiss if I didn't say something about the so-called "lucky hunter." You hear about these fellows every fall, the hunters who consistently come home with venison. There will always be the amateurs who occasionally down a good buck with the help of blind luck, but the men who have trophy antlers in their dens or garages make their own luck. Knowledge of the things we've discussed in this chapter is all important to deer-hunting success, but the payoff comes when they're combined with other factors having little to do with hunting skills.

Physical stamina, or lack of it, is almost bound to be a factor in how lucky you are at hunting whitetails. The problem today is that modern civilization has spoiled us. Man-made conveniences have done away with much of the every-day hard work of fifty years ago. I'm all for easy living, but it makes us soft, too soft for the hard work that's often required to score on whitetails.

Smart bucks get smart by figuring out

JOHN O. CARTIER

the ways of hunters. They learn early that most sportsmen don't hunt very far from roads. The deer don't realize that this situation results from the average hunter's lack of physical stamina, but they make the most of it. They head for the most remote and rugged country they know about, and that's where some of them are killed by the "lucky" hunters who can work hard enough to go in after them. How far you go and how many deer you see depends a lot on how much physical stamina you have.

This is especially true for hunters who use the driving technique. The most successful group I know are hard-working farmers. They think nothing of staging six or eight long drives per day through rough timber. Such activity is just too much for the average city-bred hunter who doesn't keep himself in good condition.

There are two other factors of "luck" that play important parts too. I call them perseverance, and faith-in-your-ability.

The half-hearted deer hunter is licked before he starts. In any phase of hunting the enthusiast wins. It's the same principle that applies to every activity in life —the harder you work the more successful you're likely to be. There are plenty of deer hunters who don't particularly care whether they get a buck or not. Such types put greatest emphasis on just being in the woods and getting away from the rat race. That's all well and good, but the man who consistently drags in a buck never gives up.

This type of logic ties in with my last subject on luck—faith in your ability. You may have perseverance, but you need one other thing too. You have to expect to score. You have to feel sure that you have what it takes to nail a buck. All of the best veteran whitetail hunters I know share this one common trait; they believe in themselves. They believe in their skill that took years to hone to a fine edge.

"Faith in your ability," said a friend who has taken many whitetails, "is no more than remembering the details of past successes." The man who has outsmarted a lot of bucks is going to outsmart some more, and he knows it. He hunts with an enthusiasm that's born of knowledge and experience. He doesn't worry about missing a shot, because he knows his rifle as a familiar tool. He knows how whitetails will react to given conditions because he learned their habits the hard way. He may get skunked today, but he's forever confident that he'll get a buck tomorrow because he knows he's a good hunter.

From the time George Marzek first pinged a tin can with a BB gun at the age of six, while living in Chicago, he has never lost his ardor for the shooting sports. He has hunted extensively throughout the Midwest, utilizing every type of weapon legal for the taking of game and at one time he made all his own archery equipment. George is now wrapped up in the art of shooting muzzle-loading rifles.

While he tends to concentrate much of his hunting in Iowa where he now lives, he has covered practically every state in the nation and has virtually lost count of the number of whitetails he has brought down. His experiences also include bagging a Barbary sheep in the foothills of the Atlas Mountains in North Africa.

George not only hunts with various types of weapons but is just as apt to shoot a camera, which has won him national honors for a number of his outdoor photographs. His outdoor writing, which he's been doing for fifteen years, appears not only locally, but has been published in regional and national publications. In 1968 he received the Award of Merit from the American Association for Conservation Information. Some of his art work has also had national exposure. Most of it is done on special commission for private individuals, some of whom are prominent sportsmen.

George is a Life Member of the Izaak Walton League of America, the National Rifle Association, and the Iowa Academy of Science. He is also affiliated with numerous other sportsmen's groups, both on local and national levels.

9

HUNTING WHITETAILS IN THE MIDWEST

George L. Marzeck

No OTHER ANIMAL provides so much challenging sport, so many healthful outdoor hours, for so many Midwest big game hunters as does the whitetail deer.

While I intend to concentrate mainly on the techniques for hunting the wily whitetail in the Midwest, I believe this task can best be done by reviewing the essential fundamentals of deer hunting in general, and by bringing out some of the pertinent aspects of Midwest whitetails as they relate to what actually is the Number 1 big game animal of the entire country.

Essentially, bringing home the quarry —and the Midwest has recently produced some outstanding record-book bucks— depends a lot more on our understanding basic traits and habits than it does on our

ability to merely follow each and every hoofprint along a trail. This is not to say that I think the study of tracks (and other signs) is not important. On the contrary, it certainly is important, and can be particularly so when trailing a wounded deer. But more about that later.

Relative to the success of the hunt, nothing will insure it more than being able to properly cope with any given situation within the specific area being hunted, and having a solid working knowledge of the legal method (both weapons and mode) that we are employing. The really successful hunter, the one who brings back the venison year after year, doesn't believe in luck, nor does he resort to so-called hunting secrets. What the successful hunter does have

Central Wisconsin typical whitetail buck. PHOTO BY WISCONSIN NATURAL RE-SOURCES DEPT., MADISON, WISCONSIN

down pat are the basic fundamentals and a thorough knowledge of the terrain he is hunting.

I. General Characteristics

The nature of the whitetail deer has enabled it to survive the agricultural expansion of the Midwest. It has demonstrated its ability to live nearby well populated areas, and in many cases multiply to the point where some farmers consider them pests. They are smart and more than once I've seen them pull a vanishing act that would put Houdini to shame. They can be found feeding at the open edges of farmlands, but tend to lay low in concealment when danger is present. Get a little too close for comfort, and you better be prepared for what resembles an explosion as they burst from cover. I've found that, once on the move, whitetails are more concerned with what is in back of them than what is in some other direction.

While the Midwest whitetail is often found in open farmland (I have seen them grazing with cattle), he is a brush-area animal that spends almost his entire life span in or near scrubby, swampy or heavily forested regions. He does not migrate

GEORGE L. MARZECK

from summer to winter ranges. Once he finds an area to his liking, he will generally stay within this territory, and it will often be only a few miles in radius.

If I were to lay odds on the special physical advantages a deer has over a hunter, I'd have to say that they're 3 to 1 in favor of the whitetail. I don't know of a single hunter that he can't outhear, outsmell and outrun. The best thing we have going for us is the fact that a whitetail does not see too well. If he had keener eyesight, I'd hate to predict what we would be up against.

There are a few other fundamentals that can help us outwit the whitetail, but they have little significance if we fail to observe the previously mentioned factors. The deer is not a long-distance runner. It makes its dashes in short, fast spurts and prefers to circle within its area rather than run out of it. Further, like so many other wild creatures, whitetail deer will on rare occasions show signs of extreme curiosity almost too incredible to believe. And, during the rutting season, bucks are prone to throw caution to the wind.

Taking all these things into account, the whitetail can still have the hunter wandering around befuddled—maybe completely flabbergasted—without a chance at a good shot, because of the way he might pull some peculiar, unexpected trick.

A lot has been said about the whitetail being shy and furtive, sometimes even curious. But little is mentioned about

their being mighty unpredictable. Some folks might insist that what I call "unpredictable" is really just a sign of curiosity, but I believe it's different.

I don't know for certain why such things happen—and they're not at all common—but it's quite possible that some of the antics of specific Midwest whitetails are prompted by their close proximity to agricultural activity. They literally get used to seeing people, yet they remain wild, and trying to catch one would bring us right back to trying to outrun one. It can't be done.

In all my dealings with Midwest whitetails, I've had three encounters I consider somewhat extraordinary. As one example, take a situation that occurred not too long ago.

Earl "Easy" Wright, my good friend and a great sportsman, owns a dandy little cabin right on the edge of several hundred acres of woods in a real hotspot for big deer—Clark County, in northeastern Missouri. One day the two of us set out from the cabin to do some pre-season scouting of the woods in his old four-wheel-drive Jeep. We wanted to get a better idea of the lay of the land, but weren't looking to find a deer behind every tree. It was the latter part of September.

As we suspected, there were plenty of tracks, but no deer were actually sighted —yet. Turning back after a while, we neared the cabin where Easy had a bushel of apples outside the small storage shed.

Talk about coming upon a picnic! There were deer all over the place! We stood there, in plain sight, just watching, but we could have been in Timbuktu for all the attention we got. And remember, these were wild deer, not pets. Finally, when the last apple was gone, the deer slowly began sauntering away, as though they had all the time in the world. It was then we viewed cleanly a magnificent buck amongst them.

It was September, so his antlers were already fully formed, and doggone impressive, but the color of his coat hadn't changed from the reddish-brown of summer to the grayish-tan of winter. In the sunlight it glinted like burnished copper. "Sonofagun," was all that Easy said. I couldn't think of a word to add to it.

Another time, Jerry Johnson, one of my closest hunting buddies, called me to come down to his farm along the Skunk River in southeastern Iowa. Since his place is only nine miles from my house, it didn't take long for me to get there.

Jerry and I cut through the back pasture, past the cornfield, where we came to the edge of a nice stand of trees. We intended to check the condition of several tree stands built a while back, rather than look for signs of deer. We know they're around by their tracks which are everywhere, but actually seeing a whitetail is another matter.

After assessing that a little rebuilding of the tree stands was in order, we headed back toward the farmhouse. I can't remember who looked back first, but when we did, there, as big as life and right out in the open, was a large doe following us not more than fifty yards away. From her manner it would have been difficult to prove that she wasn't a pet. She trailed right along with us, all the way to the farmyard when, apparently frightened by Jerry's romping collie, the doe suddenly scampered off to return to the woods.

My most memorable experience came when I was out duck hunting. It was a slow day and I was about half asleep, leaning back against some rushes and pin-oak branches we used to make a shore blind at a pothole. Suddenly, without warning, a big buck poked his head right into the blind. I could've sworn we bumped noses! He just about scared the daylights out of me—it certainly woke me up, anyway. If it hadn't been for the uproarious laugh my buddy gave out, I'm inclined to believe that buck might have stayed for lunch. But I guess he figured things weren't that funny, so the old buck hightailed it for parts unknown.

Now, the incidents just related aren't meant to give anyone the impression that Midwest whitetails practically fall in the hunter's lap. Far from it. In fact, as I said earlier, these are the only three times I've ever been that close to whitetails without their seeming to be afraid of me, and I have a half notion they somehow knew they weren't being hunted.

What I do know, however, is that things change considerably once the deer season begins and things are in full swing. But don't bet against peculiar behavior

George L. Marzeck

Jerry Johnson, Southeast Iowa (Des Moines County). Tree stand, near Skunk River.

on the part of any wild whitetail. In fact, quite often, while stalking, I try to remember the sage advice of an old-time deer hunter who once said, "Look back now and then. That something that may be following you could be just what you are looking for."

II. Areas and Terrain

Anyone not familiar with the Midwest may think of it as flat, agricultural land, and much of it is just that way. But there are also plenty of woods and forests, hills and gullies, and even some fair-sized mountains in the Ozarks of Missouri. In other words, there is a good variety of wildlife habitat, and much of it is very suitable for sustaining whitetails of fine quality in good numbers.

A good example of a heavily wooded section is Shimek Forest, over seven thousand acres of mostly evergreen trees, bordered by brushy areas and cornfields. This ideal setup for whitetail deer is located in the southeastern Iowa counties of Lee and Van Buren, just east of the Des Moines River, and not too many miles north of Clark County, Missouri.

If anyone were to ask me my all-time favorite area for deer hunting in the Midwest, I'd have to admit it's on Jerry Johnson's farm. In addition to Jerry being a grand guy and a fine hunter, he's got a piece of land with whitetail habitat as good as you could ever hope for. It is composed of scattered cornfields, criss-

crossed with small gullies and ridges. Throughout the area there are fine stands of trees bordered with brush and second-growth saplings.

A particularly good spot on Jerry's farm is at a juncture of two ridges that gradually slope off into a gully. One of the cornfields comes almost to the edge of one ridge, while the slope has just the right kind of brush and tall grass. Bordering this, and actually descending into the gully, is a fine stand of trees with a good number of oaks. Running at the bottom of the gully is a small spring-fed creek that stays at least partially open even in the coldest weather.

When you consider that all of the aforementioned is almost within walking distance of my home, you can hardly blame me for calling it my favorite. Yet, strangely enough, the biggest buck I've taken to date was bagged just north of Black River Falls, Wisconsin, back in 1954. Biggest in terms of body weight, it dressed out at 220 pounds. It did have a nice ten-point rack, but it wasn't of any exceptional size. Anyway, the region around Black River Falls is different than that in southeastern Iowa. If anything, it's more akin to the kind of country you'll find in northeastern Iowa with its Yellow River Forest. Both, in most respects are rougher regions, with higher hills, steeper gullies, and somewhat different wooded areas. Come to think of it, Shawnee Forest in extreme southern Illinois can be likened to them. And, of course, I've already mentioned the Missouri Ozarks—

Central Missouri, whitetail country. "The Ozarks."

some of that country can be really rugged.

But, getting back to Illinois, a fine area can be found in and around Peoria County, in the lower portion of the northcentral part of the state. A mixture of agricultural flatland, gullies that are in all likelihood part of the Illinois River watershed, and a scattering of just the right kind of brush-bordered woodlands, all combine to attract and hold some fine whitetails.

All in all, of the specific areas mentioned, many are similar in some ways to regions found outside of what is generally considered the Midwest. In any case, the following is a slightly more

comprehensive rundown on where we're most likely to have the most success in bagging a good whitetail deer in the four-state area covered:

In *Illinois,* the best areas will be found in the northwestern, west-central and extreme southern counties.

In *Iowa,* almost all of the southern section of the state is good, with three exceptional areas in the northeastern and southeastern corners, and in the extreme southwestern portion around Council Bluffs.

In *Missouri,* the Ozarks region is considered best, but don't overlook Clark County in the northeastern corner of the state. Right now it is probably one of the hottest spots in the *entire nation* for trophy bucks.

In *Wisconsin,* the best whitetail hunting has moved from the northern counties down to the southern two-thirds of the state, with the central counties carrying the highest deer concentrations.

I'd like to recommend that anyone contemplating a deer hunt in any of the above areas, learn the terrain by actually getting out in it, preferably with a native deer hunter. Spend a couple of days, or several weekends if you can, just camping in the chosen area. Do this prior to the hunting season, of course. Because regulations, seasons, fees, etc., change from year to year, it would be wise, before planning a deer hunt, to first check with the appropriate game agency. Regarding the four-state area in this section, up-to-date detailed information can be obtained by addressing inquiries as follows:

Illinois—Department of Conservation, State Office Building, Springfield, Ill. 62706

Iowa—State Conservation Commission, 300 Fourth Street, Des Moines, Ia. 50319

Missouri—Department of Conservation, P.O. Box 180, Jefferson City, Mo. 65101

Wisconsin—Department of Natural Resources, Box 450, Madison, Wisc. 53701

III. Signs

Finding deer tracks is, naturally, an almost absolute guarantee that whitetails are in the area. And if we're going to look for them initially, they are most likely to be found at trail crossings, along the edges of brushy ridges bordering forests, and near woodlots adjacent to crop fields, corn especially. A very good place to look for deer tracks is at a narrow pass through a ridge, particularly if it includes any of the above.

There are many other signs besides hoofprints that we can look for, but they are of such a general nature that it doesn't seem necessary to elaborate on them here. The same can be said about the kinds of food that attract deer, except that the whitetail's diet is more varied than some folks might imagine. Deer have even been known to eat fish which they've managed to paw from some small creek. However, they are basically vegetarians. They don't eat every kind of plant, under normal conditions, though. Nor is a whitetail apt

to eat what seems impossible or perilous to obtain.

When hunting in the Midwest we have to take into account the kind of food deer find appetizing, readily accessible, and relatively free from danger. For example, in my neck of the woods, whitetails dearly love corn, but I surely wouldn't go out in the middle of a thousand-acre flat cornfield to look for them. Not if I were hunting alone, that is. It's almost impossible to be as quiet as necessary while walking through a cornfield, standing or picked. However, I would recommend quietly scrutinizing border areas of such fields if they contain plenty of brush and trees, or maybe have an old orchard nearby. The Midwest has many such spots, so don't overlook them.

The sounds deer make can be included among the signs that indicate whitetails are present. But they can vary all over the lot, depending on what may be going on. Once again, this is general, no matter what section of the country we might be hunting. As one example, if you've ever heard two pugnacious bucks trying to knock the stuffings out of each other during the rutting season, you've heard them all.

IV. Hunting Methods

Driving. Along with still-hunting and standing, driving is regarded as one of the three standard methods of hunting whitetails. It is the method most often used where a deer population is pretty well known and numerous hunters are in the area.

A good case in point is the annual drive hunt held at the Iowa Army Ammunition Plant, seven miles west of Burlington, Iowa. Here, largely through the fine efforts of the local Long Creek Conservation Club, this twenty thousand-acre compound is maintained as excellent habitat for whitetail deer and other wildlife. Each year a biological survey shows an abundance of exceptionally fine specimens of whitetail deer. Because of the vastness of the area, and other limiting factors, driving is by far the best way to conduct any kind of deer hunting at IAAP. The well-regulated and organized drive hunt provides good deer hunting for a large majority of the sportsmen in the area. At the same time, the deer population is held within the bounds of good conservation practices.

There are those who consider deer drives the least thrilling of all forms of whitetail hunting, and, frankly, I tend to agree. Then, too, it's probably the most hazardous, due to the number of hunters that may be involved. But properly conducted, it enables many a deer hunter to bring home some choice, corn-fed venison, whereas he might otherwise have no other opportunity to do so. Further, as far as hazard is concerned, there's more good fellowship than danger at all the IAAP hunts I know about.

Extra safety and good sportsmanship have always been greatly stressed at all IAAP drive hunts, and prior to each annual hunt a clinic is held where all participants are clearly instructed as to just what they are supposed to do. Anyone who does not attend these preliminary meetings, although a qualified hunter, is not permitted to participate.

In all the years that drive hunts have been held within this huge compound, I know of only one minor accident occurring, and that happened before the "standers" and "drivers" even began to hunt. Regardless of a specific individual's attitude about the thrill of the chase, such a safety record speaks highly for the sportsmen involved and for the manner in which the authorities conduct these hunts at the IAAP.

Standing. This mode of bagging a whitetail is based on what we know about the various traits and habits of specific deer in a given area, and, next to stalking, is my favorite way of hunting. It is particularly suited for anyone who may wish to hunt with a bow and arrow or with a muzzle loading rifle, and can be done from concealment on the ground, although I tend to prefer working from a properly constructed tree stand. In fact, when I'm out shooting a camera only, a tree stand is invariably where you'll find me.

Tree stands (and they need be no higher than ten feet from the ground) have the advantage that a deer generally never looks upward unless it hears an unusual sound or commotion. Camouflage is not nearly as critical as when hunting at ground level, so, by remaining reasonably quiet in my tree stand, it's very likely I'll never be noticed.

But whether I'm hunting from a tree stand or concealed on the ground, I try to keep in mind that the deer's eyesight is relatively poor, it has a habit of staying within a localized area, it prefers using trails along certain ridges and crossings, and it tends to be most active during the very early hours or late in the afternoon.

Except for occasional movement on cloudy, overcast days, whitetails are rather inactive during midday; they're usually bedded down somewhere. We'll hardly miss a thing if we take a noon break ourselves, and save our energy for the more productive hours. Combining all this information will enable us to place ourselves at the right spot, at the right time, in the best possible way, and more often than not create a better-than-normal chance to outwit our quarry.

To elaborate a little on the phrase "in the best possible way," in standing it's necessary to have the ability and patience to remain concealed and very quiet, sometimes for long periods of time; that's why I think the noon break is so important. It gives us a chance to stretch our legs and get rid of any kinks that may have developed. Further, if I'm stand-hunting from the ground, I try to post myself so that the deer have to come past me downwind. This is not quite as critical when hunting from a tree stand, where we're above the deer and wind currents will tend to dispel human scent without arousing the white-

tail. But it doesn't pay to be careless. I learned my lesson long ago about smoking, especially my smelly old pipe. Ridding it of ashes by knocking the pipe against a tree does not sound like a woodpecker, and, believe me, it certainly doesn't smell like one.

So, whether stand-hunting from the ground or from a tree, I try to remember that deer can outhear me and outsmell me any day in the week.

Stalking or still-hunting. Now we are getting down to what I feel is the most thrilling and satisfying form of whitetail deer hunting. And I venture to say that a great majority of veteran deer hunters will agree with me. Here, we are playing the game of hide-and-seek in the deer's own bailiwick, and what he doesn't know about every nook and cranny in the area isn't worth mentioning.

The best way I can explain stalking a deer is to be extremely stealthy and employ all the strategy you can. I think of myself as the one being hunted, instead of the other way around. What would I do if someone were sneaking up on me, and my very life was at stake? How would I go about outsmarting my pursuer?

At first, I'd probably lay low, try to conceal myself in such a way as to make it seem that I'm nowhere around. And I'd remain as motionless as possible. If I thought I could hold my breath for any great length of time, I'd probably even include that.

But, what if my pursuer was really "hot

GEORGE L. MARZECK

Jerry Johnson checks hoofprint of wounded whitetail. Southeast Iowa (Des Moines County).

(Iowa) stalker/still-hunter (bow and arrow) -camouflage.

on my trail"? I'd take off in a direction that, hopefully, would be entirely different from the one I'd be expected to take, maybe circling around completely. In some respects, I would then be following the follower. (Remember about looking back now and then?)

I try to keep myself camouflaged to look like a natural part of the surroundings, to the extent legally permitted. Some states require that a deer hunter wear some article of clothing which is either bright red or blaze orange. This might appear to be a handicap, but it doesn't have to be if the stalker moves very, very slowly. The "out of place" color has proven to be of inestimable value as a hunter safety measure.

Even when totally camouflaged, the greatest disadvantage a stalker can place upon himself is to move too fast, to make noises unrelated to the natural sounds of the woods. I tend to walk so slowly that a casual observer (if he could spot me) might figure me for an old man who will never make it to the other end of the pass. But precisely because moving very slowly enables me to see better, I'll take the added benefit of not tiring myself needlessly and becoming an "old" man before my time.

Relative to unusual sounds, let's keep in mind that the deer itself isn't always completely silent. Maybe the sharp crack of a snapping twig or the skittering of pebbles along a creek bed indicates a deer

Central Wisconsin deer-hunter camp.   PHOTO BY WISCONSIN NATURAL RESOURCES
DEPT., MADISON, WISCONSIN

on the move. What about rustling sounds on a windless day? It pays to keep our ears open.

The thrill I get from outsmarting a whitetail while stalking—getting close enough for a good, well-placed shot—satisfies me more than the actual shooting.

But to get that clean shot, I'm prompted to repeat: When I start out to stalk and initially find fresh tracks, I try *not* to keep my eyes glued to the ground. Seeing tracks may help keep my adrenalin flowing, and the study of tracks can tell a lot about what the whitetail may be doing,

yet I concentrate on looking ahead, to the side, occasionally back, but very seldom down.

Buddy-hunting.   I don't know how well-known the expression "buddy-hunting" is, even in the Midwest, but it's a local term we use that simply means two people hunting as partners. Actually, all it is is a junior-sized version of a drive hunt. The difference lies in the fact that you're not hunting with a large group; the rest is basically the same. It's the old technique where the deer moves to protect itself from the sight and sound of one hunter,

144

GEORGE L. MARZECK

all the while unintentionally coming into a position where the other hunter might get a clean shot.

Among my best friends buddy-hunting is a very popular form of going after whitetails. In fact, I enjoy it almost as much as stalking.

With a good partner, buddy-hunting is a pleasant, cheerful and satisfying way to go after the wily whitetail. There's none of the sometimes hectic hustle-bustle associated with big drives, yet there is fine companionship and the feeling of relative safety and assistance, should any be required. More than once I've had the grateful pleasure of some extra muscle to tote a deer out of the woods. And it's nice to know a good buddy is fairly close by to lend a helping hand, should you twist an ankle, or lose your bearings slightly—not unlikely possibilities, but all part of the sport.

In wrapping up methods, I can't help re-emphasizing the whitetail's keen sense of smell, because of an incident with a novice hunter. When I picked up the young lad the morning of our hunt, he had just shaved. The aroma from his after-shave lotion was more likely to attract a "dear" than a "deer." Maybe the bottle said "Pine Scent" but you can't fool a whitetail. I won't make any claims one way or another about commercial scents used to lure bucks, but I will strongly advise against getting one's "deer" mixed up. Basically, avoid any odors that are not consistent with the na-

tural scents found in the woods and fields. That might mean taking a good shower with the mildest, most scent-free soap obtainable, just before starting out to hunt.

V. Weapons

Because the many kinds and variations of weapons that can be employed in the taking of deer amounts to a sizeable subject in itself, I'm going to touch on this only briefly.

Rifles. As of this writing, Illinois and Iowa prohibit the use of rifles but they are legal in Missouri and Wisconsin.

A note of possible interest might be that my deer bagged near Black River Falls, Wisconsin, was dropped with a single shot from a Winchester Model 94 lever-action rifle using a .30/30 cartridge. The whitetail collapsed completely about seventy-five yards from where it was initially hit.

Being an Iowan, more prone to use a shotgun, in all honesty I don't hunt much with a rifle. Yet I've been told by folks who know what they're talking about that the combination I used comes about as close to being the ideal for whitetails as can be put together. Considering the outcome, I can't help but believe it. After more than eighteen years, my biggest buck is still the one bagged in Wisconsin.

Shotguns. Illinois, Iowa, Missouri and Wisconsin all allow shotguns. There was a time when a choice could be made between using buckshot or rifled slugs, and it still may exist in some areas, but I'd recommend the rifled slug every time. It's much more accurate, is lethal over a longer range, and packs a more solid wallop, leaving less chance for crippling. The most preferred shotgun is a 12 gauge pump or semi-automatic.

Muzzleloaders. Illinois, Iowa, Missouri and Wisconsin permit the use of muzzle-loading rifles or muskets.

My good buddy, Jack Taylor of Gulf-port, Illinois, shot a dandy "spike" buck that dressed out at 109 pounds. This whitetail was dropped on the spot with one shot from his .45 caliber Hawken rifle, while hunting from a tree stand near Oquawka, Illinois, in Henderson County.

I own a .50 caliber Hawken muzzle-loading rifle, and feel it's best suited for stand-hunting; yet, as in archery, it can be used while stalking. If there's any draw-back to stalking with a muzzle-loading rifle, it might be the extra weight of the gun. If we miss with the first shot, we have to consider "time out" for reloading. But neither the weight nor the reloading need detract from the sport.

Handguns. In the Midwest, only Missouri allows the use of a handgun for taking whitetails.

Bow hunting. Illinois, Iowa, Missouri and Wisconsin permit the use of bow and ar-row, but to be successful as an archer, we must recognize that we're faced with a very short-ranged situation.

Around my neck of the woods, about the only method archers use to hunt whitetails is solitary stand-hunting (either from the ground or from a tree stand), or by solitary stalking. Complete camouflage and utter stealth are of paramount importance. Even a standing target can be a difficult proposition, so every effort is made to keep the whitetail from making any sudden moves.

Even if we get within thirty or forty yards of the deer, there is almost always a chance that some obstruction will prevent a good clean shot. Some of the smallest branches and twigs can deflect an arrow from its intended flight. And contrary to what some folks might think, an arrow is nowhere near as quick a killer as a bullet. It is absolutely essential that the arrow strike a vital spot.

In bowhunting for whitetails, I'd rather go home empty-handed than take a chance on a risky spot. And shooting at a running deer is strictly taboo in my book.

VI. Vital Shots and Trailing

Anyone interested in bagging a whitetail is after some choice venison, a trophy buck, or both. It makes sense to know how to field-dress a deer properly, or have someone along who does. As far as cooking recipes go, my choices may not be to your liking. There are others far more

146

proficient in the culinary arts than I, so I'll leave the subject at that.

Now, to bring down a whitetail for keeps, I aim at the heart-lungs area if at all possible, or, if at short range, the next best spots (if they're the only ones exposed), which are at the neck or spine.

A deer, though mortally wounded, can still put a lot of distance between himself and the hunter if it is "pushed." I'm always grateful for the ones I drop on the spot, but when it happens otherwise, I've trained myself to wait at least twenty minutes before shagging after a deer known to be wounded. I'll mark the spot where I believe the deer was when first hit (in case I have to retrace my steps and start all over again), then I'll lean back and relax.

Now comes the real art of tracking, and every effort should be made to locate the deer. There is no reason in the world to allow a mortally wounded deer to go to waste; yet, if the deer simply cannot be found, hopefully the wound was so superficial (it happens with the best marksmen) that the whitetail will survive with little or no problem.

A wounded deer will move slower, pause more often, actually lay down quicker, if it is not followed up too soon. Usually it will also leave a more discernible trail of blood. If it's bright red, the shot has hit the lungs, and the whitetail won't travel too far. Dark, heavy blood comes from muscle tissue, and could mean a relatively longer trail to follow. Any signs of greenish fluid indicate a gut

Carl Barnett of Salem, Iowa (Henry County). Hunting near his home and close to "Big Cedar Creek." This photo took third place, adult-in-outdoors, 1972 Garcia Photo Awards.

Though hit in the spine (or very near to it), this fairly large doe managed to move almost a half-mile from where it was hit (12 ga. rifled slug) and was finally located near the bottom of a gully, under a cedar tree. Southeast Iowa.

shot, unfortunately, and the trail to follow could be quite long. In addition, a gut-shot deer can be in real agony and potentially dangerous when it's finally located.

Frequent, large spots of blood, regardless of color, usually mean the deer has been hit pretty solid. If a distinct drag mark shows along with the hoofprints, it's almost a certainty that one of the legs has been hit. Deer that have been hit hard have a tendency to head downhill sharply and generally drop their flag promptly as they run off. If we notice this, we can feel fairly sure our shot was well-placed.

Even after I begin trailing the wounded deer, I make it a point to never hurry, and constantly look ahead carefully. Not only do I keep my weapon ready to finish off the deer quickly when necessary, but I never approach too closely while he is still alive. A wounded deer, in its desperation to escape, can inflict some pretty serious wounds with its hoofs.

VII. Weather and Clothing

Weather can be unpredictable anywhere, at any time, but somehow it seems to delight in being downright contrary in the Midwest during the whitetail season. I recall one three-day stretch during December in particular, when it went from a bright, mild high of 60° down to a cold, blustery low of 10°. To hunt in any kind of comfort you have to be prepared for such extremes, and it really begins before you leave the house.

I'll start off with some good, lightweight, insulated underwear and socks—they don't necessarily need to be heavy. Then I'll stick with soft wool or flannel outer garb that won't swish, rustle or scrape when I walk or move about. I wear a number of thin layers rather than wrap up in one or two heavy coats. I can stay just as warm, if not warmer, even when it's really cold, have more freedom of movement, and it's a relatively simple matter to adjust for any changes in temperature. If I'm hunting in really wet weather, I prefer a waterproof poncho with a parka hood over anything else.

Good footwear is a must. Soft-soled shoes make for more silent stalking, but don't go for the smooth-bottom type. Cleats of some sort are required for surer footing. Some hunters are known to wear sneakers, but they're not for the Midwest.

I prefer soft leather boots whenever the weather is relatively mild and dry, and switch to insulated, waterproof boots only when it's wet, snowy and extra cold. In both cases the boots are nine-inchers, and I invariably take both kinds along. Whether it's rain or shine, I never leave without my poncho.

Regarding accessory clothing, such as caps or hats, gloves or mittens, vests, etc., I feel this is a matter of personal preference, and leave the choice to the individual. The same can be said for such specialty items as battery-heated socks.

To conclude this section, I'd like to mention the possibility of having to travel in some rather nasty Midwest weather.

It's not unlikely to run into freezing rain or a good snowfall. Be sure your vehicle is in tip-top shape for winter driving, and it certainly wouldn't be a bad idea to have snow tires installed.

VIII. Some Outstanding Examples

Considering weight alone, a Midwest whitetail buck is capable of reaching nearly 400 pounds, but more often than not, it is apt to go around the 140-pound mark. Does and fawns (when and where legal) will, of course, be considerably smaller. With all the emphasis on prompt field dressing, the live weight of many deer is very often never known but a good approximation can be made by multiplying the field-dressed weight by 1¼.

Yearling bucks normally do not grow the full racks so often portrayed by artists until they are older. In the Midwest a whitetail buck with four points on each of the two main beams will be called a "typical" eight-pointer, whereas in the West, a mule deer would be known as a three-pointer. Only the points on one antler are counted, and the brow point is disregarded. Any odd number of points would classify the rack as "non-typical." An average, mature Midwest buck may have from six to ten points, including the two brow points, also called the brow tines.

Now for some of the outstanding examples:

Illinois: The largest deer on record had a live weight of 370 pounds. In 1965, a rack

came out of Peoria County that scored 204-4/8 points and presently holds second place in the Boone and Crockett ranking, just two points under the all-time record of 206-5/8. In 1972, Mercer County yielded a whitetail that field-dressed at 259 pounds.

Iowa: The largest deer on record had a live weight of 345 pounds and came from Iowa County. In 1964, a 281-pound field-dressed buck was taken in Lyon County and its rack is listed in the national big game records. In the same year,

Author with large whitetail buck. Normally a ten-pointer, but note lack of L. H. brow tine. Was not shot off, but missing beforehand and likely broken off in struggle with another buck. Southern Iowa. Contrast of dark clothes against white background of snow covered with white sheet at time of hunt.

Bill McManis, formerly of Fort Madison, bagged an eight-pointer in Lee County with bow and arrow, which weighed 175 pounds field-dressed. In 1967, Craig Field of Burlington shot a buck in Des Moines County that had a live weight of 291 pounds and a rack that held the all-time Iowa record for "shotgun-typical" until 1971. In that year, Marvin Tippery of Council Bluffs shot a buck in Harrison County, which became the new all-time Iowa record replacing that of Craig Field. In 1969, I came mighty close to at least equalling my Wisconsin kill with a ten-pointer from Des Moines County that field-dressed at 212 pounds.

Missouri: In 1969, Jeff Brunk shot a buck in Clark County whose antlers totaled 199-4/8 official points and presently holds fourth place in Boone and Crockett ranking. In 1967, Allen Courtney shot a buck in Clark County whose antlers totaled 178-0/8 points and it is also listed in the official Boone and Crockett records. In live weight, the largest known is a 369-pounder from Livingston County, taken by Cliff Davis. In 1971, Larry Gibson of Moberly shot a buck in Randolph County whose rack scored 201-5/8 points, according to official Missouri sources. It is not yet known if this has been officially accepted by the Boone and Crockett Club. Should it be, then it looks like the record book is due for another change, and Gibson's buck will be mighty close to the top.

Wisconsin: According to Boone and Crockett scoring methods, the largest

Larry Gibson, Moberly, Mo., killed buck 1971 Randolph County, score 201⅝ First Place 1972. PHOTO CREDIT TO MISSOURI DEPARTMENT OF CONSERVATION, PHOTO BY DON WOOLDRIDGE

buck ever taken was shot in Polk County in 1937 by Homer Pearson of Almena, and scored 288-7/8 points on the non-typical list. The largest deer on record, by verified weight, was a 321½-pound dressed-weight buck taken by Richard Kay of Washburn in Bayfield County in 1938. The live weight of Kay's deer was estimated at 406 pounds.

And so it goes. Many other fine examples of Midwest whitetails have been omitted—not that they don't deserve to be mentioned, the listing would simply be too long! Weight, in itself, is only one measure of trophy quality, and is affected by many variables. Most, if not all, states are now relying on antler measurements exclusively for the purpose of establishing records. And don't forget some of the biggest and most recent of those record-book racks have come from the Midwest.

Trophy hunting requires skill and determined effort, not to mention loads of

GEORGE L. MARZECK

patience and perseverance, and so it follows that standards of excellence and recognition have been established, both on a statewide basis and nationally. The Boone and Crockett Club is the national organization responsible for deer taken with a gun, whereas the Pope and Young Club is the national organization responsible for deer taken with bow and arrow. For a listing of official scorers from both groups you can contact the game agency of the state where the "possible record" whitetail buck was taken. I am grateful to many people, including some grand hunting partners, who enabled me to put this whole thing together, and I'm particularly indebted to the following fine friends who helped me to verify some of the facts and figures contained herein:

John C. Calhoun, Chief of Forest Game, Illinois Department of Conservation

Lee Gladfelter, Game Biologist, Iowa Conservation Commission

Dean A. Murphy, Assistant Chief of Game, Missouri Department of Conservation

John A. Beale, Deputy Secretary, Wisconsin Department of Natural Resources

As hunters, let's continue to do our part by showing a sincere respect for the outdoors, and by adhering to the laws, written and unwritten, that indicate the mark of real sportsmen.

The territory normally considered as the Midwest certainly includes more states than the four specifically covered in this chapter. For example, it would hardly be proper to omit reference to Minnesota and Nebraska. Address any inquiries to these two states as follows:

Minnesota—Department of Natural Resources, Centennial Office Bldg., St. Paul, Minn. 55155

Nebraska—Game and Parks Commission, P.O. Box 30370, Lincoln, Neb. 68503

Wherever in the Midwest we may choose to hunt the whitetail deer, it would pay us to keep in good physical condition. And our hunting equipment, regardless of the methods and weapons we may prefer to employ, should be maintained in tip-top shape.

"Off-season" practice is great for sharpening our skills, even if at times we intend to shoot only with a camera. In fact, a camera shooter, aiming for some good photographs, requires considerable savvy as a stalker—he's right in there with the successful archer who prefers stalking to stand-hunting.

During an actual hunt, our gear should be convenient, not arranged to clutter up the works. We don't want to take along something we can readily do without, but don't overlook some small but vital item that can spell the difference between a good hunt and a bad one.

Whitetail records continue to be broken, and some huge racks are coming from Midwest farmland that not too long ago wasn't even thought of as deer country—in fact, some states of the Midwest had no open seasons until recently. If that doesn't speak well for good game management, I'll eat my blaze orange cap.

Bob Gooch started hunting at the age of five, stalking English sparrows with a BB gun on the family farm in Virginia. Since those tender years he has roamed much of North America, hunting such game as turkeys in Alabama, geese in North Carolina, moose in Newfoundland, pheasants in South Dakota, squirrels in the Ozarks, rabbits in Idaho and grouse in Nova Scotia. However, his favorite big game animal is the white-tailed deer, and he lives close to some of the best deer hunting in America. There he has successfully employed the various hunting methods he describes here.

A freelance writer, Bob has contributed over one hundred articles to leading outdoor magazines, including *Outdoor Life, The American Rifleman* and *Field and Stream.* For ten years he has written the widely syndicated column, *Virginia Afield.* He is also the author of two books, *The Weedy World of the Pickerels,* and *Squirrels and Squirrel Hunting.* He is a past president of the Mason-Dixon Outdoor Writers Association of America and the Virgina Outdoors Writers Association. He is also a member of the Outdoor Writers Association of America, and holds life memberships in the National Rifle Association and the Virginia Wildlife Federation. He was the 1969 recipient of the Virginia Conservation Communications Award.

He was born at Troy, Virginia and took his Bachelor of Arts degree from the University of Virginia. He now resides in Troy with his wife and two daughters. In addition to hunting, he enjoys fishing, canoeing, camping and trapping.

10

MANY METHODS
TAKE SOUTHERN DEER

Bob Gooch

IT WAS LATE November in Virginia. The light breeze out of the northwest was chilly, threatening to usher in the wintry blasts of December. Already a light snow had dusted the countryside, melting quickly under the warm rays of an autumn sun. But winter was officially several weeks away, and a few red and gold leaves still clung to the maples down in the swamp. Here and there specks of green served a reminder that autumn still reigned.

The deer season had been in progress for several weeks now, and some handsome bucks had been cleared through the local store, the official checking station for the Commission of Game and Inland Fisheries. Johnny had been envying those lucky hunters, and had even missed a couple of days from school in hopes of

bagging a good buck for his own family freezer. However, time was running out. After all, a fellow who plans to make a place for himself in the world needs an education—even more than he needs a bragging-size buck.

From his stand near the edge of the clearing, Johnny had an excellent vantage point covering a well-used deer escape route. His hopes were high as he settled down to wait.

Johnny's father, a veteran deer hunter, had dropped him off there and moved on to place other members of his hunting party along routes a fine buck might possibly travel. The hunters placed, he turned down a rutty logging road to the far side of the dense thicket, and released his pack of deer hounds.

A good thirty minutes ticked by, ever so

slowly, and Johnny was getting impatient, but he did not dare move. To do so would violate a cardinal rule of the hunt; once placed on a stand, the hunter does not move until the hunt is over, or he is picked up by the hunt master.

He glanced at his watch. Now an hour had passed. And then he heard it—ever so faintly at first, chop-chopp-choppp! Then silence. Seconds passed and there it was again but much louder this time! Ole Jack's bass voice rose above the melodious music of the pack. Johnny tightened his grip on the battered shotgun. Would he get his chance this time? Suppose another hunter got a shot first, or the deer veered off and passed out of range of his stand!

The commotion was getting closer. Johnny shifted to a more comfortable shooting position. He nervously checked his gun, and for the umpteenth time, surveyed his field of fire. A flash of movement in the thicket caught his eye. The rustle of dry leaves placed the deer close by. Johnny leaned forward, straining his ears and eyes.

Finally the big animal, gleaming magnificently in the bright sunlight, burst from the swamp! Stately wide antlers rode its proud head, the countless shiny points glistening in the November sun. The big deer hesitated momentarily, but then made a powerful bounding leap, intending to span the little clearing.

Johnny was ready. He slammed the shotgun to his shoulder, keeping his eyes glued to the fleeing target. The muzzle of the gun popped into his line of sight, and he swung with the big target. The old scattergun barked and the deer stumbled.

The schoolboy hunter did not remember pulling the trigger, but as he prepared for a second shot the deer collapsed near the far edge of the clearing. The shot had been well placed—just behind the massive shoulder. Apparently a buckshot or two had hit the spine, dropping the animal almost instantly.

Following the often repeated instructions of his father and other older hunters, Johnny, satisfied the deer was dead, proceeded to field-dress his kill. He removed the musk glands from the legs and then slit the fat buck from the apex of its chest cavity to the crotch. Rolling it on its side, he removed the viscera. He carefully carved out the heart and liver and placed them in plastic bags he had been carrying all season for that purpose.

Just as he was finishing the job, his Dad rolled up in his pickup truck. There was probably not a prouder father in the world at that moment. Together they admired the son's kill, and the boy excitedly detailed the high moments of the hunt. Finally they loaded the field dressed animal in the truck and headed for the checking station. Later they would butcher the meat and divide the venison with other members of the hunting party.

Although this is a typical story in deer rich Dixie, such a hunt calls for a good deal of planning, a sizeable chunk of hunting territory, a party of hunters, and a pack of deer hounds. It also demands discipline among the members of the

154

party. However, all of these ingredients are not always easy to come by, and as a consequence, many southern hunters are shifting to more conventional methods such as still hunting and trail watching.

The organized deer hunt, still preferred by a large number of southern hunters, traces its early growth to a number of factors. For one thing, southern hunters have always placed a premium on their hunting dogs; pointers and setters for bird hunting, beagles for rabbits, and trail hounds for fox, 'coon, bear, wild boar and deer. The whitetail puts down a strong scent and is a natural for the trail hound —American foxhound, black-and-tan coonhound, Walker hounds, and others.

In recent years the plodding beagle has become popular among deer hunters because it does not press the deer so hard. Most foxhounds will also chase deer, and this has created problems for fox hunters who suddenly find the deer populations have expanded tremendously in their favorite hunting haunts. They may find it impossible to keep their hounds off deer trails.

Deer also have a habit of breaking up rabbit hunts. An ambitious little beagle can hit a hot deer scent and lead an entire pack of the little hounds into the next county. My first deer was a wise old buck that broke up a Virginia rabbit hunt on a bright day in November. Two friends and I were working the thickets along a meadow creek for cottontails. Suddenly, a hundred yards down the creek, the dogs hit a hot trail in a little swamp and bed-

Bowhunters in a Tennessee deer camp. PHOTO COURTESY TENNESSEE GAME AND FISH COMMISSION

lam broke loose. Within seconds the dogs were headed up the creek in our direction, and we quickly spread out to intercept an escaping bunny. I was stationed on a narrow stretch of creek bottom near a point formed by the junction of two small streams. Beyond the point was a sharp dropoff to the bed of the creek.

As my eyes swept back and forth in search of a flash of fur, I suddenly realized a handsome set of deer antlers had materialized out of that creek bed—pointed right at me! The range was not twenty-five yards. Beneath the antlers the buck's head and neck presented a clear target.

I was armed with a light 16 gauge shotgun and size 6 shot. Still, I felt I was close enough to deliver a killing shot. My gun came up and I leveled on a point just beneath the buck's nose. At the crack of the gun, the antlers disappeared. I ran to the point, figuring I had scored an easy kill, but by the time I reached the creek bank, the deer was bounding off downstream—back in the direction of the dogs. My two companions, hearing the shot, joined me in time to also get a glimpse of the fleeing buck.

I was sure I had not missed at that close range, so we decided he would not go far. We found him stone dead, about three hundred yards down the creek. That buck boasted a beautiful, well-proportioned, eight-point rack that rests on the wall just above my desk as I write this.

I learned a couple of lessons from that kill. One was to pass up shots at deer in front of beagles if you do not want to convert them to deer hounds. The other was to refrain from shooting deer with light shotgun loads, regardless of how tempting the shot. Deer populations have expanded tremendously in my hunting country since that first kill long ago. In the interim I have had many opportunities while hunting birds, rabbits and squirrels, but now I shoot at deer only when I am properly armed.

In much of the top deer country in the South, dense vegetation and swampy areas make it just about impossible for the hunter to enter the whitetail's favorite cover. Dogs are needed to route the game out of the impenetrable thickets and this is probably the strongest justification for the deer hound. The Great Dismal Swamp of Virginia and North Carolina is a perfect example of this kind of deer cover.

Other contributing factors are the popularity of the shotgun as a hunting arm in the South, and the effectiveness of the deer drive in hanging venison from the game pole.

A variation of the deer drive described above is the one in which fellow hunters replace the dogs and drive the game to their companions waiting on stands. The drivers must remain alert for they often score on deer doubling back and attempting to sneak through the line of drivers. This type of drive is usually limited by the terrain, and is by no means unique to the South.

These days a lot of "deer hound" type hunting is done by clubs that hold leases on large acreages of hunting territory. The dogs are club property and membership fees cover the care of the dogs, cost of the lease, and other incidental expenses. Rarely does the lucky member who bags a whitetail keep the entire deer. The antlers are usually his, but the custom is for all members of the party to share in the venison.

Many hunting clubs prohibit the use of the deer rifle, because of the large numbers of hunters involved and the safety factor consideration. Shotguns and buckshot are common, even in areas where there are no legal restrictions on the hunting rifle. Probably one of the strongest rules in "drive hunting" is the one which prohibits the hunter from leaving his stand until he is told to do so by the hunt master. This, too, is primarily a safety precaution, and a sensible one.

A handsome Tennessee whitetail buck. PHOTO COURTESY TENNESSEE GAME AND FISH COMMISSION

Many deer hunting principles go out of the window on a big, organized deer drive. Since the hunter is placed on a stand, he has no way of combating the breezes that may carry his scent to the deer, and so, the prevailing winds should be considered when planning such a hunt. The stand hunter must keep quiet and remain well concealed, and, because he is not too concerned about other hunters, he can dress in camouflage clothing for these controlled drives.

The well planned and well executed deer drive is an effective and accepted producer of venison. Properly handled, it neither abuses property owners nor endangers the lives of other hunters. It can also be rich in hunting experiences. A big buck bursting out of a thicket into the bright fall or winter sunlight is a sight the hunter will never forget.

Unfortunately deviations from the legitimate drive have evolved in many parts of the South and given deer hunting a black eye. The problem is the result of a desire to use dogs, but the lack of sufficient hunting territory. Unscrupulous hunters release their dogs on small tracts of land where they have hunting privileges, hoping the hounds will move deer from surrounding posted land or other prohibited hunting areas. They may even have hunting rights along normal escape routes, but if they do not, they simply take up stands along public roads. In so doing, they raise the ire of landowners and the public in general.

Because I grew up in the South in an area where deer hounds were popular, I was initiated to whitetail hunting by this method. It is an easy way for the inexperienced hunter to get a deer and learn some of the fundamentals. But such hunting is much like fishing the ocean for marlin. The hunt master supplies the knowledge and experience, just as the charter boat skipper uses his knowledge to put his client over a marlin. If the hunter remains on his stand and is a reasonably accurate shot, a kill requires no great hunting skill.

After taking a couple of deer by this method, I developed a desire to try something else. I bought a good book on deer hunting and read a number of magazine articles during the learning process. Deer populations were just beginning to expand in much of America, and good deer hunting literature was in demand. Both the outdoor magazines and book publishers responded with good material.

I suspect many other southern hunters followed the same route. The deer drive, either by dog or man, leaves a lot to be desired in the way of a complete hunting experience. The true hunter eventually needs a greater challenge, one that calls for a deeper understanding of his quarry, its habits, habitat and way of life.

Hunting with hounds is not conducive to a thorough development of this kind of knowledge. This is not intended as a reflection on the many fine deer hounds and the hunters who follow them. Successful hound hunting also requires a mastery of certain techniques such as dog handling, knowing when and where to release the hounds, and anticipating the deer's moves once he is jumped.

In my book, however, the ideal deer hunt pits the lone hunter against a big buck, probably the wiliest big game animal in America and a joy to hunt.

The successful deer hunter recognizes his quarry's habits and his tendency to feed mostly at night, or early morning and late afternoon. In the South, the whitetail beds down during the usual hunting hours, seeking the protection of dense vegetation or the heavy laps of a freshly harvested hardwood or pine forest.

Assuming that just the hunter and the deer are afield—admittedly a rare situation—the hunter's best chances come early in the morning as the deer move from feeding to bedding grounds, or late in the afternoon when the movements are re-versed. Locating these areas requires scouting and the ability to read deer sign; beds in the grass or snow, droppings, tracks, deer hair on barbed-wire fences, and barked trees where a buck has rubbed its antlers. Complete familiarity with the country and an opportunity to observe deer movements on a day-to-day basis is a tremendous help. This is the reason so many rural boys bag their trophies the first day or so of the season.

I live in a rural area, and much of my pre-season scouting is incidental to other outdoor activities. A particularly delightful combination of forest, dancing meadow brook and lush hayfield, once furnished me with venison for three seasons in a row. It was by pure accident that I discovered that hotspot. A well used trail leading from the hardwood forest, across the creek and into the field, marked it. Whitetail deer, like most animals, are creatures of habit. I made it a point to watch the field for a number of evenings, and almost like clockwork, each day a small herd of deer worked its way slowly and cautiously down that trail and into the field to feed.

An hour before feeding time on opening day, I posted myself about one hundred yards downstream from the field. As anticipated, movement deep in the woods soon caught my eye. I practically held my breath. Like shadows they drifted into full view, moving alertly down the trail. There were four of them. Their pace was painstakingly slow, almost as if they suspected something was

A big buck bedded down in prime Kentucky whitetail country. PHOTO COURTESY KENTUCKY DEPARTMENT OF FISH AND WILDLIFE RESOURCES

wrong. I watched those deer for a good hour, and it was almost dusk and near the end of legal shooting time when the first doe stepped into the field.

It did not start to feed at once. As is usually the case, the does were in the lead. The bucks hold back until the coast is clear. That doe was obviously nervous. Once, she moved back into the edge, but then reappeared, followed by two more does.

I waited in vain for the buck, and finally settled for a fat doe. We had either-sex hunting that year, and a season limit of two. I would get my buck later. A doe produces excellent venison—in my opinion, much better than the meat of a buck.

That was an easy kill, requiring about two hours hunting time at most. However, I had spent plenty of time in pre-season scouting, much of it in conjunction with other outdoor pursuits. I took a whitetail at this same spot each of the following two years.

The deer hunter who does his homework well and knows his territory can almost assure himself of a shot within a matter of hours on opening day.

Once the hunter has established his quarry's living pattern, he must equip himself properly for the foray after his favorite game.

Clothing is important. The most important characteristic of the deer hunter's clothing is the finish of his outer garments, particularly his jacket and trousers. It must be soft. Wool is ideal. However, since southern deer seasons may open as early as August 15 in South Carolina, wool is often too warm. Well-worn denim is a fair choice, but any loose weave clothing is satisfactory. The sharp ears of a deer will quickly pick up the harsh noise made by hard finished clothing rubbing against brush. Upland hunting clothing made of duck or similar material is a poor choice for the deer woods. Still, I see deer hunters so dressed every season.

Shoes should have rubber soles, preferably soft rubber. Some hunters even wear tennis shoes, but I do not like them for woods wear.

One of the most conspicuous features the deer hunter takes into the woods is his "pale face" office or shop complexion. A good growth of beard helps. Some hunters use camouflage paint or wear headnets. In cold weather, soft gloves should cover the hands, another give-away feature. For late summer or early fall, light cotton gloves or camouflage paint will conceal the hands from the wary eyes of a whitetail.

Loose items that rattle or get caught in the brush should be kept to a minimum. The hunter needs a knife, possibly a compass if he is hunting strange country. A dozen rounds of ammunition will suffice. A light rope will be needed to string up the downed deer, or to drag it from the woods, and a plastic bag or two for the heart and liver. These items can be tucked into convenient but separate pockets so they will not rattle. Binoculars should be swung around the neck and tucked into the shirt or jacket front.

His scouting done, properly clothed and equipped, the hunter is ready to chose his weapon and head for the woods.

The choice of firearms varies widely in the South. Many hunters, the old timers particularly, stick to their shotguns loaded with buckshot or slugs. However, the deer rifle is growing in popularity with the 30/06, .270 and 7mm all popular calibers. Most are fitted with telescopic sights. My favorite weapon for woods hunting is the little 30/30 carbine fitted with peep sight. It is a light and handy little rifle with plenty of punch for whitetails. The peep sight provides fast sighting and permits quick shooting in woods hunting. However, if I expect to do my shooting in a meadow or open field, I prefer a telescopic sight. A variable scope rides my light .243 which also gets heavy woodchuck duty.

If he is to successfully outwit and bag his deer, the hunter must overcome the three senses the whitetail uses in his defense, the senses of smell, hearing and vision.

The sense of smell is the strongest and the deer's first line of defense. The nose of a wise old buck is amazingly sensitive, and human scent will spook him for sure. The hunter overcomes this by working into the wind whenever possible. This means constantly checking the wind direction and being guided accordingly. Even on seemingly windless days, there are usually light breezes that shift willy-nilly through the hills and valleys. These are the kind of winds that give the hunter a fit. A steady wind blowing out of the northeast is predictable. Ideally, the hunter should work directly into the wind, but just about any direction except downwind from the hunter is acceptable. Crosswinds present no problem unless the hunter unknowingly gets abreast of a deer.

Right behind the animal's sense of smell is his hearing. It is here that proper clothing plays a vital role. Also germane is the manner in which the hunter moves through the woods. The approach should be quiet and stealthy. The Indians perfected the stalk and the modern deer hunter has learned much from these early American hunters. The most successful

BOB GOOCH

North Carolina hunter used a shortgun to down this fine Tarheel whitetail. PHOTO COURTESY NORTH CAROLINA WILDLIFE RESOURCES COMMISSION

whitetail hunter moves just a few steps at a time, placing each foot carefully so as not to snap a twig or small stick underfoot. When he moves, the hunter should concentrate on doing so quietly. The long pauses between moves are reserved for looking.

The stand hunter should clear the area around him of leaves and debris so he can shift his position noiselessly.

The sense of vision is the deer's weakest sense. Like many animals, the whitetail is color blind. However, colors that blend into the terrain or woods are less conspicuous than those that contrast with them.

Camouflage patterns that break up the hunter's outline would help conceal him from the mediocre eyes of the deer, but for reasons of safety (by law in many states), the hunter should wear orange or bright red. But even in safe, bright colors, a camouflage pattern helps break up the hunter's outline.

A deer picks up sudden or unusual movements more quickly than it does color. Movement of the hands is particularly noticeable. The whitetail knows his home country like the hunter knows his backyard. He may not recognize a hunter in an open field, but he knows that object was not there yesterday. He becomes wary. When stalking a deer the hunter should freeze—motionless when the deer looks at him. Once the deer resumes feeding, the hunter can move again.

Still hunting has become my favorite way of taking whitetails, and this popular method took my largest buck. By still hunting I mean moving slowly through known whitetail cover in an effort to get within range of a deer. Dressed properly and working into the wind, using the stop-and-go method described above, the hunter can get surprisingly close to his game. I like still-hunting because it provides more action and more of a challenge.

The big buck I took in this manner was on the move early one morning in November. It was about 8 A.M.—past the effective time for trail watching. I was working slowly through a mixed pine and hardwood forest and a light snow covered the ground. I had moved less than a quarter of a mile when I got my chance.

Just as I was looking up from a cautious move across a leaf-covered forest floor, I spotted the animal moving toward me. Its head and tail were down, and at first I thought it was a big dog. I spotted the deer before it saw me or suspected anything. I froze and waited for a shot. As I was shifting into a shooting position, moving my left foot and twisting my body slightly, the big buck stopped and looked right at me. For a moment or so we stared at each other. The deer was alerted, but he had not figured me out as yet. This was a head-on shot, much like the one I had taken years before on that rabbit hunt. This time the distance was greater, about seventy-five yards, and I was armed with a Marlin 30/30 fitted with a peep sight.

Slowly I brought the rifle up and centered on the buck's chest, trying for a heart and lung shot. Surprisingly, I had plenty of time. I slowly squeezed the trigger. The little carbine roared and the buck reared, whirled in his tracks, and dashed out of sight over the hill! I was sick. How could I have missed at that close range? And at a stationary target! True, I had shot offhand, but at that range there was no excuse for missing.

Working another round in the chamber, I ran to the spot where the deer had been standing. There was no blood, but picking up the trail in the snow was easy. I topped the hill, and there, just over the crest, was my buck. He was down, but

not quite dead. Another shot finished him off.

My first shot was more accurate than I had thought. It was a little high, but it had hit the boiler room, destroying the heart and lungs. How that buck ran as far as it did was a credit to the stamina of this popular American big game animal.

I dressed my prize and dragged it through the snow to the edge of the woods where I could pick it up with my car. I was completely sold on the merits of still hunting.

Field dressing a fine whitetail buck bagged in the George Washington National Forest in Virginia.

Bob Gooch

Another popular method employed by successful southern deer hunters is the tree stand, or elevated stand. The white-tail has few enemies that attack from the sky, so he seldom looks up. I have taken several good deer from tree stands, and find it an interesting and productive method of hunting. A stand can be as simple as the lower branches of a sprawling oak into which the hunter climbs, or as elaborate as a tree house overlooking a deer trail or feeding area. Since I like to hunt a number of different areas, I seldom invest a lot of time in building a tree stand. I usually climb into a convenient oak, get about fifteen feet off the ground, and wait for dawn. A light ladder helps, but is not always necessary if the tree has low hanging branches.

When climbing to a tree stand I leave my rifle or bow and arrows on the ground, fastening a long cord to my weapon and taking the other end of the cord with me. Once settled, I pull the weapon into the tree. I reverse the procedure when leaving. Climbing with a rifle or bow and arrow is dangerous.

The tree stand places the hunter above the deer's normal line of vision, and often sends his body odors breezing over the animal's head. And in a tree the hunter can rest quietly, well above the rustling leaves or loose twigs that alert the quarry.

While the laws vary from state to state, there are generally no regulations that prohibit a hunter from floating quietly down a stream in anticipation of surpris-ing a big buck watering at the edge of the stream. A light canoe and winding stream can carry the hunter to prime hunting territory, and a deer dropped on the banks of a stream is easy to slide into a canoe and carry out.

I once took a fine young spike buck in this manner, dropped it with a neck shot just as I rounded a bend in the stream. Actually I was jump shooting for ducks, but a heavy load of magnums at close range gave me all the punch I needed.

The hunter who plans such a hunt should steal a few tricks from the duck hunter, hugging the banks of the stream and anticipating shots as he rounds a bend in the river. Shooting a deer *in* the water is illegal in most states, and un-sportsmanlike in all. But floating a stream is a deadly method of getting within range of a good buck.

In most southern states, the archery season precedes the firearms season by at least a month. This special season puts the deer hunter in the woods at a delightful time of the year. Even if he fails to arrow his deer, he learns a good deal by the time the firearms season opens, and probably knows exactly where to go for that trophy head. In my book, the tree stand is by far the best bet for the bowhunter. It is about the only method that will put him within the limited range of the bow. Still hunting will rarely get a bowhunter a whitetail.

In many states the deer and small game seasons run concurrently. Small game hunters rarely disturb the deer hunter. In

A pair of happy Tennessee bowhunters. PHOTO COURTESY TENNESSEE GAME AND FISH COMMISSION

shot rifles. However, it does give the deer hunter a chance to bag an unusual trophy without traveling a great distance.

Back in 1966 the Tennessee Game and Fish Commission secured some blacktail deer from Oregon and released them in seemingly suitable Tennessee habitat. The deer from the Far West show promise and are now being introduced to other new areas.

Seasons are long in the South. South Carolina deer hunting starts as early as August 15 and continues well into January. The Alabama and Virginia seasons also run into January, though they do not usually open until November. The Mis-

Captain Robert L. Baker of Portsmouth, Virginia, took this handsome sika deer on Assateague Island. PHOTO COURTESY OF BUREAU OF SPORT FISHERIES AND WILDLIFE

fact they can improve his chances by keeping the deer moving.

In the South the whitetail and deer hunting are synonymous. However, a couple of other species add a little variety, though it is extremely limited.

The Chincoteague Island National Wildlife Refuge on Assateague Island off Virginia's Eastern Shore boasts a small herd of sitka deer. These little members of the elk family were accidentally introduced there years ago. The herd has grown to the point that limited hunting is possible. In recent years the Island has been opened to bowhunting and single

164

North Carolina bowhunter examines maps of state deer hunting areas. PHOTO COURTESY NORTH CAROLINA WILDLIFE RESOURCES COMMISSION

sissippi season is another one that continues into January. Add the archery season and special primitive weapons sea-

sons, and the Southern deer hunter has lots of time in which to bag his venison.

Deer herds are flourishing throughout the South, and liberal bag limits reflect this healthy picture. The Alabama deer herd is estimated at 500,000 and the Mississippi herd in excess of 400,000. Virginia biologists estimate their deer population at 200,000. Annual harvests are good; 40,000 in North Carolina, 45,000 in Virginia, 8,000 in Kentucky and 30,000 in Mississippi.

Bag limits are liberal in most states. In Alabama, for example, deer hunters may take one whitetail per day. Virginia and South Carolina hunters are permitted two deer per season, and in parts of South Carolina, the season limit is five bucks. Most states permit some antlerless hunting.

The mild climate of the Southland favors both the deer and the hunter, and the sport is growing rapidly. The long seasons and liberal limits permit the hunter to try a variety of hunting methods—and a chance to invent some of his own.

Dean Wohlgemuth writes a twice-weekly column, "Woods and Waters" for *The Atlanta Constitution,* covering hunting, fishing, boating, camping and related outdoor subjects. He has hunted deer, quail, waterfowl and turkey over much of the South and is an ardent angler of bass, trout, panfish and saltwater game fish. The Kansas native has lived in the South for nearly twenty years.

Wohlgemuth was formerly chief of public relations with the Georgia Game and Fish Commission and editor of *Georgia Game & Fish* magazine. He is a freelance writer and has been published in *Field & Stream, Outdoor Life, Sports Afield, Southern Outdoors* and several other magazines. He is a past president of Southeastern Outdoor Press Association and a former board member and past national convention chairman for Outdoor Writers Association of America.

He has also been outdoor editor and assistant sports editor of the Lynchburg, Virginia, *Daily Advance;* sports editor of the Rock Hill, South Carolina, *Evening Herald;* and aviation editor of the Wichita, Kansas, *Eagle.*

He served in the U.S. Air Force at Shaw AFB, South Carolina, where he was editor of the base newspaper. The Kansas native is married to the former Kay Hilton of Kershaw, South Carolina. They have three children.

11

DEER IN DEEP DIXIE

Dean Wohlgemuth

"If I even see a buck in the woods today, it'll be a first," Grady Cook asserted as we rode with Frank Cox in his pickup truck in chilly Dixie pre-dawn darkness.

Of course, these words in themselves weren't completely unique among deer hunters, but what he had to say next added considerably to their weight. "Yessir, I've hunted deer for forty years or more, and I have yet to see my first buck in the woods."

"Forty years? How in the world did you manage to stay with deer hunting that long without success?" I asked.

"Well, now," the retired telephone company executive from Atlanta pointed out, "I didn't hunt every year and I didn't go completely without success. I killed one doe a couple of years ago during doe season."

To make a long story short, this was the day for Grady Cook. Even after forty long scoreless years, the losing streak could be broken. Two hours after he took a stand, one shot put a beautiful eight-pointer on the ground with barely so much as a twitching muscle. When you've waited this long, you can't afford buck fever and a muffed chance. Grady finally had his buck.

Later, when we were dressing out the deer, Grady fumbled around in his pocket and brought out four shells, loaded with buckshot. I noted them, and did a double take—they were roll crimp shells! I hadn't seen shells like those in years!

The old gentleman could read the question in my eyes. I didn't want to ask it, because I couldn't really believe those were what he had used to put down a deer with one shot.

"I bought those five rounds when going

167

on a hunt twenty-two years ago, back in the forties." He grinned. I counted. Sure enough, there were only four rounds in his hand. Was he really going to tell me that's what he was using? "Apparently they're still good," he went on evenly. "It just took one to bring that buck down."

It took awhile to answer that, but I finally did. "Well, at your current rate, you'll have to live a long time to use up the rest of those," I smiled.

Grady didn't live that long. A couple of years later those four shells lost their chance to put another deer in the cooler for him.

I think back on his forty-year-buck now, and ponder the changes of the deer hunting picture in the South he saw during that time. His first deer hunt would have been in 1928, a time when it was certainly no surprise to go deer hunting in Dixie and fail to score. In fact, in those days, Georgians who even *saw* a deer, any time of the year, could usually count on getting their name in the local newspaper.

A few short years later deer management programs in the South really got rolling. It was slow at first, beginning with some law enforcement—not enough, but at least it was a start. Soon after, stocking programs began. About this same time there was a considerable change in land use across Georgia, one that was to play a highly important role in the great comeback of the whitetail.

Farmers began to realize that growing row crops was a certain road to the poor house. One tale still goes around the heart

A major deer-stocking program which begin in the late 1930's has brought back deer in abundance through most of the South. Live trapping and release still continues in areas where needed. This deer is released on a new State Game Management Area in South Georgia, which was leased to the State Game and Fish Department by a forest industry.

of Dixie. It seems there was a man who was selling eggs on the roadside for thirty-five cents a dozen. A mile farther down the highway, his wife was buying them back for forty cents a dozen. One curious customer couldn't resist the obvious question: "How can you make any money like this?"

"Well," drawled the old Southern gentleman, "it ain't much, but it's a heap better'n farmin'!"

With conditions like this, many a farm was left to do as it would, which was to grow pines. The pines became attractive to forest industries, who soon moved in en

168   DEAN WOHLGEMUTH

masse and began to put money in once empty pockets, and more trees on previously unprofitable land. Now the South is a highly important timber producer. Coupled with sound game management, these forest lands are producing deer like never before.

That statement was not just a figure of speech. I've been told by game biologists that there are now more deer in some areas of the South than there were before the first white settlers ever saw this country! That's hard to believe, but then, those who understand deer management have it all figured out. Controlled hunting, good game management and law enforcement mean a healthy herd, the maximum that the land can support. Good forest management is also highly important, because habitat is so often the key limiting factor on the populations of any game species. Properly managed forests, like properly managed game herds, are healthiest when they are correctly harvested. And healthy forests provide quality game populations. It's a ham-and-eggs combination. That simple.

The best example I can give of what has happened to deer herds in the South is the recent record of the state where I now live, Georgia. For the past several years, the annual legal harvest has increased about 5000 deer a year. One year it was 20,000 (estimated), the next year 25,000. Then it was 30,000, 35,000 and most recently, it hit the all-time high of an estimated 40,000 legally harvested deer.

Game censuses indicate Georgia's herd has reached 120,000 deer, and it's still growing. There is little if any doubt that the herd has reached record proportions. All this points out that Dixie deer have

This deer is one of an estimated forty thousand legally harvested during a recent Georgia season. Deer harvests have increased dramatically in the Deep South over recent years due to stocking, better game management, better law enforcement, and improved habitat. Larger harvests indicate a vast increase in deer populations, attested to by liberal bag limits in Alabama and South Carolina. Alabama hunters may take one deer per day over a season that, combining archery and gun season, may span more than one hundred days.

Deer in Deep Dixie

come of age. There now is excellent hunting in the Deep South. Quite a change since Grady Cook's first hunt!

Figures and statistics are great, but then comes the question, Where and how can I get my deer in Dixie? Methods are simple enough, but they do take skill and determination. Two major techniques are used, but of course there are as many ways to hunt deer as there are imaginations to dream them up. One of the most important means to bag a buck is generally frowned upon throughout the remainder of the world's deer hunters. That is hunting with dogs. The other is stand hunting. Let's talk dogs first.

Dog hunters are as serious about their sport as anyone. And it really isn't as unsporting as it sounds, when you consider all the facts. In terms of results, it can't be considered the most productive means of getting venison, when you weigh it equally with all other areas of the Southeast. But you can't measure apples by oranges. Dog hunting is done in areas where other methods might fail dismally.

It's like this: the low lying country of the South has a high percentage of swampland. Few people know enough about the swamps to have any business in them, and those that do know enough treat them with a great deal of respect! Even where there is no swamp, poisonous snakes are very common in the thick underbrush of this area. Not many knowledgeable people are willing to stalk deer in this kind of habitat! If they were, the heavy understory and limited visibi-

lity of the thick timber make it indeed unlikely that even the most skilled Dan'l Boone could ever tiptoe within range of a wary buck.

Hunting from a tree stand isn't terribly productive either, because with thousands of acres of swamp and dense forest to hide in, deer don't have to move about to where you'd want to put a stand. If you want to get deer in swamp counry, you have to bring the game to you. There's only one satisfactory *and* legal way to do it. Dogs.

One of the fringe benefits of dog hunting is a type of companionship unique to deer hunting. Other forms of deer hunting may provide solitude, or comradeship with a chosen few, but to be a dog hunter you've got to be gregarious. The hunting party may number as many as fifty or even a hundred persons. Add to that approximately the same number of dogs and you have a situation that can hardly be described as solitude! Even so, actual hunting time is usually all your own, with ample breathing space.

The selected area will have definite natural boundaries. Usually a main road forms one line of demarcation. Invariably a swamp or river acts as one barrier. And there just about has to be a logging road to provide an open area to bag your quarry.

Let's say our "ideal" hunting area is bordered on one side by a deep swamp, and on the other by a large river. The starting point for the dogs is a highway which forms the third side of the rectan-

170

Dog hunting is popular in coastal regions of the South where thick, swampy woods make this the only successful method of hunting. Ancestry of the dog is usually far less important than his ability to hunt. An outstanding dog may be worth several hundred dollars.

gle. The hunters are scattered on the fourth, a logging road deep in the woods. Because we have quite a good number of hunters with us today, some are stationed along the edge of the Big Swamp.

The hunters are in position, just after sunrise—all stomachs bulging with sausage and ham and eggs and grits—standing about two hundred yards apart, and armed with 12-gauge shotguns loaded with number 1 buckshot. (In some instances, hunters may use rifled slugs, but generally these, and almost without exception, high powered rifles are considered too dangerous.)

Once everyone is on his assigned stand,

the dogs are turned loose. They won't be seen again until they make the logging road at the far end, but their presence won't be a secret if there are deer in the area. Once he's on the trail, a dog will sing out with a bawl that is symphonic beauty to a genuine dog man. This is important. It tells the hunters that a deer is moving, and the baying outlines the direction of his travel. When he's headed your way, you'll know it! And you'll be ready.

Standing shots in this type of hunting are indeed rare, though it doesn't necessarily follow that you're going to see deer only on a dead run. I know of some instances where deer are run hard, but it usually isn't the case. Deer that have been run hard don't taste as good because the adrenalin coursing through a hard-run deer affects its flavor. Shots are harder, too, and there's some danger of shooting a doe by mistake. For these reasons good sportsmen prefer dogs that don't push the deer hard, but instead simply keep the deer moving. This type of hunting is, in my experience, much akin to hunting rabbits in front of beagles. I've had time to look over a herd of three or four deer which had stopped for several minutes to look back over their shoulders to see how far behind the dogs were. The dog handler might well be the first man to get a shot. After he has put the dogs down, they might jump a deer which will get back through the pack and head straight for the handler.

As you move a bit farther from the coastal plain into hillier country, you won't see dog hunting. It usually isn't legal, nor would it be as productive on a regular basis. Here the deer hunter may have scouted the woods for weeks before the season began, searching for an area used heavily by deer. If he's an experienced hunter he may well be in quest of a trophy buck, and he'll have the habits of a particular deer all mapped out.

His stand probably is at the edge of a thicket or overlooking a creek bottom. It's probably high enough on a hillside that if a deer crosses the ridge, he won't look the hunter right in the eye—even though the stand is built twenty feet or so off the ground. Yet the stand won't be right on the ridge. There will be at least one heavily traveled deer trail within a few yards of the stand, but expert hunters seldom select a spot that doesn't have at least two crossing trails. Three or four trails intersecting within range aren't uncommon. Some open area is preferred, especially for early morning and late evening hours, but to get a smart buck, there has to be heavy cover nearby, too.

When a doe wanders out into the clearing, the hunter should sit tight and move nothing but his eyes—even to the point of blinking as quietly as possible—for the next forty-five minutes to an hour. His eyes should be busy, however, combing through the brush, because there's a good chance that where there is a doe, a buck can't be too far behind.

Though a few Dixie hunters may take stands on the ground, the vast majority prefer tree stands. Whitetails naturally look ahead and look down, but they don't expect enemies to come from above. Also, and perhaps more important, a man's scent won't carry as well to the deer from the tree stand as it will at ground level. Even so, I normally watch more closely to the upwind side.

I can't promise you a deer won't spot you if you're sitting well up in a pine or oak tree. Deer become familiar with the hunters' methods, too, and a wizened old trophy buck may have been shot at from a tree stand during a previous season. I've been spotted in a tree stand by deer on several occasions. One very young deer spotted me in an unusually high stand while I had the string on my bow drawn. I tried to hold the string long enough for him to glance away. It was no use. I had to release the arrow, and it missed by five feet. What made the situation worse was the fact that my stand was a quarter of a mile from the landowner's home, and that he was watching me through binoculars. I still haven't lived it down!

Because archery season usually precedes gun season in most southern states, many gun hunters have taken up the bow for two reasons. First, it extends the amount of time that the hunter can enjoy his favorite sport. Second, he can hunt while he does his scouting. Thus, archery hunting has boomed in popularity in the past five to ten years.

Most archers rely on tree stands, testing out the area where they'll sit with a gun later on. Others have special stands for bowhunting and different locations for rifle season.

One major difference between a gun stand and a bow stand is the height from the ground. A rifle hunter may get twenty or even thirty feet off the ground where he is sure he's out of sight and scent of a buck, but the archer would be at a distinct disadvantage at such dizzy heights. Thus, his stand may be only six feet or at most ten or twelve feet off the ground. He's more easily seen, but it's much easier to shoot accurately. The trajectory of an arrow from a high stand would take an engineer to figure out.

Some archers like to stalk whitetails, but those who put a deer in the bag this

Everyone pitches in and gives a hand when a lucky hunter bags his buck. Often that help consists largely of advice.

Hunters bound for renowned Blackbeard Island off the Georgia coast must load hunting and camping gear into a boat for a twenty-mile cruise to the whitetail hunting grounds. Small size of the island, which is part of the Savannah National Wildlife Refuge for waterfowl, dictates that deer hunting is by bow only. Deer hunts are necessary to control a heavy population.

The beauty of Blackbeard is allure enough to get an outdoorsman to visit this semi-tropical island. Rich in history and tales of the old pirate who used it for a hideout, the island now has abundant wildlife in a primitive type habitat.

way must have some kinship to Dan'l Boone himself. It takes a great deal of skill to get within bow range of a deer on foot. Stalking is usually done during the mid-day hours, after spending the early morning on a stand. Late evening hours will again find the archer sitting it out. The reason for the mid-day stroll is because the deer won't be moving much at this time, and he can scout the area for gun season. Even if he pushes the deer out of hiding and doesn't get a shot, he knows where his quarry is for a later hunt. Whether hunting with rifle or bow, the stalker doesn't run foot races.

Stalking and still hunting are interchangeable words with most deer hunters. The stalker spends more time standing still than he does walking. If the hunter walks continuously, the deer will know from the sound of his movements that the noise doesn't come from a wild creature. The hunter who moves constantly will seldom see a deer, and if he does, it will be at some distance and speedily departing. The good stalker will take two or three steps, then stop for a minute or longer, looking about in all directions. He's never in a hurry.

Recently, primitive weapons, such as muzzle loading rifles and shotguns, have

174

become increasingly popular in the South. Like the archer, the muzzle loader hunter will spend most of his time on a stand. And like the archer, he must wait for a closer shot than the hunter with a modern firearm. The archer has little business shooting more than twenty-five or thirty yards. The muzzle-loader shooter can't reach a great deal farther and should limit his shooting to seventy-five yards. Beyond that distance power and accuracy fall off rapidly.

One reason that both archery and primitive weapons are growing rapidly in the South, however, is that because of cover, shooting ranges will not extend beyond seventy-five yards anyway. Also, the short-range weapons add more sport to the hunt. The same factors explain the popularity of the shotgun among many southern hunters. The scattergun, loaded with buckshot, is a deadly weapon within forty yards, every bit as deadly as a high powered rifle (if not as accurate). Most

shots the hunter gets that are clear and sure enough to warrant pulling a trigger or drawing a bow string are within the forty-yard limit. Slug shooting shotguns will permit sure shots a bit farther than this.

The modern rifleman isn't restricted by range, however, and he can often find it to his benefit to station himself near a powerline clearing, clear cut area in a forest, or over an open meadow. If he knows the terrain well enough and the location of other hunters, he can safely take shots of one hundred to two hundred yards, but he will rarely have the opportunity to reach that outer limit in this section of the country.

The argument of the low country man that the high–powered rifle is far more dangerous than the shotgun doesn't really hold water when applied to the hunter using a stand in rolling country or in the mountainous regions of the South. The rifle hunter using a tree stand will gener-

State managed deer hunts provide opportunities to hunt for thousands of city dwellers and out-of-state visitors as well as local hunters. Variety of hunts include buck-only gun hunts, either-sex hunts (when high populations dictate), archery hunts and hunts for primitive weapons (muzzle loading rifles and shotguns). Hunter is wearing a blaze orange vest, required for managed hunts in some states.

Deer in Deep Dixie

ally be shooting toward the ground. Of course, there is a remote chance of a ricochet should the bullet strike a stone, but the thick woods will stop most bullets before they get far. In all cases, hunters should endeavor to put at least a quarter mile between them and the next hunter. This isn't hard to do when hunting private land with a party, but when you're hunting a national forest open to the public, industry-owned land or state managed areas, you just have to rely on careful scrutiny. Hunters normally take their stands a half-hour before daylight, so you can watch for flashlights and listen for the sounds of another hunter when heading for a stand. If you're already in your stand and another hunter comes by, you had better let him know you're there, either by a quiet yell or a whistle. Coughing is not always recognized as a human sound.

Firearms for the southern deer hunter should vary sharply from those used by the western hunter in the wide open spaces. Flat trajectory and high speed over long ranges are not worth much to the Dixie deer man. He would be far better off with a heavy, slow bullet that is accurate up to about 100 to 150 yards. Beyond this range he won't be seeing deer well enough to see horns anyway.

The fast, light bullet of the westerner that covers long, open country to get to its target might be pretty useless in the southern forest. Should such a bullet hit a twig, it could veer far off target and maybe even shatter. The southerner

Lush forests operated by forest industries provide excellent habitat for deer. A change in land use over the past several decades, from farming to forestry, has been a factor in the great increase in southern deer herds. Some experts say there are now more deer in the South than when the first settlers came to this country.

chooses a heavy, slow bullet to buck the brush. It will be far more accurate through heavy cover at short ranges.

Keep your .270 on the rack if you're coming South for venison, and save your .243, too. If you have a .30/06, you have what is in my opinion a fine rifle for southern hunting, as well as an all-around firearm for most North American game. Use a heavy bullet, such as a 180-grain soft nose, but you don't need a heavy load. I load my own and usually use forty-five grains of 4895. This is ample power, and for my rifle, it is highly accurate to two hundred yards.

The old .30/30, credited with so many pounds of venison in the locker, is still a

176

DEAN WOHLGEMUTH

good cartridge for the southern deer hunter who works the heavy brush and who realizes its limitations. Rifles chambered for this cartridge are generally light and handle easily in thick stuff, and their lighter recoil make them pleasant to shoot. They will get on target quickly and go to your tree stand with less effort and danger. (You should use a sling to climb the tree, and please remember to leave the rifle unloaded until you are in the stand.) The .30/30 will put the deer down—if you hit him where you ought to.

The rifle hunter should wear some article of bright red, orange or yellow clothing, such as a hat or vest. My preference is blaze orange, because this color is the most visible for the greatest distance. Yellow can be seen for a great distance, too, but to my way of thinking, can probably be seen better by a deer because of its proximity on the color scale to white, a danger sign to a deer. Red is least visible to a deer, but also to another hunter. It is still much better than drab brown.

The archer can get away with camouflage, and he will need it because he must let the deer get considerably closer to him. Muzzle loader hunters also wear camouflage, but many are going to a new style these days—or should I say old style? They're dressing like Daniel Boone.

Choosing a place to hunt in the South may not be an easy task. Finding the areas that have the most deer also means finding more hunting pressure. Locating land open to the public is sometimes a problem. Land in the hands of small private owners is rarely opened to a stranger, particularly in the more populous areas.

National forests and state game management areas are safer bets for the city dweller or out-of-stater. Lists of these along with local regulations may be obtained through government agencies. Wise advance planning would have to include writing a few letters to obtain this information. State conservation agencies can answer any questions on management areas as well as those regarding regulations, license fees and seasons, while the U.S. Forest Service offices can usually provide maps and details on their lands. Many management areas are within national forests, while others may be on forest industry land. While all southern states have good acreage of national forests, they are nowhere near as vast as in the West.

Outside of these public and closely regulated areas, the visiting hunter will most likely have to rely on forest industry lands. The best source of information about these properties would be the individual companies. In order to save time and get good general information along with specifics on whom to contact, write to the Southern Forest Institute, 1 Corporate Square, Atlanta, Georgia.

The Piedmont region of Georgia would have to be considered the top deer producing area of this state. The Piedmont is the low rolling hill country that leads up to the Blue Ridge mountains. The mountains themselves are fine places to

A page from history seems to be pulled out by this group of hunters enjoying a managed hunt set aside for only blackpowder enthusiasts. They have proof that their means of hunting can and does produce venison.

hunt, and contain much of the available national forests and state management areas. Mountain land is not as abundant in Alabama or South Carolina as it is in Georgia, and in these states has less deer.

The geographic center of Georgia would have to get the nod as the best section for deer. South and east of Atlanta, all the way east to the South Carolina line, is a belt of forest land, including the Oconee National Forest, which is perennially the top producer of the most and biggest deer in Georgia. The mountain counties would rank second best. Coastal counties in the southeast corner usually rank third. The southwest portion of the state has too few deer to be worth going any great distance to hunt. This is basically farm land and plantation country,

with very little land open to the hunter. Quail are much more prevalent than deer here, as this is the Quail Capitol of the World!

Along the Georgia coast there is no national forest land, but there are a few game management areas on timber industry land. The "flat woods" country here is used mostly for commercial purposes, and it is largely owned by industries. Permission to hunt this land can be obtained easily enough from the owners, but be careful to stay off land that is leased by a local hunting club for dog hunts. Additionally, I'd have to recommend that you leave your rifle home and bring only a 12-gauge shotgun and No. 1 or No. 0 buckshot, if you want to be welcomed.

The shotgun advice would pertain to South Carolina's low country, too. This is largely swampland and woodland of the commercial variety. Virtually all the hunting in the southern half of South Carolina is done with dogs, in large groups and primarily by hunting clubs. South Carolina enjoys its position of having the longest deer season in the nation. The season here normally opens in August and runs well into January. The deep swamps are generally overpopulated with deer in spite of dog hunting and heavy pressure throughout the long season, and limits are very liberal. In contrast, most of the upper half of the state has no open season, though some game management areas in certain locations have good hunting.

DEAN WOHLGEMUTH

The Alabama-bound deer hunter would do well to go as far into the southwest corner as he can. Deer here are too populous for the carrying capacity of the range, and the limit is liberal enough —one deer per day throughout the long season! This limit is statewide, but the length of the season varies. In some sections, the season may be more than one hundred days long, thus you can legally harvest more than one hundred deer a year, if you were to stay for the entire season! This would include both archery and gun season, incidentally. In most sections of Alabama, archery season begins in mid-October, while gun season opens about a month later. Both seasons run well into January over much of the state.

Other areas of Alabama have more deer than the range can adequately support. These are generally in the middle of the state or in the southeastern corner. If you were to start in the very southwest corner of Alabama and head northeast to a point about two-thirds the way northward toward the Georgia border, you'd stay in excellent deer country almost all the way.

The state of Florida is experiencing a great increase in human population and a big influx of hunters. Foresters tell me that the woods have been pretty well hunted by the end of the season. Game commission people concur that pressure is heavy.

The timber-growing region of northern Florida is one of two good regions for Florida deer hunting. Vast acreages of timber produce the habitat, and these areas have good deer populations. There are quite a few state management areas in this region. The Ocala National Forest is open to public hunting, and industry lands are generally open to the public as well.

By the time one is as far south as Orlando, dairy and truck farming and orange growing predominate and deer aren't as prevalent. Continuing south to the Everglades one is back into deer hunting country. Populations are good enough here, too, but terrain dictates a dog hunting situation, and the visiting hunter will need some connections to get invited on the hunts. Considerable dog hunting is done in northern Florida, but still hunting is increasing in popularity throughout this area.

Let's drop back for a moment to Grady Cook. Forty years of Dixie deer hunting passed before he saw his first buck! During most of that period deer populations in the Deep South were lean—darn lean. That's the main reason Grady had such poor luck. Today the Dixie deer has made his comeback and then some. Because of modern forestry practices, law enforcement, an enlightened public and knowledgeable game managers, whitetails are flourishing. As a deer hunter, I'm glad. Grady Cook would be, too!

Clyde Ormond was born at Rigby, Idaho, and has lived in the Upper Snake River Valley most of his life. He is married and has a son and daughter. From 1926 until 1938 he was a teacher and principal in the public schools, and then turned to professional writing, which is still his livelihood. He has written hundreds of outdoor articles and stories for all the outdoor magazines, a newspaper column now in its twenty-eighth year, and eight books on outdoor subjects. Clyde has also co-authored other books, and does his own photography for illustrations.

Gathering pictorial and text material for books and articles has taken him over the best hunting areas from Mexico to the Arctic. He has taken most species of North American big game from Kodiak bear on down, and has hunted mule deer for over forty years in the states of Idaho, Wyoming, Montana, Colorado, New Mexico, and Arizona.

12

HUNTING MULE DEER

Clyde Ormond

THE MULE DEER *(Odocoileus hemonius hemonius)* is one of North America's most populous and popular big game animals. The hunter who takes one in fair chase, during the crisp autumn days when the seasons are normally set, not only obtains a prized species but also, usually has a thrilling experience with mountains, magnificent scenery, fresh air, and allied benefits of the chase.

My own biggest lesson in mule deer hunting came when I was just a youngster. Two of us, entirely innocent of hunting big game, decided to go deer hunting in central Idaho.

At that time, the entire Salmon River country held a fine deer population. In the area where we went, mule deer were especially concentrated. There was difficulty in getting deeply enough into the

region, but this was accomplished by "herding" a Depression-type car to the end of a certain Forest Service dirt road.

We made camp on a sparkling, tiny creek, and immediately the prospects for deer heightened. All about the camp area in the dust left by mild October weather were valentine-shaped tracks indicating that deer had recently been there. These tracks continued on all the game trails leading up the canyon, and the various slash canyons.

The next morning, opening day of the season, we were up and ready before daylight. To us, who were experienced only in small game, the hunting procedure was clear. Those fresh tracks were made by deer, and at the other end of the spoor would be the prized animals.

That entire day, from daybreak to

dusk, was spent *tracking* those millions of hoofprints. We sneaked up the game trails paralleling the creek and moved slowly down the same chattering creek, on the trails and nearby. We repeated the same technique on the incoming creeks, tinkling into the canyon. Like Dan'l Boone, we cautiously studied areas around every pine tree, alder bunch, and rock pile, for any sign of the Big Buck.

We must have covered at least fifteen miles that first day, up and down the creek bottoms. It was hard, in any trail we covered, not to step upon fresh deer tracks, some going up the creek, some coming back down. How we could miss seeing at least one deer during the day was a mystery. But noiselessly as we moved and carefully as we scrutinized everything in the pine forest, we saw nothing.

That night as we sat around the open fire, several other hunters who had been hunting in the same area came over to talk in friendly fashion. As we listened, awed by their apparent wisdom about deer hunting, one word kept running through the conversation. They'd been *up* such and such a ridge. *Up* at the head of such and such a creek they'd jumped a whopping buck. *Up* here, *up* there. *Up* seemed the key word.

The one smart thing my partner and I did was to listen. And the first thing we did at daylight was not to comb the creek bottoms again, but to start climbing a certain half-open ridge to the west of our camp.

We hadn't covered more than a half-mile of the spiney ridge when I spotted something that didn't quite belong, standing under a small pine tree and half covered by shadows. The more I looked at it, the more one shadow became the form of a leg. Certain branches slowly evolved not into a tree, but the antlers of a big buck deer. Then, for the first time I saw clearly what was in the plain open—the big ears, black-patched face, and staring eyes of the biggest "picture-buck" I'd ever imagined.

I raised the old borrowed .25-35 Winchester and let him have it. The great buck jerked his front feet under his chest, sprung violently upward, and bounded off down the side of the mountain.

We found him, a few rods beyond, dead. The Ranger told us going back home that a thirteen-point mule-deer buck was "pretty good for a kid."

Had I been asked at the time what fundamental rules I'd learned of mule deer hunting, I could have answered with the innocence of youth, something fairly accurate: "Go climb a ridge," and "A buck won't necessarily drop dead when shot through the heart."

Mule deer hunting is an art, and is learned, as any other art, by study, intelligent observation, practice, and the capacity to learn not only from one's own experience, but from the experience of others. The very best way of learning how to hunt this species is first to learn something of the animal's basic nature, traits, habitat, and reaction to instincts. From

CLYDE ORMOND

this knowledge and a growing hunting skill will come an understanding of the basic hunting techniques.

The mule deer is generally a mountain-type, broken-country, sparse-forest animal. The lower-country, plains habitat which he once used has now been inhabited by man, causing this species to move to the rougher, more elevated areas. The distribution of mule deer today is essentially contained within the western United States, with overlapping areas into Alberta, Saskatchewan, British Columbia, and Manitoba on the Canadian side, and areas of habitat reaching well into Old Mexico. States having the greatest mule deer populations are Colorado, California, Utah, New Mexico, and Oregon, in that order. Other states having vast mule deer populations are Arizona, Wyoming, Idaho, Montana, Nevada, and Washington. States having relatively few mule deer are South Dakota, Nebraska, Texas, and North Dakota. There are an estimated two million mule deer currently within the forty-eight contiguous states.

The mule deer moves within the areas of rough, broken, mountainous rim-country, and "breaks" areas in this part of the continent. The species is nocturnal in nature, and a browser. Food ranges from various shrubs, aspen, mountain mahogany, and bitter-brush to sagebrush in winter. The animal feeds mostly at the daylight-dusk periods, which is a key to successful hunting techniques.

In summer, as with many other species of big game, the mule deer will stay with the higher elevations within the general range. The muley likes the high mountain ridges and sparse-timbered promontories where he escapes heat and flies during the summer months. During this season his coat is reddish in color. When the snows of winter come, or threaten to come, he moves downward. During mid-winter, the animals range out into the forest-fringe country, and during severe winters will feed and live in broken, sagebrush areas, living on bitter-brush and the more unpalatable sagebrush. During fall and winter, the color of the hair turns to a dark gray.

The mule deer is distinctive in appearance. Its generally gray coloration during fall hunting season blends well with foliage barren of leaves, and the carriage of the animal is one of grace. The bucks have large antlers which are bifurcated and rise high above the head. There is no wild animal that has more pride manifested in its stately appearance than a big mule deer buck. In addition, mule deer have dinky little rope-like tails, and great forward pointing ears, from which the name mule deer derives. Also, the metatarsal, or musk-glands, appearing on both sides of the hind legs on both sexes are considerably larger than on whitetail or blacktail deer.

Big bucks may run to 300 pounds and over. But the hunter who bags a 200 to 225-pound muley buck has a fine big buck. Four tines, or antler points to the side, plus a brow point on each side represents a "standard" buck. Six-pointers and over, if they have good symmetrical heads, are exceptional trophies; and "brush-heads," or non-typical antlers in some bucks may have as many as two dozen small tines.

The biggest antlers coincide generally with areas of good limestone formation—the deer getting the mineral from its food, and thence into the antlers. Some of the best trophy heads, for this reason, come from such areas as the Kaibab Forest, the area overlapping Wyoming-Idaho in the Star Valley-Swan Valley region, and the Jicarilla Indian Reservation in New Mexico.

Does of this species will run about sixty per cent of the weight of adult bucks, and have the same general characteristics as the bucks, except for antlers. The gait of both in flight is a high bounding jump, well adapted to carrying the animals over the broken terrain it inhabits.

During the fall migrations downward, generally coinciding with the hunting seasons, the big bucks of a small herd will descend a day or more after the smaller males and does and fawns. This fact, like the others, can be of great importance to the observing hunter. Another basic generality for the late-season mule deer hunter is that a good place to look for this game is at the snow line, if in mountain country. Again, during late-season hunting and when the rut or mating season is on full blast, the big bucks are less wary and more easily approached by the hunter.

This hunter got his buck as it fed along a ridge, just before going into the pine cover to shade up for the day.

There are several successful methods of hunting mule deer, based generally on the habits and characteristics of the game.

One of the most used and successful techniques is that of stalking. Stalking means, basically, that the hunter sets out from camp or place where he leaves his vehicle and locates the game on foot. One of the first things to do, if not previously done, is to find out if there is game in the area. Check for spoor left by the animals.

If the hunting is done in mountainous country, the hunter best strike off up a handy ridge and climb all the way to the top. Most any ridge in game country will contain the tracks and droppings left by the animals.

The tracks of mule deer vary with the size of the deer, its sex, and whether or not it is alarmed or feeding. In general, the tracks of mule deer will be valentine-shaped. The tracks of big bucks may reach 3½ inches in length, less the dew-claw tracks. Does and smaller bucks leave smaller tracks, and the tracks of huge bucks are apt to be blunt, partly because of the great weight the animal leaves, thus spreading the imprint. Tiny V-shaped imprints, with no great amount of pad showing, indicate the tracks of fawns and small does.

In addition to the tracks, piles and scatterings of dung will appear if deer have used the ridge trails. The kernels of deer droppings are dark in color, are shaped like hazel nuts, may run to one-half inch in diameter, and depending upon the feed, are usually segregated from each other. Their freshness can be ascertained by stepping on the pellets. Fresh kernels will still be comparatively soft.

Such spoor, if it appears on the ridges, will also show in the canyon bottoms along the game trails. But the game will not, as I learned in that long-ago experience, be along the creeks or canyon bottoms during the daylight hours. Mule deer will descend from the ridges, promontories, and "breaks" during the night to drink at the available creeks. At daybreak they will ascend again to feed on the slopes and alps, and during the middle of the day shade up in the thick timber or mahogany copses.

There is a protective instinct in this rhythm of movement. Cool air descends and warm air rises. At dusk the currents of air are gently moving downward. If the game descends at generally the same rate, then it takes its own scent in a general "area" of air downward with it. When it moves upward with the morning thermals, its scent follows with it. In either case, no amount of animal scent is left far behind for enemies to follow.

When spoor is found, the mule deer stalker than proceeds to hunt. The amount of spoor and its freshness will indicate the amount or presence of game. In light snow, spoor is easy to read. If the base of the tracks is unfrozen, and if the dung is not frozen, then the game is not far ahead. In dry dirt, the same tracks may look fresh after several days. And again, after any rain, the dung will soften.

If no sign is found, then the hunter best leave that ridge and hunt either another ridge or higher up.

In stalking mule deer, the hunter should be dressed in color as near the same coloration of the foliage and country as possible. That is, color should be drab, not gaudy. Mule deer can spot gaudy coloration far beyond rifle range and will move off. Where game laws require bright orange color to keep the hunter safe from others, then it must be worn.

Any deer in the area will be found at that optimum hunting period, daybreak till sunup, along the upper ridges of mountainous country. The game will still be in the open, feeding or moving about.

The fringe or "edge" country of any timber should be especially watched for game. Mule deer love edge country; it gives them feed in the open areas, and the protection of timber in case of danger.

The sunny south slopes of ridge-timber country are where the game may be found until well into sunrise. Then the game will gradually move to the north slopes of the ridge where the timber normally grows thicker, to shade and rest for the day. After the heat of day, during a normal fall season, the animals will again move out into the open edge country to feed during the evening. The evening dusk-till-dark period is the second best period to hunt mule deer via stalking, especially if the hunter hunts close to camp. The morning period is best for the stalker, as it gives him all day to find other game, to dress out an animal if he gets one, and to get back to camp.

The stalking technique is gradually learned. It is basically a process of sneaking up to where game is suspected, or has been spotted. Generally the hunter must move very slowly, make no noises such as stepping on or breaking twigs, coughing, or talking. The mule deer's special senses of sight, hearing and smell are far keener than the hunters, and he will detect the hunter's presence far quicker than the novice hunter suspects. Neither should the hunter smoke while stalking, nor hunt downwind. He should keep inside cover when possible.

The reason for moving more slowly than the beginning hunter may feel is necessary, is simple. Slow-moving or immobile animals will spot *fast* movement very quickly. Conversely, if the hunter is still, or very slow-moving, he can spot moving or immobile game easier.

As the hunter moves along the ridges, he should watch both sides for game. A big reason mule deer "use" the ridges so much is for safety. While on a ridge an animal has three avenues of escape—its back track and the two sides of the ridge. A few jumps, depending upon where danger suddenly appears, will put the animal on one of three courses of escape. While feeding, the animal can use both sides of the ridge, only a few rods down, and still have the same built-in safety factor.

While ridge-hunting, the hunter should watch both adjacent ridges across the valleys or canyons on either side of him. Game is as often located on an opposite ridge or hillside as on the one the hunter hunts. In such a case he should circle, so as to get completely out of sight and hearing, then stalk the game from the area where it is.

If in his slow moving he comes upon game within range, he then should assume the most solid shooting position, wait until the game turns to offer a broadside shot or nearly so, then shoot. The most solid field-shooting position for mule deer is the sitting position. It is nearly as solid as prone position (which most of the time can't be assumed), and will usually place the line of sight above intervening brush.

CLYDE ORMOND

A fine mule-deer buck once taken by the author in typical sagebush-aspen, pine edge country.

If game is located and startled, it will run—usually in a long-circling arc of travel alongside the opposite side of the ridge from which it has spotted the hunter, and then come out higher, at the canyon apex. It is useless to try to pursue and overtake startled game. It's better to cross to the opposite ridge, work upward just under its far side, then circle down to where the game is expected to pause, approaching it from the upward side. The mule deer hunter should always try to carefully work his way to the game so that he may get a standing shot, or a shot at slow-moving, unalerted game. One such shot,

taken from a solid position, is far better than a half dozen shots at spooked and running game—even if it's out at two hundred yards or more.

A second, increasingly popular method of hunting mule deer, especially in the West, is from horseback. This is especially true in tough mountainous country where it's physically hard for the foot hunter, and where long distances to the game country must be covered.

This is a pleasant, thrilling way to hunt. The horse does most of the heavy work, and the hunter can look for game and enjoy the scenery. When one hunts on

Horses and a light camp are often taken into back country, where hunters then hunt deer on foot.

horseback, he should make sure the saddle fits, the stirrups are correctly adjusted, that he packs a raincoat on the saddle, and that his rifle rides in a suitable saddle scabbard.

The problems are the same as for stalking, except for the fact that a saddle horse or two, if one hunts with a partner, will make more noise and can be seen easier by the game than the foot hunter. This is more than offset by the fact that one covers far more country on horseback, and can get into places beyond the range of the average foot hunter.

A basic trait of mule deer is that they habitually watch their back tracks, and generally expect enemies from below. The horseback hunter takes advantage of this. At daylight he leaves camp and proceeds to climb to the highest ridges, alpine "saddles," and crests within the country he wishes to hunt. As he rides he utilizes the old game trails up the ridges, realizing that the game has routed the trails through the easiest terrain.

Going upward the hunter watches adjacent country for signs of deer. Often he will spot one or more on some opposite

CLYDE ORMOND

canyon or gulley. In such a case he continues riding until the horse or horses are out of sight, then ties them firmly to an available tree. Then he stalks the deer, utilizing the stalking procedures mentioned before, until he comes within shooting range. In stalking he tries always to keep cover between himself and the game.

If game isn't seen on the way into high country—and good binoculars are a must for this type of hunting since game may be seen a mile or more away—then the hunter slowly works his way downward, along some other ridge known or expected to have deer. He stops often, scouts all surrounding country, and many times will lead his horse while studying both sides of his own ridge as well as opposite ridges.

There is one great advantage in this type of technique. All game watches for enemies from below, looking back on their own tracks made while coming upward. By hunting on horseback and getting *above* the game for most of the day, the hunter has the advantage of coming to game from the *unsuspected* direction. That factor is a key rule for any form of hunting!

During the noon period, most deer within any area will be shaded for the day. The horseback hunter utilizes this fact. He dismounts on some high point or promontory overlooking as much basin and valley country as he can, ties his horse out of sight, then eats his lunch while glassing all lower country. Often he can spot deer as they stand in adjacent timber patches below, or, if during the rut, as the big bucks move about in search of does.

Horseback hunting for mule deer has two further advantages. If the hunter bags a big buck, say in the two-hundred-pound class, he has the aid of the horse to get his deer to camp. Generally, there is no "uphill pull" to drag or pack out the carcass.

Many western horsemen and hunters can pack a buck onto a saddle horse in a professional manner. Balance him across the saddle, lash down both halves with a swing-hitch on each side, pull the antlers back across the cantle, and tie the entire load down with a diamond hitch—that's the proper way.

The amateur horseman can't do this. But if he is familiar with horses, has a gentle animal, and will use care, he can "button-hole" the buck onto the saddle and haul him safely into camp. Briefly, this means to lift the buck onto the riding saddle, belly forward. Then, in the abdominal flesh just below the rib cage and upward from the belly incision (as the buck was dressed), a two-inch slit in the flesh is cut. This slit is slipped over the saddle horn, and this keeps the carcass from slipping sideways.

Next the feet are tied down to the saddle-cinch rings on each side, and the antlers are swung back up on the saddle's cantle, and tied securely, with absolute certainty that no antler tine can in any way gouge the horse. Lastly the lucky hunter then picks up the reins and slowly leads his horse back to camp, going by the easiest, most level trail possible.

Big bucks killed late in the day by the horseback hunter, should be hung by the head to cool until the next day. This allows them to drain well, and the grain of the hair will shed rain or snow.

Partner hunting is another successful technique for hunting mule deer. Partners offer companionship, and can often bag a mule deer when a single hunter could not.

Briefly, when partner hunting, one hunter will hunt on top of the ridge while the other hunts the bottom areas, thus, paralleling each other and eventually coming out at the apex or bottom of the canyon. In this way, two areas are covered instead of one, and at least one of the hunters is apt to see or move game. If the one hunting the ridge jumps game, it is apt to circle downward, giving the lower hunter a chance, and vice versa.

This type of stalking is good for hunting the mid-day period when the deer have gone downward from the ridge tops and are resting or shading themselves for the day, normally in trees, brush, or other cover.

Often, when working a canyon or gulley from the lower end, neither of the hunters may see game until they have moved nearly to the top or canyon apex. This may be because the game has detected them and moved quietly ahead towards the top country. Either or both

Horses are often used to take hunters to the head of a canyon. Then one hunter brings them back while others hunt the ridges back down.

the hunters may get their chance near the apex of the gulley, where the game normally will remain until they identify anything rising from below, and then bolt over the top into another gulley or canyon.

The biggest mule deer buck I've ever taken was bagged in this manner, and my success was due in part to a characteristic of this species—the habit of old fat bucks to lie close in cover until they feel themselves detected and must make a break for it.

Three of us had been working a huge canyon in the above manner, on a late-season hunt where the light snow at the bottom of the canyon gradually increased in depth to knee-level at the top. There were big buck tracks winding about the canyon side, but we'd not been able to see or jump him.

CLYDE ORMOND

When we reached the top where the high saddle dipped away into another great canyon, we stopped to debate whether to return to camp. We talked perhaps three or four minutes while standing there. Then suddenly, from a tiny knot of pines just to the left, a huge buck with a thirty-inch antler spread couldn't stand the pressure any longer. In a flurry of snow he bounded out, heading back down the canyon.

"Take him!" I told my partner, who had never taken a huge buck.

In the sudden excitement, he missed, but as the gray form bounded, two jumps from out-of-sight over the crest, I got lucky with the 7 m m and rolled him. He's in my trophy house today.

A trick for mid-day hunting in large canyons having heavy foliage such as pine and aspen groves will often work for the single hunter. Normally any deer in the canyon will be somewhere down towards the bottom or canyon sides, shaded in the timber or aspens. If the hunter will work the ridge above quietly, then throw a rock far downward into the trees or brush, he can startle a deer into moving and showing itself. If the rock hits and rattles between the hunter and where he suspects deer to be, a deer is apt to break out and move downward across the canyon, climbing upward along the opposite side. If, however, the hunter heaves his large rock far out and *beyond* where a buck is thought to be shaded, the subsequent noise is apt to move the buck upward towards the hunter.

A final method of hunting mule deer is tracking, or trailing. This is most easily done after fresh snow, when tracks are easily read. To the novice hunter, this may seem the best possible way of hunting.

This is generally erroneous. Over the many hunting years I've spent in the field, I cannot think of many occasions when I could track down a mule deer buck, even in snow.

The basic reason this cannot be consistently done is that game fights for survival against enemies, and the principal one is man. In its normal field behavior, game has found by instinct that enemies follow its spoor. The defense then is to watch, and plan its back track so that any pursuing enemies can be detected long before actual danger occurs.

In studying the spoor of big bucks I have attempted to follow or track over the years, I have found that the strategy of any deer, whether it suspects it is being pursued or not, is to plan its back track so that it can look back periodically from points of vantage, and see or detect any pursuers. This is done in an ingenious manner.

For instance, a huge buck will be traveling up a certain canyon. In foliage it moves slowly. Where it must cross any opening, the pace quickens, sometimes breaking into a mild run until it enters the next patch of foliage or timber.

But once into the protection of any cover, the animal will abruptly change course, perhaps heading up a side of the

Three of the author's long-range mule-deer rifles. Top to bottom, custom-stocked Model 70 Winchester .264 Magnum, 7X61 Sharpe & Hart in Schultz & Larsen rifle, and custom 7 m/m Remington Magnum.

Some popular mule-deer cartridges. Left to right, 7 m/m, .284, .270, .308, and the old 30-30 of an earlier era.

canyon until it reaches a position above, and a point where it can look back and *see any pursuer* coming over its tracks *where they cross a previous opening.*

That is the basic strategy. And from the new vantage point, the deer will plot a new segment of its course, repeating that deception by leaving some open spot in its back track over which a pursuer must pass, and which spot the animal can watch from another new vantage point.

For this reason, even in snow, it is far better to parallel a mule deer's tracks than to directly follow them. It is far better to try to anticipate where the buck may *now* be, then circle unseen so as to come upon it from the unsuspected direction.

In addition to the proven methods of hunting mule deer, there is always the chance that the hunter, if he hunts noiselessly and in good game country, will simply blunder into game. Many a huge muley buck has suddenly become venison and trophy, only because he happened to be in the wrong place at the right time.

Because of the big-country, open-spaces nature of the West, neither driving nor still-hunting, which are so successful with whitetails, are fruitful methods of mule deer hunting. Unless in an actual concentration of mule deer, the hunter cannot depend upon still-hunting from a deer stand, or on enough hunters in his generally big area to make a drive successful.

Because of the same factors—big, mountainous, rough, open country—the best weapon for mule deer is the rifle.

192

CLYDE ORMOND

Such a rifle should be flat-shooting, accurate, reasonably light in weight, and scope-equipped. Any action that suits the hunter is fine. Two hundred yards is a good sighting-in range.

Some of the very best calibers for mule deer hunting are the .25-06, .270, .284, 7 m m Mauser, .300 Savage, .308, .30-06, and the 7 m m Remington Magnum. The best all-around scope-power is 4X, though some of the compact variables, such as the 2X-7X variable are fine. Among the very best rifles for mule deer are the Winchester Model 70, Remington Model 700, Ithaca LSA 55, Ruger Model 77, Savage Model 99, and Weatherby rifles, using the above or comparable cartridges. A sling, for the long miles of rifle-carrying while foot hunting, is one of the most important parts of any hunting rifle.

A group of experienced handgunners currently hunt mule deer with the heavy six-gun. Where handgun hunting is legal, only the most high-powered six-guns should be used. There are three calibers currently suitable—the .357 Magnum, .41 Magnum, and the husky .44 Magnum, all shooting suitable bullets. Because of the current rash of propaganda against handguns, which is responsible for the mistaken view that their elimination will stop all crime, handgun hunters are up against stiff opposition.

Lastly, there are a few tips of value to the mule deer hunter:

Get the hunting regulations annually for the region in which you expect to hunt. Get them early, along with the hunting license—some are sold out in a matter of weeks, and some are on a permit-drawing basis only.

If you expect to hunt with a guide or outfitter (and some states and provinces require it of the non-resident hunter), be sure to contact and book him early. The best packers and outfitters book well ahead of the season. Some of them fill up with "repeaters" from the year before, who make reservations at the close of the previous hunt.

If you are lucky and bag a whopping muley buck which you may want for a trophy, don't rush up to him, cut his throat, and whack his head off behind the ears. Your modern rifle bullet will have killed him, so leave the bleeding for when you dress him out.

First take some "bragging" pictures. Then begin at his withers and make a cut up the *back* of his neck to a point between the ears. Next, from the withers, make a cut down each side of the shoulders and bring the two cuts together far down behind the brisket. With only these three cuts, peel out his neck to the point where it joins the head behind the ears. Cut and twist off the head, and take it with the antlers and cape to the taxidermist. Salt the wet skin heavily if there is any delay.

Next dress out the buck. By saving the trophy and dressing out the carcass, you can have trophy and venison both—a way of having your cake and eating it too. That's what all mule deer hunters strive for.

Judd Cooney is an avid sportsman who has been bowhunting since high school, and has taken deer, elk, bear, antelope and wild turkey with bow and arrow plus most of the small game species in his area. He has a degree in wildlife management and lives in Colorado, where his job keeps him out-of-doors constantly. When time allows, Judd studies and photographs wildlife of all types. He is Bowhunting Editor for *Archery World* Magazine and has articles on bowhunting in most of the archery magazines.

13

BOWHUNTING THE MULE DEER

Judd Cooney

MULEY, BLACKTAIL, BUCKSKIN or just plain Mule Deer, call him what you want, but this big, gray member of the deer clan is a trophy that most bowhunters dream of hanging on the den wall.

The Mule Deer (*Odocoileus hemionus*) is found throughout the western part of the United States from the prairies of South Dakota and Nebraska to the brushy slopes of California and Oregon; from Mexico's rugged canyons and cactus arroyos to the high, majestic Rockies of British Columbia and Alberta. The highest population and best bowhunting for mule deer are found in Colorado, Utah, Wyoming and Montana, with New Mexico and Idaho also providing a good number of muleys each year.

The mule deer's most distinguishing characteristic, and the main reason for his name, is a set of ears that won't quit. Those ears may look a little ridiculous standing out like twin radar screens, but when the muley tunes them in, he can hear a mouse tiptoeing through a pile of duck down at fifty yards. The mule deer's antlers, unlike those of his cousin, the whitetail, branch into two main beams which each branch again into two more points, whereas the whitetail's antlers have single points projecting from one main beam.

The antlers of the mule deer are also more majestic and awe-inspiring than those of the whitetail. It is not uncommon for a mule deer buck to sport a rack with a width of thirty-six inches or better, and most of the "average" four point muley bucks will be far larger than a trophy whitetail rack.

Generally the heavier animal of the two, the muley appears much blockier in build than the whitetail. This blocky build may give the impression that a mule deer buck is somewhat slow and awkward on his feet, but any hunter who has watched a big, mossyhorn buck on the run wind his way up a rugged mountain canyon, will surely tell you that this is not the case.

In late summer and early fall, the mule deer is usually reddish brown but gradually changes to gray as the fall progresses. He is further distinguished by the dark U-shaped patch of hair between the antlers, or on the forehead between the eyes, which is more pronounced on the bucks than on the does. The brisket is dark brown or black and the underbelly is a soft white. The mule deer has only a short, sparsely haired tail that is white with a black tip, hence the name "blacktail" in some areas. The muley does not carry his tail like a flag when spooked like the whitetail, but clamps it down between his hindquarters and moves out.

Habitat-wise, the muley buck is as likely to be found bedded down in a rocky arroyo as on a sagebrush flat with no timber for miles around. He might be peacefully snoozing under an alpine willow at twelve thousand feet, or in a dense patch of golden aspèn alongside a bubbling mountain stream. In other words, the mule deer's only hard and fast rule about habitat is that he has to be in the western half of the country. I guess he just naturally takes to the best part!

Small mule deer in winter.

Many a bowhunter, especially those that haven't had much experience, will claim that a mule deer is much easier to hunt than a whitetail buck. For my money there isn't much difference, and what difference there is stems not from intelligence or lack of it, but from a difference in habit patterns.

An old whitetail buck will live and die in a given location, usually a couple of square miles in area. Not so the muley buck. He is migratory in his movements, sometimes moving as much as thirty miles from the high mountain meadows where he spends his summers, to his wintering area in the foothills.

The lack of set patterns within a small area can create a new set of problems for the bowhunter who thinks that he can successfully hunt the mule deer with the same methods he used on the whitetail.

Judd Cooney

Another factor that makes hunters think the muley is easier to hunt is the fact that a lot of mule deer country is fairly open and the deer can often be seen in fair numbers during a day's hunt. Many hunters report having seen numerous deer and state firmly that had they been hunting whitetail, they certainly wouldn't have spotted that many deer in a day's outing. This is true enough, but the mule deer isn't quite as sneaky as the whitetail, and he seems to sense that if he is in the open where you can see him, then he can also see you. The same hunter will also relate how he almost got close enough for a shot, but not quite, and herein lies the truth. That "dumb ole muley" didn't *let* him get close enough. A muley buck is a master at assuming complete nonchalance until the last moment. Then he calmly steps around a tree or bush and disappears.

Mule deer are not much different from other big game animals with their feeding and moving habits. They are most active during the early morning and late evening hours. However, it is quite common to find the deer up and actively feeding during midmorning, especially in the higher elevations.

Awhile ago, when checking over my records of bow kills on mule deer, I was amazed to find that I had not made a single kill earlier than 10:00 A.M. "Ah ha," you say, "that's because he never gets out of that nice warm sleeping bag until midmorning." Well, I will admit that I do relish the warmth and comfort of good down-filled bag on those cold, frosty mornings. However, I have made my share of tracks in the frost-covered grass and leaves just as the sun was gilding the mountains with its golden rays, and I must also admit that I have seen plenty of deer at this time. But for some reason I haven't scored during the early hours as much as I, or anyone, should expect.

There must be a reason and this is my theory. Mule deer start feeding several hours before it gets light. Shortly after it is light enough to see, they begin moving to the area where they are going to bed down for the day. This means that they are traveling in a fairly straight line, and at a semi-rapid pace, even though they may be browsing on the way. Consequently, the bowhunter hasn't much time, if any at all, to make his stalk. Muleys moving from feeding area to bedding ground will move about as fast as a man on foot. They are just looking for desert type browse on their way to their daytime beds.

After the mule deer have bedded down for the day and as late afternoon approaches, they again get the feeding urge and start to move. At this time they are more interested in feeding and finding good browse than they are in finding a place to bed, so they are much more intent on what they are doing. The fact that they are fully engrossed in filling their bellies, and are not moving around much, makes them less wary and easier to stalk or still hunt.

On many of my night patrols, I have watched mule deer busily feeding along the edges of meadows until 9:00 or 10:00 P.M. Then they bed down right on the feeding area and don't get up until a couple of hours before daybreak to resume feeding again.

The mule deer is mainly a browsing animal, and in most of the mule deer range they have a plentiful supply and choice of vegetation. They usually do not have regular feeding areas, as whitetails do, which, at best, makes a touch-and-go proposition of trying to get between them and their feeding area, and waiting them out. In some of the dry mule deer ranges of the southwestern part of the country, these animals use waterholes with enough regularity to make setting up a blind worthwhile.

To be a successful mule deer bowhunter, you will have to have the right kind of equipment to do the job properly. Quite naturally, in order to bowhunt for mule deer you must first have a bow. The muley is a tough animal to keep down, but above and beyond this, he is also a magnificent and worthwhile adversary and deserves the quickest and cleanest kill you can make. You should use a bow of at least forty pounds with arrows that are spined for the bow.

Another factor of bowhunting mule deer is that the range at which they are shot is usually a little longer than for whitetails. The average shot at a muley will be in the neighborhood of thirty to thirty-five yards. I have shot mule deer as close as fifteen feet and as far as eighty yards—and missed a good number at all distances in between. I feel that a good forty-pound bow will do the job for most bowhunters. My bow is a sixty-five pounder, but I also use this bow for elk, which are considerably tougher to grass.

The arrows should be spined for your bow and your bow properly tuned with those arrows, be they wood, glass or aluminum. I much prefer aluminum shafts because of their speed, consistent flight and their accuracy. I figure that what is best for the target shooters is good enough for a trophy mule deer buck. In my own experience, aluminum arrows also hold up much better in the field, and their long life more than offsets their original cost. My own personal arrows are a mixture of homemade three-fletched Easton 2020's with five-inch feathers, Red Wing 2020's and Bear Magnum No. 316's. All my arrows are equipped with screw-in adapters to take the threaded points. This, in my estimation, is one of the greatest innovations in arrows since arrow makers started using feather fletching. The points can be presharpened at home and taped up (more on this later). When you take to the field after mule deer, you can untape several of the broadheads, screw them into the shaft and you are ready for business. If you slam a broadhead into a rock or tree instead of behind a buck's front shoulder, you can unscrew the damaged head and replace it with one that is razor sharp and be ready to go.

While we're talking about arrows for mule deer, let's take a minute to discuss color fletching. I used to be of the school

Author hunting from above on muleys.

Author glassing a lower ridge.

Looking over some high country mule deer range in hopes of spotting that big one.

that thought you needed everything camouflaged to be successful, but I have changed my mind somewhat. I used arrows painted flat black with black or natural barred feathers for some time and found that this was not the answer. When I shot at a deer, regardless of the range, I had no idea where the arrow went from the time it left the bow, because it was almost invisible in flight. I did kill several deer with this combination, but even when in a deer, you couldn't pick out the arrow easily. I now use arrows with fluorescent yellow or orange feathers for all hunting and have little trouble following the arrow in flight and several times have actually had the feeling of "looking the arrow into the target." I have found that the color doesn't seem to make the slightest difference to the deer or elk.

Besides your bow and arrows, the next most important piece of equipment for bowhunting mule deer is a good pair of

7x35 or 8x30 binoculars. Ninety per cent of successful mule deer bowhunting is spotting the animal *before* it spots you. Any bowhunter can see the obvious need for binoculars in the open sagebrush country and the rugged open canyons and alpine mountain meadows, but for me, the most valuable time for good glasses is in the heavy, thick timber. Many times I have stood my ground and glassed an object fifty yards away, an object that just didn't seem to fit in the surroundings; pretty soon I would make out the outline of an antler tine or maybe an ear or even the edge of a rump patch. That feat would have been impossible without good binoculars. Get a good pair and *use* them. You'll be surprised at how much more game you will see a shade before it sees you. Remember, spotting a mule deer first is 90 per cent of the battle.

Camouflage clothing is old hat to most bowhunters and to deer hunters in general, and I think that it is of real value in hunting mule deer. Camo helps you become a part of the scenery and makes stalking and getting close a much easier accomplishment.

One point to remember when getting your camouflage gear together is to match it with the type of cover in which you will be hunting. A bright green camo outfit is not going to blend with the dead leaves and brush of a late fall deer hunt, nor will a predominantly brown outfit mix with the lush alpine foliage of a mountain slope in early August. Deer cannot distinguish colors, but they damn well can

200

recognize color intensity, so try to match your camouflage with the terrain. A good test for camo matchup is to run a regular camera light meter first, next to your clothing, then, next to the foliage in which you are hunting. If the meter needle jumps very much as you pass over your gear, or as you pass the meter next to surrounding brush, you can bet that a deer is going to have a relatively easy time spotting you.

Another point on camo gear is to buy the softest and quietest type you can, then wash it a couple of times in fabric softener to make it even more noiseless in the brush. A mule deer has good eyesight, but those big antennae-like ears don't miss anything, especially something like a stick or twig scraping along the back of a shiny new, nylon ripstop camo jacket.

Footgear is another mighty important piece of hunting equipment that can have a real bearing on the success or failure of your mule deer bowhunt. For the most part, you are going to be hunting in rough, rugged terrain that is usually quite rocky, so get some good boots that will take a beating—preferably a pair that has a good lug sole for gripping the rocky ground and keeping your feet on terra firma—not sticking up in the air as you careen down a steep slope.

If I am hunting rough country, I like to wear a good pair of lug-soled hiking boots and also carry a pair of sneakers or moccasins for super-sneaking if the occasion warrants it. The sneakers are also mighty handy to have around camp to slip on in the evening when you come in tired and footsore after a day's hunt. Make darn sure you break your footwear in long before the hunt so that you don't start sporting a set of blisters the second day of your week-long hunt.

Now we come to the most important part of mule deer hunting, and for that matter, any type of bowhunting—the broadhead. I have used most of the broadheads on the market today and all of them are good *if* they are *razor-sharp*. By razor-sharp, I don't mean file-sharpened or sharpened with Mom's kitchen knife sharpener; I mean a head that will smoothly and cleanly shave the hair off your arm with one stroke. I know that many deer have been killed with all sorts of dull broadheads, but that doesn't excuse *you* from taking to the field with one in that condition. I know of several deer that have been killed with blunts, too, but I damn sure am not advocating that you go hunt mule deer with blunts on your arrows.

A razor-sharp broadhead is an extremely lethal thing that will provide you with a clean, almost painless kill. Isn't this what a trophy like the mule deer deserves?

The edge on a broadhead should be *in* the steel and not *on* it, as it is on the edge of a file-sharpened head. A file-sharpened broadhead is far better than one that is not sharpened at all, but still not in the same category as a stoned and honed head. If a serrated, feather-edged broadhead is supposed to do a better job of cutting and slicing, then why don't doctors use scalpels with serrated edges for operations? I'll bet if they did, their business would fall off in a hurry.

To get a sharp edge on the broadhead, take a file, and with a few strokes, remove all the tool marks from the head, trying to keep the broadhead blade angle the same. Take a medium grit Arkansas stone, either oiled with good honing oil or dry, and try to take a thin slice off the stone with the broadhead, first pulling it toward you, then reversing and pushing it away. When the edge feels sharp, with no flat spots, switch to a fine Arkansas stone and repeat the process for several strokes. Finally, take a piece of smooth leather, an old belt or better yet, an old razor strop, and strop the head a few times on each side of the blade. A short length of arrow shaft, tapered to fit the head, will make these steps easier. When you are done, you should be able to shave the hair off your arm or leg with one easy stroke. If not, do it over until you can. Once you get the knack of the proper technique, it should only take you a minute or two to renew an abused head to one you will be proud to show your bowhunting buddies.

Now you have all your gear and are ready to take to the woods. How do you hunt the muley so that you can get close enough to make that good clean kill?

Mule deer can be bowhunted by all the methods used in hunting whitetails, but for my money, the most challenging and personally successful has been still hunting and stalking. I don't much care for the term "still hunting," because I think that

Photo showing difference between razor-honed broadhead and file-sharpened broadhead. Note the feather edge on file-sharpened head. Right side of photo. Both heads unretouched.

even though you haven't yet seen your game, you can still be stalking it in every sense of the word.

In the early mornings I try to pick out a spot with a good vantage point where I can thoroughly glass the area. In glassing for mule deer, don't try to spot the whole deer. Train yourself to look for anything that doesn't fit the surroundings; watch for movement, a tail flickering, an ear, or maybe the tip of an antler over a bush. Anyone can spot a whole deer on a hillside covered with green grass, so get used to looking for a small portion of the critter. Glass each area thoroughly, then come back a few minutes later and do it again. As you glass the area, try to memorize each suspect object so that when you come back and look it over again, if it has changed at all, you will notice. Don't waste time on the obvious things.

Concentrate on those that don't fit. Pretty soon you will find that you are unconsciously doing this and you will start seeing a lot more game.

Mule deer will normally bed down under a bush or rock and watch downhill, because that is the way most danger approaches, namely man. When you are hunting in mountainous or rugged country, always try to do your looking from above the animals. It is much easier to work from above a mule deer than from below. Usually a spooked mule deer will run up hill, so even though you spook him, you may still have a chance to get a shot.

Once you have spotted a deer, the stalk begins. Take your time and move slowly, keeping the wind in your favor. If you happen to spot a muley that is in the open with no cover for a stalk, don't give up. I would rather sneak in on a deer that I can see plainly at all times than any other. Since a mule deer cannot see when he has his head down grazing or browsing, this is the time to move. Watch his ears for a telltale flicker that will indicate he is going to raise his head. When he does look up, make sure you don't move a muscle or even blink. Another thing of which I am convinced is the importance of eye contact. Don't look directly at an animal you are stalking in the open; something about the direct look seems to trigger a sixth sense, so watch him out of the corner of your eye. As soon as he puts his head down, move fast and quiet. This way you can get within mere feet of a feeding deer.

I once stalked a doe that was browsing and got within ten feet of her. Even though she was nervous as all hell, she didn't break and run until I jumped up in the air and let out a yell. She ran practically without hitting the ground for fifty yards, then stopped and walked back within twenty yards of me to check things out. To this day, I don't think she ever knew what happened for sure.

If two bowhunters are working together, one can stalk the animal while the other picks a spot in hopes that a spooked deer will pass close by. A mule deer normally will go up hill when frightened, so if the terrain is suitable, one hunter can try working his way above the deer, while his partner stalks them from below. Two hunters who are familiar with the country can work together very effectively in moving deer toward each other.

I remember one hunt where an outfitter, who is also an ardent bowhunter, and

Some of the good broadheads author has used. Left to right. Black Cooperhead Slicer, Bear Razorhead, Ben Pearson Deadhead, and Super Hilbre.

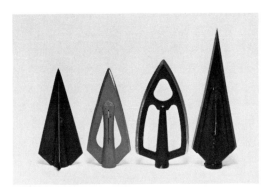

I were working an old burned-over area. Dan was working the far side of a half-mile wide strip, staying up the hillside and doing a lot of glassing, while I worked the other sidehill. We both spotted two nice bucks about the same time and Dan began the stalk, since he was closer than I. He spooked the bucks and it was as if they were on a string that I was pulling, because they both worked their way toward me. The reason, though, was that I was on a good trail, one that they used often to get from that particular pocket. One of the bucks was a nice four-pointer with about a twenty-six-inch spread, and the other was a "dream" buck. His rack would go thirty-two inches or better and was a perfectly balanced four point, the kind that really score. The smaller buck worked his way up and stopped about twenty yards below me, a perfect broadside shot, as he stood looking back down the trail. Unfortunately, I didn't want him, at least not with his big brother so close. As luck would have it, the big buck came almost abreast of the smaller buck and stopped right behind the only damn spruce tree on the hill, completely eliminating any chance for a shot. The smaller buck, meanwhile, ambled up within ten feet of me. All this time I was trying not to shake the feathers off my arrows but not having much luck. With the small buck that close, the status quo didn't last very long. He evidently winded me and took off in high gear. The big buck came around that tree on the dead run right at

me, and to this day I don't know where I shot—probably straight up, because I sure didn't get the deer. Luck, knowledge of the trail's whereabouts, and a hunting buddy who knew what to do gave me the chance for a shot I would never have had otherwise.

Mule deer can also be successfully hunted from stands or tree blinds, but here a thorough knowledge of the deer's movements and the terrain are vital. As I stated earlier, a mule deer doesn't have the cut-and-dried patterns of the whitetail, so the job is much tougher.

Well-used waterholes, salt licks and good game trails are the best bet for a stand. Tree blinds seem to work the best on mule deer, but don't be surprised to find a buck standing back forty yards and casually eyeballing you as you sit perched in a tree. A whitetail will very seldom look up into a tree stand. Not so the muley! They are used to looking in the trees and on ledges for two of their natural enemies, the mountain lion and the bobcat. They think nothing of looking up into a tree if they see any suspicious movement.

Many guides and outfitters in Colorado used salt licks with blinds over them to put their hunters into bow range, but this practice of baiting with salt was outlawed recently. In some of the higher country, deer develop a habit of moving through a certain pass or along a certain trail when spooked from below. Hunters who are familiar with the area and the trails can station themselves along these crossings, and have their hunting partners move through the timber and slopes below, in hopes of moving deer up to them.

In this type of hunting, I have found it is important to always make sure that you drive from below and move the animals up to the hunter and not the other way around. Mule deer, especially bucks, are hard to move down slope even though the hill may be only a couple hundred feet high. They want to get *above* all trouble, then see what is happening. This is one of their habits that is consistent no matter where they are hunted, and one that can pay off if you take advantage of it.

During the late fall and winter seasons that some states have for bowhunting (such as South Dakota and the Sandia Mountains in New Mexico), driving, when used properly, is an extremely effective method of taking deer. The bucks at this time are usually in the rut and with snow on the ground, finding well-used deer trails is much simpler. A group of hunters can push deer back and forth to each other and greatly increase their chances of success.

Several winters ago Colorado had a late season hunt, starting late in November and going through the middle of December. The deer were bunched up on their wintering areas and extremely hard to stalk because of the low sagebrush cover and snow. Several members of the AMO, or Archery Manufacturer's Organization, came to Kremmling where the hunt was held, in hopes of getting a

Author with mule deer, exceptionally heavy antlers 7 inches around base, but was only three on one side and four on the other. May make Pope and Young with velvet removed—twenty-seven-inch spread.

Author with Pope and Young buck shot in winter season.

trophy muley for the book. Mule deer were everywhere and it wasn't at all uncommon to see five hundred in a day and not get a shot. We finally figured out how to make use of the lay of the land and a muley's tendency to head uphill, and started to put on drives. Several of these took in an entire draw several miles long, with hunters standing on the upper ends on deer trails leading out. By the end of the week, everybody had shots at record book bucks at less than thirty yards, and Jim Dougherty and I had two nice bucks that both made the Pope and Young Record Book. That wasn't too bad for hunting in knee-deep snow and 20 below zero weather. Knowledge of the country and of the deer's habits were the main factors

Jim Dougherty of Ben Pearson Archery Co. with buck shot during winter season. Hunting method—driving.

that swung the scales our way on this hunt.

Probably one of the hardest things for a neophyte mule deer hunter is to judge a "trophy" buck over an "average" buck. All of us dream of getting a buck for the record book, but each year there are hunters who return home with a buck that seemed like a tree on legs on the mountain but didn't measure up when the time came.

As I said earlier, the rack of an "average" mule deer buck with a twenty-four-inch spread will be much larger than a trophy whitetail's rack. In fact, most average muley racks are far bigger than a good whitetail, mainly because of the antler conformation and width. The things to look for in a real trophy head are width and height, but most important for a good measuring head is the length of the antler tines and evenness of the antlers overall. A deer with an average spread of twenty-four to twenty-six inches with long tines and even lengths will outscore a deer with a thirty-two-inch spread and short uneven points. Add to this the velvet on many bucks taken during the August and September archery seasons in the West, and you have a real problem in self-control. A buck in velvet looks twice as big as one not in velvet, but to be measured for the Pope and Young record book bucks must have all the velvet off—so don't overestimate.

You must judge for yourself what a trophy deer is. If you decide a doe or a

JUDD COONEY

Record book mule deer: Note long points and symmetrical antlers.

small three-point buck is the trophy that you want, then don't let anyone tell you different. There have been times when my wife would have gladly traded a big buck rack for a tender, juicy steak from a nice dry doe.

Whether you are stalking that muley buck with the magnificent antlers in the Blackhills of South Dakota, sitting on a waterhole in the Arizona canyon country, or maybe glassing a high alpine meadow in the Colorado Rockies, bowhunting the mule deer is a challenge and well worth the effort. When you combine the aura of the hunt with the spectacular country these deer call home, then add a batch of good old-fashioned western hospitality, you can't fail to have a hunt that will be long remembered.

Jim Tallon has been fishing ever since he was old enough to sneak down to the south bank of the Ohio River with a make-shift rod; hunting ever since he managed to rake up two dollars to buy a rolling block Remington .22. That was back in the Depression.

Born in Newport, Kentucky, he cut his hunting teeth in the Kentucky hills, usually in pursuit of small game such as cottontails and bobwhites. In the late 1940's he made a trip west, and got hooked on the greater hunting and fishing possibilities. After several vacation trips, he moved to Arizona permanently in the 1950's. He lived at Grand Canyon for eight years where the mule deer was his everyday neighbor.

Jim worked on a ranch near Flagstaff where nearly every morning, when he opened the bunkhouse door, he spooked muleys away from the watering trough. Most of his mule deer hunting has been concentrated in northern Arizona.

He started freelance writing while at Grand Canyon and sold his first story in 1954. In 1964 he went to work for the Arizona Game & Fish Department as writer-editor of the department's publications. He also received law enforcement training, and annually acted as a "game warden" during deer seasons. He considers his stint with AG&F invaluable, but after three years, he made the break to full time freelancing, and that's where he's been ever since.

14

THE MULE DEER IN THE SOUTHWEST

James Tallon

THE RANGE OF the mule deer extends from southern Yukon Territory to Saskatchewan, touching on southeastern Manitoba and the extreme northeastern tip of Minnesota, then, in the West, spreads southward into Mexico. But nowhere within this great expanse is the mule deer more sought after or considered more important than in the Southwest. Here, the saga of the mule deer is a slice of outdoor Americana. Interwoven with overhunting and underhunting, over grazing and politics, grand illusions of stockpiling mule deer, disregard for game regulations, general wildlife ignorance and mismanagement, and finally, modern management, it is likely to be remembered in wildlife circles as long as Texas remembers the Alamo and Massachusetts remembers the Boston Tea Party.

The Southwest, arbitrarily defined, is the states of Arizona and New Mexico, a 235,085 square mile rectangle that runs the gamut from barren desert to lush pine and fir mountain highlands, and embraces six of the seven climatic conditions of the world. Only tropical is missing. In Arizona, elevations range from just above sea level to 12,670 feet atop the San Francisco Peaks near Flagstaff; in New Mexico, from 3000 feet above sea level to 13,161-foot high Wheeler Peak in the Sangre de Cristo Range. With a few small exceptions, mule deer abide everywhere in this two-state complex, even in sun-baked, treeless hills and vegetated flats—not with pine forest, but with the thorny plants of the desert.

The Lewis and Clark expedition of the early 1880's "discovered" the mule deer along the Missouri River and dabbed it

Rocky Mountain mule deer with antlers in velvet.

with the moniker because of its mule-like ears. No doubt Lewis and Clark crossed trails with *Odocoileus hemionus,* the Rocky Mountain mule deer, and the largest of the family we commonly call deer. There are other mule-deer members of the genus *Odocoileus,* however, subspecies that should be mentioned. In California there lives *O. inyoensis* and *O. californicus.* On Mexico's Baja Peninsula roam *O. fuliginatus* and *O. peninsulae.* And on the Mexican mainland, *O. sheldoni* and *O. crooki. Crooki* is widely distributed not only in northern Mexico but also in Arizona and New Mexico. Perhaps not one hunter in a thousand knows this deer by his scientific name. In the Southwest he has been referred to as the "gray mule deer," but most hunters recognize him simply as the "desert mule deer."

Until fairly recent times, some Arizon-

ans believed that their state harbored at least four full species of deer, two species of mule deer and two species of whitetail. In 1897, Edgar Mearns, the noted doctor-naturalist, examined an unusual deer taken on Emory Peak in the Dog Mountains of New Mexico. He identified it as *Dorcelaphus crooki,* a new species. In the early 1900's, another example, this one from the Bill Williams Mountains just south of Williams, Arizona, was also identified as *Dorcelaphus crooki* by Mearns. About a decade ago, Donald F. Hoffmeister of the Museum of Natural History, University of Illinois, was hired by the Arizona Game and Fish Department to solve the mystery of deer species in Arizona. Hoffmeister's revelations give rise to the theory that what Mearns thought to be a separate species of deer was actually a hybrid, part mule deer and part whitetail. In further studies Hoffmeister showed that only two distinct, separate species exist in the state, the mule deer and the whitetail. However, the desert mule deer is recognized as a subspecies and is now tagged with part of Mearns' identification, *crooki.* Essentially it is the same as the Rocky Mountain muley, but it has slight differences. The Rocky Mountain muley has been known to top 500 pounds hog-dressed, while the desert mule deer rarely weighs over 160 pounds field-dressed. The desert mule deer is also lighter in color, generally sort of a grayish-yellow. The rump patch is smaller, the brow patch is a lighter brown, and the tail tends to be more brownish than white. An occasional animal will have a tail with a dark line down the middle.

My first contact with the desert mule deer came more than twenty years ago, on the Apache Trail about sixty miles northeast of Phoenix. Fresh from Kentucky, I lived under the illusion that you would always find mule deer near conifers or in a recently logged-over area. But here stood a small band of does and fawns in a desert landscape, fully at home and nonchalantly flicking their ears at me. The first Rocky Mountain mule deer I encountered were kicking up volcanic cinders in the weird lava-land of the San Francisco volcanic field northeast of Flagstaff, Arizona, but at least a pine forest was nearby. Just a kid of seventeen then, I worked on the Swanson Ranch near Sunset Crater, and the foreman, Harry Bell, and I scoured for suitable deadfalls to cut into firewood for the coming winter. The deer were trophy bucks, muscular and big-racked. This was the start of a keen interest in the muley that continues today.

The original range of the mule deer stretched across two and one-half million square miles of mountain, foothills and adjacent plains. When the white man thrust westward, mule deer numbers were calculated to be around the 10 million mark. Meat and hide hunters, a total absence of game rules or regulations, ignored regulations at a later date, and other factors reduced the great American mule deer herd to 175,000. In 1897 the New Mexico territorial legislators set up the "buck act" which permitted hunters to take bucks only during a three month deer season. Two years later the state decreed a bag limit of one buck deer per hunter annually, but records show that few hunters paid any attention to the new ruling and poaching was rampant. Deer and other game continued to decline, and the legislators got tougher. They closed New Mexico to all deer hunting (and antelope, elk and bighorn sheep) for a period of five years, re-opening seasons in 1903. But this measure failed to give salvation to the decreasing number of deer. By 1924 only an estimated 19,488 deer remained in the state. New Mexico had reached its all-time low deer population.

Meanwhile, across the border in Arizona, game managers were having an entirely different problem with deer herds. In an area that today combines the Grand Canyon National Park's north rim and the Kaibab National Forest, the deer population was exploding in contrast to New Mexico's overhunting. During the 1870's some five hundred Kaibabit Indians had called this area home and annually harvested about eight hundred deer. These Indians ate venison all year long, but some balance between herds, range and Indians was apparently in effect. In 1906 the "Kaibab North," as we call it today, carried between three thousand and four thousand deer. On June 29 of that same year, an act of Congress gave President Theodore Roosevelt the authority to set aside this region for the total

Cactus country is home to the desert mule deer.

protection of game animals, and on November 28, Roosevelt created the "Grand Canyon National Game Preserve." This move set the stage for an unprecedented wildlife disaster.

From the estimated 3000-4000 deer, total protection boomed the herd into an incredible 100,000 deer in 1924. The muleys devoured everything available that they normally eat, then went to work on plants entirely foreign to their diet. Even today scars remain from that range abuse. By 1931 starvation had decimated three-quarters of the 1924 herd. In other words, about 75,000 deer died lingering deaths. One observer, prior to the die-off, reported seeing 1028 deer in a one hour and ten minute drive from VT Park to Grand Canyon, about twenty-six miles. Others claimed to see as many as 100 deer a day while afield. Furthermore, at a time of year (summer) when deer should have been in perfect shape, they were boney and bedraggled. After the great winter die-off, one man counted 87 head of dead deer in one quarter of a mile.

At the peak of the population high of 1924, some well-minded sportsmen came

212

up with the idea of driving deer from the Game Preserve down through Grand Canyon and up the South Rim. Included in the plan was the intent to take these deer on to Arizona locales that had poor deer populations. But the basic reason for the move was to relieve the deer-congested Grand Canyon Game Preserve. The sportsmen hired one George McCormick who was to deliver no less than three thousand and no more than eight thousand head of deer to the South Rim. For this he would be paid $2.50 per deer.

With federal permission the drive began—and ended—on December 16, 1924. One hundred twenty-five men on horseback and on foot banged on anything that would make noise. Pots, pans, bells, tincans, you name it. Barely underway, a wintery storm swept across the Kaibab and with each step the drive became more muddled. Some men got lost in the inclement weather; others figured they had had enough and dropped out. At Saddle Canyon, just a short distance from the drive's point of origin, not a single deer had been seen. Though undernourished and sickly, the deer managed to elude their harassers and had slipped back into the pine and firs of the Grand Canyon Game Preserve where death would claim most of them. As for Mr. McCormick, he didn't make a dime, and the "greatest deer drive of the century" was abandoned in frustration.

Until 1924 the rule of the Grand Canyon Game Preserve had been *no hunting*.

Now, with deer covering the landscape in frightening numbers, a public hunt was authorized for the preserve. But that first hunt barely grazed the surface of deer control. Rumors came out of that hunt that some hunters had killed as many as six or seven deer trying to find one with enough meat on it to take home. By 1926 deer were being found dead on the summer range as well as on the winter range. Then, in a move that bordered on outdoor insanity, the government eliminated 403 coyotes, 111 bobcats, and 11 mountain lions in a predator control program on the Game Preserve. With deer keeling over by the hundreds from starvation, they cut back the predators, the one natural element trying to check deer herd growth.

In December, 1928, a more aggressive move was made toward control when government hunters were ordered to reduce the deer population of the Game Preserve. The 1124 animals they killed caused a furor with the hunting public. Why not open a liberal season on the Game Preserve for deer hunters? Finally, public pressure and a flicker of good sense did open up the preserve, and subsequent hunts reduced the herds to a point where the range improved noticeably by 1938. Despite new management regulations, deer populations exploded again. Between 1945 and 1949 deer increased from 12,000 to 57,000 head. In 1954, twelve thousand permits were authorized to reduce the Kaibab North herd, but it was too late. Deer numbers had gone up, and range quality had gone down. Dr. Wendell G. Swank of the Arizona Game and Fish Department estimated that 18,000 deer died of starvation during the winter of 1954-55.

As a result of the Kaibab North tragedy, or Grand Canyon Game Preserve as it used to be called, a number of deer management basics were learned. Deer have a tremendous reproductive and survival potential; and depending upon the area, can almost double their numbers every two years. However, taking of bucks alone is not a sufficient controlling factor, and on productive deer range like the Kaibab North, does must be taken as well. As deer herds increase, lowering the carrying capacity of a specific region, the animals must be reduced—preferably by the hunting public—to fit that specific region. We know now that high deer populations spring from misuse of the land and the plants that grow on it. Heavy harvesting of deer eliminates the possibility of permanently damaging the range. Deer herds can be built up in a relatively short time, but it may take a lifetime to repair damage to the range.

When I moved to the South Rim of Grand Canyon in the early 1950's, I found high deer populations there as well. Inside the National Park I regularly counted up to fifty bucks (during the time they carried antlers) on the twenty-six-mile stretch of rim road between Grand Canyon Village and the Watchtower. I accumulated eight years of guiding tourists in the park and when I called it quits for good in 1968, I saw few deer along the rim drive. Where did they go?

I've asked a number of conservation agencies that question and have yet to get a satisfactory answer. A National Park biologist blames the reduction of deer numbers inside the park to hunting outside it. Of course I cannot speak as a trained wildlife biologist, but after three years as writer-editor for the Arizona Game & Fish Department and hobnobbing with their top research men, I find this hard to believe. My personal observations revealed that during hunting seasons, greater numbers of deer were present inside the park, evidently seeking sanctuary from hunters. Was there a deer die-off in Grand Canyon National Park, South Rim? I have found the National Park Service expert at keeping such things quiet; even hard news items sometimes worth the front page were reduced to a few column inches and tucked away deep in newspapers.

I have personally known national Park employees that would like the general public to think that their total protective policy on wildlife is keeping harmony with nature. Plenty of park mule deer have died on the bumpers and grills of vehicles, and over the years probably hundreds have died from junk such as cigarettes, cigars, bread, cookies, candy, paper and other foreign matter fed to them by the tourists. When cars pile up in "deer-jams" eager motorists rush non-digestibles to the wild and semi-wild deer. Fortunately, the wild deer head for the

JAMES TALLON

deep forest, while the semi-wild (or perhaps semi-tame) become reduced to beggars that spend more time foraging around the park's hotel and restaurant garbage cans than they do eating natural browse in the woods.

One evening while crossing the Santa Fe track below the El Tovar Hotel, I encountered such a beggar that was emaciated but sported a big rack. I carried a bag of groceries that contained some fresh vegetables, and evidently the buck had gotten wind of them. When he came within a few feet of me, I yelled and tried to flag him off. But he walked in close and hooked at me like an unruly bull. With a hand against his forehead, I tried to push him away. If I had been thinking straight, I would have tossed him a stalk of celery and got the heck out of there. Now he snorted and hooked at me more strongly. I backed up. He came at me again, and this time I popped him right in the snoot with a short, hard jab. He bleated like a goat and trotted off. I was lucky. He could have gotten rough.

During the years I lived at Grand Canyon the fall and winter human population was around three hundred. I found most of the male residents to be "gung-ho" hunters, and some of them didn't bother to go outside the national park to do their hunting. I've always been keen on playing by the rules, and my deer hunting was south of the Canyon, from the Coconino Rim westward to about Redland, a cattle camp on the Cataract Plains.

Fork horn mule deer and the animal he was named after. Mules are Grand Canyon saddle mules, and mule deer is helping himself to a bit of mule chow.

I don't remember if it was 1956 or 1957, but one day I stalked through the pinyons and junipers in the vicinity of Buck Tank, about eight miles east of Redland without seeing a single deer. In late afternoon I drove back along the rutted road toward Grand Canyon Village and spotted three handsome trophy bucks posed on a low ridge and in easy rifle range. I slid out the driver's door and stayed low behind the pickup's bed while I poked shells into the rotary magazine of my Model 99 Savage. When I tried to chamber a .300 cartridge, it jammed part way into the chamber. I turned the gun over and literally hammered the shell into firing position by pounding on the lever. When I peeped over the bed of the truck, I was surprised to find the bucks still gawking in my direction. I drew a bead on a two hundred-pound, six-point and fired. He never moved. I had missed him clean. How could I, I asked myself, when I had zeroed the gun in before deer season. At that time I could drive tacks with it. For the next shot, I duplicated this whole procedure and missed again. Neither did the third shell go into the chamber without hammering.

Meanwhile the bucks may have been thinking the third time could be a charm, and had walked out of sight behind the ridge. When I topped the ridge in pursuit, I touched off the balky .300 at the rump patch of the nearest buck. By now I was in a state of semi-buck fever. When the .300 roared, the whole sagebrush flat at the edge of the junipers and pinyon forest came alive with deer. Shades of the African veldt! I have never seen such great numbers of deer in one herd before or since. There were at least two hundred of them, and I'm being conservative on that estimate. I sat open-mouthed on a chunk of Kaibab limestone and watched as they ran out of sight, and the deer I had shot at, unscathed, along with them.

The incident was important to me because I suspect that I will never again see a herd bunched up like that one. At the same time I learned a lesson about cartridges. The shells I had carried in the 99 during my day's stalk were factory loads. When I ejected them to get into the pick-up truck for my trip home, I stuck them in my left jacket pocket. In my right pocket I carried a batch of handloads given to me by a friend, and these were to serve as emergency ammo. In my haste to load my

rifle when I saw the deer on the ridge, I grabbed shells from my right pocket. My friend had forgotten to *re-size* the cases! Furthermore, there must have been a difference in velocity between the handloads and the factory loads I had used for sighting in, and that could have affected the bullet's point of impact considerably.

The Southwest has always been a popular place for deer hunting. In 1957, some split twig figures that look like deer, bighorn sheep, and pronghorn antelope were discovered in caves in Grand Canyon's south rim. Dated by the radio-carbon method, they have proven to be three thousand years old! Some archeologists believe these fetishes were stashed in the caves to guarantee good hunting. A later group of prehistoric Indians known as the "modified basketmakers" took deer in the Grand Canyon country between 475 and 700 A.D. Nature is really a good balancer of wildlife. Left to her own devices, she maintains fairly balanced wildlife populations. The Indians of the recent past seemed to be a part of nature's plan. In plain language, they didn't screw up the deer herds one way or the other. The white man, in his ignorance, can definitely be a deterrent to controlled wildlife numbers. However, the white man has come a long way in his knowledge of such things.

As mentioned earlier, overhunting, along with other factors, had reduced New Mexico's deer population, including whitetails, to 19,488 animals. It seems remarkable that this low came in 1924, the

Prior to the rut, bucks will band together. Note velvet peeling from the rack of deer in the middle.

New Mexico's deer herds at about 300,000 animals.

The density of deer in the Southwest varies with food, water, and cover. We have no figures for Arizona, but New Mexico averages from one deer per square mile to as many as thirty! New Mexico has proven the theory that if you have sufficient food and space, you can build deer herds quickly.

In Arizona, after a population high during the mid-1960's, the state's deer herds dropped to a low point about four years ago. But on the bright side, deer numbers have been slowly increasing since then. Some areas of the state have proven to be thorns in the Arizona Game & Fish Department's side. For example, the fawn crop in certain of these areas stays generally low no matter what applications the AG&F makes. Subsequently, they remain classed as "deer poor." But speaking on a statewide basis, Arizona has approximately 175,000 deer, including whitetail.

In 1971 Arizona went on a state-wide permit system for all deer management units. An AG&F spokesman explained to me that this was an effort to get Arizona back into the "quality deer hunting" business. In prior years, for example, one hunt unit drew about 6500 deer hunters annually. That represents about 6.5 per cent of the state's deer hunters. Yet that particular unit is considered a sorry place to hunt deer, with a low population of animals available. It has been said that any deer downed in that unit is tagged by

same year the Grand Canyon Game Preserve had hit the super-high of 100,000 mule deer. Where Arizona had to cut the herds back, New Mexico had to build theirs. New Mexico had the easiest job because with such low game populations, the range was not overbrowsed. By 1926, just two years after the deer low, even the early day management techniques had a remarkable effect; New Mexico's deer herds increased to 41,000 animals. And in 1973, as this is being written, modern deer management has reasonably stabilized the guy who can run the fastest. You see more hunters than deer. By limiting the number of hunters to a specific unit, you thin out the pressure to fit the number of deer in that unit, and theoretically, hunters have a better overall outdoor experience.

The adoption of this new ruling didn't meet with 100 per cent approval, as some hunters like to hunt in several units during the deer season. Say you are driving to the unit for which you have drawn a permit, and suddenly a handsome trophy buck steps out of the forest in front of your vehicle. You just know you're not going to see such a prime specimen on your specified unit. Before the new permit ruling, you could step out of your vehicle, providing you traveled a primitive back country road, and lower the boom on the buck. However, now this action would place you in violation. So limited, a number of deer hunters say essentially, "To hell with it. I'm through with deer hunting in this state."

The AG&F counted on such reactions to a certain degree, but the drop in the state's deer hunters far exceeded their expectations. During 1972, deer hunters dropped from the usual 100,000 to 63,477, a loss of more than 35 per cent. With the AG&F in a bit of financial bind, this loss in revenie from license and tag sales has placed them in an even worse financial predicament. Now the AG&F (and other state game and fish agencies across the nation) are attempting to offset lost revenue and tight budgets by raising prices on licenses and tags. And those who continue to hunt can expect to pay more in the future.

Since both Arizona and New Mexico hunting rules and regulations, season dates, and license and tag fees are subject to change regularly, we will not discuss them here. Better that you contact these agencies directly before hunting in those states. We will deal, however, with some mule deer hunting basics, and many of the techniques will apply to both the Rocky Mountain and desert muleys.

Whether or not you succeed in taking mule deer consistently, year after year, depends largely on what you know about the habits and habitat of the animal. Generally speaking, the muley has a sharp brain, great stamina, and can be dangerous when cornered. The mule-like ears of this deer—at least one-fourth larger than the whitetail's—are sensitive sound-gathering devices that allow muleys to hear noises far beyond the range of human hearing. They also have a keen sense of smell, and vision that enables them to catch minute movements. (Yet the muley may nearly run down a hunter who makes no movement.)

Unlike the broad, defiant flag of the whitetail, the muley has a rope-like, black-tipped tail that he tucks in when alarmed. And while the whitetail's antlers are prongs rising from a central beam, the mule deer's rack forks in definite "Y's." A muley's (or whitetail's) antlers do not testify to his age. First year antlers may be a spike or two points. At five to seven years

Mule deer sit like dogs? Not really. This disturbed deer is moving from his bed in the forest.

of age, providing he has had proper nourishment, the muley is considered in his prime, and may carry many points—a trophy head. A buck in the ten-year-old class is considered an "old man" and may carry no more than two points, as he did when he was a youngster. Any two-pointer with fifteen inches or more between burr and tip of the tines is invariably an old deer; worn teeth will certify it.

Bucks usually have the velvet scraped off their antlers by September, and they are ready to battle for the favor of the does. Some hunters believe that during the rut bucks sometimes fight to the death, but others say bucks rarely engage in real battles and tend to "feint" a lot. Smaller bucks are said to recognize their physical superiors and retreat before getting their hides punctured. Although bucks become more aggressive while in the rut, fortunately for the hunter, they also grow less wary.

Some Arizona biologists believe that mule deer bucks collect harems and are polygamous; New Mexico men disagree, but rather attribute the existence of that belief to the groups of does seen accompanying the bucks during the rut.

The Rocky Mountain mule deer is a traveler, migrating from summer range of about seven thousand feet elevation to winter range that may be several thousand feet lower. When deep snow covers much of their food supply, mule deer push toward warmer climes which means lower elevations. In contrast to the roaming Rocky Mountain muley, the desert mule tends to stay put, essentially living

Caught four feet off the ground by a motorized camera, the Rocky Mountain mule deer doe heads for other parts.

Rocky Mountain mule deer fawn doesn't hesitate to use water as an escape route.

in the same kind of habitat year-round. Both varieties of deer have the general habit of feeding in the morning, sometimes before daylight, and resting in the afternoon, then eating again in late afternoon, sometimes after dark. Both also like broken, rough terrain.

To take mule deer regularly, experienced hunters either stalk them on foot or hunt on horseback. They know the best place to start is the high country where, with binoculars, they can scan the slopes, hills, canyons, arroyos, and ridges below them. They closely scrutinize groves of conifers, oaks, and aspens for the Rocky Mountain muley, and patches of palo verde, ironwood, mesquite and catclaw bordering desert washes for the desert mule deer. Two hunters, working to-

gether, can expect to have more success than one man. One takes to the higher country where he can command a great expanse of landscape, while the second acts pretty much as a driver, attempting to spook game up toward his companion. I have a friend, Tony Mandile, who considers a slingshot the most important piece of equipment on a deer hunt, next to his rifle. He shoots stones into likely looking deer hangouts from higher country and gets his buck into the open for a clear shot.

The cattle country west of Anita, Arizona, looks as deerless as the Sahara Desert, but years ago Virgil Martin, a cattle camp horse breaker, tipped me off that some big bucks were using the tiny groves of junipers out in the flats for cover. That

Photographer-writer Jim Tallon with friend, a Rocky Mountain mule deer button buck.

could get to mule deer on horseback and changed my thinking somewhat on trying to down a deer with a handgun. Comparatively speaking, the .357 is a light load. The most sporting method, I believe, is to use enough bullet to finish the animal as quickly as possible. The crippling loss, wounded deer that escape the hunter only to die later and go to waste, is rarely less than 15 per cent of the annual deer bag, and sometimes as much as 50 per cent! Of course I'm considering the average deer hunter; some riflemen have the capability of placing their shots consistently into vital spots. If you're not one of them, start putting in regular practice sessions.

Barring some super disaster, the future of the mule deer in the Southwest seems to be a bright one. Perhaps never again will we see the deer highs of a few decades ago; after all, America no longer has that kind of deer habitat. But many states have more deer than the entire country did in 1922. And that's great, when you realize that in addition to all the land that has gone under the plow, the multitude of cities and towns, and the areas under water behind dams, enough concrete has been laid to totally cover an average eastern state! With modern techniques, most of the bugs of deer management, especially that of fitting the herds to the available range, have been removed. But the continuing welfare of this great game animal really depends upon land use policies and the government agencies that regulate them.

year Arizona legalized the .357 Magnum on big game, and I rode my horse, Pelau, into one of those groves with the intention of downing a deer with my single action revolver. Right away I found myself smack in the middle of a bunch of does and fawns but no bucks. It was near the tail end of the deer season, and my original intent to take a trophy buck gave way to adding fresh meat to our freezer. Does were legal, so I picked what I believed to be a dry doe—no fawns with her—and fired. Either I nicked her or she bolted at the instant I fired. Suddenly deer were zigzagging all around me, some nearly running into Pelau and me. In seconds not a deer hair remained. My big doe apparently had left with them.

This experience showed me how close I

The Mule Deer in the Southwest

221

Sam Fadala was born in Albany, New York, but had little chance to experience that state because his parents moved him to Tucson, Arizona, when he was five. Severe asthma kept him confined, and his early outdoor life was restricted to the pages of sporting magazines. When the Arizona sunshine had done its work, the asthma departed and the boy all but lived in the desert. He met the Coues deer in his late teens and over a period of about a dozen years, hunting in Arizona and Mexico, has shot fourteen record class heads. He retired the Record Desert Whitetail Club trophy in 1970 for collecting the largest head of the membership for the third time.

A one-time high school teacher, Mr. Fadala is now in his last year of Ph.D. work at the University of Arizona and is an outdoor writer by vocation. His work has appeared in *Outdoor Life, Guns & Ammo, Gun World, National Sportsman's Digest, Outdoor Arizona, Guns Plus Hunting, The American Rifleman,* and non-sporting publications such as *Progressive Woman* and *Audiovisual Instruction.*

15

COUES IS THE NAME OF A DEER

Sam Fadala

IF A HUNTER could climb aboard a golden eagle and soar above the territory of the Coues deer, he would see below a habitat of great contrast. Tiny trees, referred to as "live oaks" by the natives, dot a rolling grassland of meandering sand washes and limestone outcroppings in the midrange section. Up higher, purple rimrocks recall "Zane Grey country," with steep mountains rising from the foothills at 2500 feet to almost 10,000 feet above sea level. Huge Ponderosa pines adorn the upper reaches of this deer's habitat. Down low, there is a zone of mesquite and cacti standing on the flats, with dry washes and pockets of catclaw dressing the landscape.

North, in country which resembles a calendar picture of the Rockies, the Coues (pronounced "cows") thrives in tall forests and thick greenery, much as his east-

ern cousin, the Virginia whitetail. The southern extreme of his range lies in Northern Mexico, his numbers being greatest in the states of Sonora, Chihuahua, and Choahuila. In fact, except for Arizona, plus a few herds in New Mexico and Texas, the Coues is a Mexican deer. His head is a rarity in even the most extensive trophy collections.

Only half the size of his big brother, the mule deer, wherever the Coues is found, from arid desert to lush peaks, he is among the most cunning and alert creatures of the land. He more than makes up for lack of size with abundance of brain. Literally, if the skull of a Coues is dissected and matched with that of a mule deer, the brain pans will be about the same size, even though the mule's head is almost twice as large. Jack O'Connor, an expert

223

This is an illustration showing the difference between the mule deer rack (left) and the whitetail rack (right). Note that the major difference is the forking of the points on the mule, while the Coues (and other whitetails) simply grow up from the main beam.

hunter who has traversed many continents in pursuit of wild animals, rates the Coues the most intelligent quarry in this half of the world. Only the kudu of Africa is granted more esteem by O'Connor. In a February, 1958, issue of *Outdoor Life,* Jack relates his encounters with the beautiful half-pint bucks in his article, "Our Smartest Game Animal." "He's a little guy, about half as large as the mule deer he often ranges with. He is, on the other hand, about five times as smart as the mule deer," says O'Connor.

Whether pursued in the golden country of southern Arizona, with its wind-cured grama grass, pink rimrocks, white-bodied oaks, and scattered agave cacti, or in the dry coastal mountains of Baja California overlooking the ocean, the little Coues,

also known affectionately as the fantail by some, or the Arizona whitetail by many, is a prime trophy, a rarity in the deer family.

I was a mule deer hunter in my late teens. One afternoon as I stood in a hallway at the University of Arizona all of this changed. Two young men were discussing the virtues of the .30-30 as a deer rifle. I was still permeated with the Red Ryder syndrome, and I would defend the old '94 to the death, so I had to cut in with my own comments. The remarks of the adversary waned under my attack, and he left. I shook hands with the remaining fellow, who told me his name was Robert Bradsher. Then *we* got into it.

Robert held the rare distinction of having been raised in an almost unknown border town—Patagonia, typical mid-range habitat for the Coues. I wanted to talk mule deer. He wanted to talk Arizona whitetail. "But the mule is twice as large," I pleaded.

"And less than half as smart," Robert insisted. "If you don't believe me, come out to Patagonia this season and get after one with me." I spent the better part of that season on the track of several bucks, all of which ended the season healthier for my chasing them. The closest I came was to chip off a bit of antler from one buck as he belly-dived into a canyon. A few other opportunities were offered across canyons at racks disappearing into the brush, but my venerable .30-30 proved about as effective as a handful of rocks. I was embarrassed.

I sold the .30-30, bought a Model 70 Winchester in .270 caliber, fitted it with a 4x scope, and sought some advice. I was told that the local Tucson taxidermist, John Doyle, was not only the finest artist at mounting a whitetail trophy, but also among the state's best hunters of the Coues. Both praises proved factual. After hours in his then tiny shop, I could tell within a few Boone and Crockett points the value of a Coues rack. I was going to do more than bag a buck; I was going to come home with a record.

Next season Robert and I were again straining up the ridges north of Patagonia. This time I was wearing a pair of binoculars with which I hoped to find feeding deer as John had instructed. I also teamed with my partner in working can-

A Coues needs little cover to disappear. Often he will be resting in an outcropping just like this, in plain sight, if only he weren't so well camouflaged and so still. A good pair of binoculars can mean the difference in locating an animal like this or passing it by. This is a representative only, and not a live animal. It is a full size mount by taxidermist, John Doyle of Tucson.

yons, one of us standing in the breeze to allow scent to permeate the little pocket, while the other waited in ambush trying to cover all exits. Many times we could hear an animal getting out on us, but could not sight it.

However opportunities began to crop up. Bucks, mostly immature ones which I would have nothing to do with, were sneaking out of those little hiding places right past us. On about the fourth day out, Robert suggested hunting a spot on the edge of town. He reasoned it was so close that nobody else had touched it. Working down a steep, deep grassy ridge that afternoon, I heard a sudden rustling in the grass twenty yards ahead of me and a big rack bounded from the growth. I pulled up with the .270 and fired when the scope filled with deer. I had my buck. And it was in the record class. He looked much heavier than the scales proved him to be. Estimates of 130 pounds and up were shouted as the local butcher hauled the animal up on the scales. Not 130, not even 100, but 89 pounds was the final verdict. Robert explained that about 90 pounds was average for a fully mature Coues, with 100 being a nice one, and anything over darn big.

I was bitten by whitetail fever. John Doyle, along with several other dedicated Coues chasers, was initiating a club in honor of the deer. It was to be called the Record Desert Whitetail Club, and the rules were simple. Take a record class buck or no buck at all each season and good standing was maintained. Shoot a lesser whitetail, or, perish the thought, a mule deer, and the member was ousted like a traitor from the ranks of the faithful. I came in second place first season out. Jim Levy, well-known Arizona hunter and guide, beat me for first place with a big bruiser of a buck from the Tumacacori mountains near Nogales, Arizona. But I was finding out about the Coues.

Two blades of grass and a baseball-size rock could conceal a big whitetail buck. And the animals were always bedded where one jump would put them in a tangled mass of canyon hideouts. Also, when a buck piled into a canyon, it was not possible to predict his reappearance, as it so often was with the mule deer. Habits of sneaking belly close to the ground were common with even the youngest two-point bucks. Still hunting was difficult. Sitting on a log waiting for a deer to stumble by proved mostly fruitless, except in mountain passes where deer might be traveling to and from water holes.

But a system eventually patterned itself from bits and pieces of experience. The hunter of a big Coues buck has to first scout for an area where large families run. Picking up shed antlers and measuring them disclosed places of big buck concentration. As a general rule, the mid-ranges and lower elevations seemed to hold the greatest number of big racks. By measuring the shed antler according to Boone and Crockett method, doubling the score, then adding 13, which is about average for inside spread, a rating could be obtained. Of course, no two antlers match alike and there was always some deduction for non-symmetry. But Coues antlers are generally symmetrical. The out-of-state hunter cannot rely on preseason area scouting, but he should require his guide to, if he has one.

By using topographical maps, the hunter can "scout," too. Usually, water holes are marked, and the lay of the land can be visualized. Access in and out of an area is readily seen on a map. Game and fish departments will often aid a hunter by marking potentially good hunting areas.

After the hunter decides on his spot, he should have three major tools in addition to his everyday hunting clothing and paraphernalia. These are: a good pair of binoculars, a flat-shooting rifle, and a walking stick.

The Coues is a master of evasion and cunning. But the really big buck survives as much for another reason; he is very, very lazy. This sloth has probably done more to keep hunter success low, not much above 10 per cent in Arizona for bucks, than any other factor. Superb camouflage with a super ability to remain patient and still as a brass monkey has kept many a buck out of the freezer.

The height of successful whitetail hunting is finding that lazy buck bedded. With good binoculars and plenty of patience, this becomes a possibility, though never a certainty. My teacher, John Doyle, showed me how difficult it is one warm October day. He was working the

Looking for shed antlers is a fine way of locating trophy country. If the other side matched, this rack would have fallen into the top three in the world records. Nancy Fadala in photo.

bottom of the draws as I walked the ridges. Presently, I glanced down to find his hand waving in the air to get my attention. I moved quickly off the ridge following his arm signal directions until I arrived at his side. "Okay," he began, "now look back up that ridge, right by the boulder you just passed." I did. There was a smallish whitetail buck staring right at me. I lowered my binocular. I had walked about ten yards from him! Yet, he was not particularly hidden, and John had managed to find the animal with his 8 x 44 glass.

We learned the virtues of binoculars from a game and fish department official who had to harvest several whitetail bucks in a matter of a few days because of a severely important experiment. He got his deer with a high power rifle, since he was against traps or poison. He was successful for three reasons: he knew what deer food looked like; he knew when the deer would be feeding; and he knew how to employ binoculars. The biologist found that late evening was the best time for finding feeding deer.

He located a vantage point which overlooked previously discovered deer fodder. After brief familiarization with the lay of the land, the little pockets of cool shade, the sunny ridges, bluffs of rimrock and patches of trees, he began to search for something, but *not* a deer. He was looking for something much smaller. Because of the deer's blending ability, this animal is tough to find until the hunter learns to segment him. That is, he tries to locate a softness that refuses to blend like a rock into the terrain, or an outline that cuts itself against a stand of trees, or an eye, ear, or antler poking out from a grassy ridge. After mastering this, the hunter has come a long way toward success with the Coues. This is the ultimate, and I insist that even a master of the glass will find few such deer. But the one he does find could be the trophy he has dreamed about.

John Doyle and I were brushed up in the shade like two lazy bucks ourselves one past Coues deer season, glassing a series of grassy ridges that looked gamey. "Hey, got a deer in the glass," John reported. He had spotted an eye, sort of a glitter three hundred yards out from us. I found it with little effort, which is usually the case when the searcher is *confident* that

an animal is out there. Not really a deer, just an outline in the grass was apparent at first. Then a buck popped into focus, appearing like a Walt Disney character from a paint-with-water coloring book. He was a small buck lying beside a grayish oak log. As we watched the buck and the "log" got up and walked away. Both of them were two-pointers. The binocular, this "Eye of the Hunter" I call it, is invaluable on the Arizona whitetail hunt.

Oftentimes I have spotted a barrel cactus that on closer scrutiny turned out to be a big feeding buck. Or what I thought was a soft gray rock lying on a ridge has suddenly risen to its feet and fled. Feeding deer, of course, present an easier target as they change position. The early morning and the later part of the afternoon are prime times for looking with the glass. We make it a practice to look until dusk relinquishes itself to darkness. Many times the flashlights in our packs had to be turned on for our walk back to camp. Often, while our fellow nimrods were home in camp cooking the evening beans, my partner and I were backpacking in the bacon.

All in all, good glasses are a must. There is little sense in carrying a three hundred dollar rifle and twenty dollar glasses, as the former is used continually, but the latter only for an occasional shot. I have seen old, inexpensive army rifles, wearing decent sights, that could keep all their bullets in less than an inch and a half at a hundred yards. But I have discovered

SAM FADALA

no ultra cheap binocular that filled all the criteria of a good optical system.

The first thing I want is that nebulous quality, *definition.* Looking the word up in a dictionary won't render the first-hand impact of experiencing this quality. Testing two glasses one evening, I found I could discern the leaves on an oak at a hundred yards with one pair. With the other I could see the serrated *edges* of those leaves. The first glass was an import selling for upwards of three hundred dollars; the second glass traded for about two hundred dollars. Price alone will not tell the full story.

The binocular should transmit light well, and its construction must be rugged enough to withstand the occasional bounce it will receive on the trail. The glass should be carried slung, not bouncing loose like a millstone around the neck.

A flat-shooting rifle is a boon to whitetail harvesting. If I were forced to carry the standard .270 Winchester for the remainder of my whitetail hunting days, I would not shed a single tear. At the same time, I find no argument with the specialist who prefers a .25-06, or .257 Weatherby. And the users of the big 7mm Magnum have their reasons for packing an arm which handles that powerhouse. I employ it myself on special occasion.

Depending on terrain and hunting style, rifles from 6mm all the way to the goliath .300 Magnums find a place in Coues hunting. Where stalks are possible after long range sightings on bucks with binoculars, the little 6mm with its 80 grain bullet at almost three thousand feet per second is adequate. The shot will be at less than 200, probably under 150 yards, and the hunter will not have to suffer under the burden of a nine-pound riflescope combo all day.

If cross canyon shots, with wind playing its bullet-swaying powers, are the rule, a big gun comes in handy. Plenty of energy remains at extreme range to dispatch quickly and humanely. In this kind of hunting for Coues, I use the 7mm Magnum with either a 140 grain bullet propelled by a stiff charge of 4831 powder, or the wonderfully accurate 160 Nosler driven at 3200+ feet per second.

But the only really long shot I ever had to make was with the mundane .270. Spotted through binoculars across a steep and wide gorge was a nice whitetail buck. He sensed detection, so he froze on the spot. There was a wind striking from the left. I held what I thought was nine inches above the deer's spine, and about two feet into the wind and touched off. The buck toppled. The cartridge was loaded with the far-flying 130 grain Remington Bronze Point; backed by 62.5 grains of 4831 the bullet dropped probably less than thirteen or fourteen inches. I feel the shot was a true 400 yards.

The final tool of the tripart set is the walking stick. The finest type I know of is often called a Moses Stick in the Southwest due to its possible origin with the Bible people who covered miles on foot with aid of their staffs. Made from the balsa light, oak strong, agave family of cacti, the sticks will help carry a two hundred-pound man through years of hiking.

Aside from the obvious asset of a walking aid, where the stick allows a man to cover more territory, plus saves him from a few bad falls over broken ground, the staff is also invaluable in two other departments—steadying both rifle and binocular.

Very little will be discovered by the hunter who does not rock-steady his glass while viewing. And here is where the Moses comes in. There is not a trace of heartbeat in that stick to upset the magnified image viewed in the glass. By sitting, back rested, arms propped on knees, with the stick dug in, a hunter can glass for hours in comfort. The leather handle of the staff serves to cushion the glass as well as support the hand for non-slip walking. If a hunter should have to stand to see over brush, the stick can be used again. There is nothing which shows up on an amateur binocular man faster than his standing on hind legs with the glass unsupported. If he thinks he will optically ferret out much game that way, he is badly mistaken.

Shooting cross-canyon presents many problems. Aside from having to correctly dope out the range and the ballistics of the cartridge, steadiness is difficult to attain. By wedging the stick in between the legs while assuming the sitting position, a near benchrest solidness can be gained. Either end of the stick can point down. By using the top of the staff, the soft deer hide

handle, the gun is protected and cushioned. If a standing shot is necessary, again the stick comes through.

I would not want to venture into a serious Coues hunt without the three tools mentioned. The Moses Stick helps get the hunter to the spot safely, then, coupled with the rifle or binocular, it performs its steadying tricks. The glass is an extension of the legs as it looks into far country, bringing it into the lap of the hunter. The well-sighted rifle of long range quality is the tool of dispatch.

There are, of course, many ways to add a Coues to the trophy room, sheer luck being one of them, but a bad one to bank on. Perhaps the most gentlemanly style of chasing the Coues, however, is from the back of a well-trained horse. I have seen more deer on foot, with a big glass in hand, such as the Bushnell 10 x 50, and in the same country I had horsebacked through only a day earlier. During the warmth of the day, when the deer are enjoying a siesta, walking in and out of cool canyons can be productive, but looking is best the remainder of the day.

When John Doyle wanted to show his son, John Jr., the ropes of whitetail hunting, he took him into the low country of the beautiful Huachuca mountains on the Arizona-Mexico border. I was along. The season was hot, as it so often is at the outset of the October schedule. The deer were bedded by early morn and not up again to feed until near dark. We found a few critters, but little John had been around head hunters too long. He didn't

SAM FADALA

The Moses Stick in walking. The bottom portion sports a rubber bumper which allows good grabbing potential over the rocks. The handle is glued on and consists of tanned buckskin, applied either in one long piece rolled on, or two pieces, a top portion and a handle section.

This is another method of using the stick to steady the big binocular for top notch viewing.

The Moses Stick as a shooting rest. This position offers near benchrest stability and long hits are possible because of it.

want a two-point, or young three. He wanted a big boy.

Scent runs up canyon on warm days, and we took advantage of this by posting the lad so he could see any bucks that might sneak out ahead of us as we slowly wormed around the canyons. At one point, John Sr. poked around the mouth of a small cut, while the younger shooter and I looked on from a rock bluff. Tail tucked between its legs, a big racked buck fled like a spirit through a brushy draw as the scent-giver, John, milled below him. The deer hugged the brush, offering no target until he was four hundred yards away. John Jr. did not feel he could execute a hit at that range, so he urged me to try. I did. After three .270 bullets whined harmlessly by the now running animal, I gave up, but not before following the animal through my 10 power glass until he bedded. Usually, a big lazy buck will go only as far as he feels is necessary to escape his pursuer.

We waited for about one hour. When we were sure the animal's nerves had calmed, we went after him. The buck had entered a patch of land that resembled a six-fingered hand. The palm of the hand was a thicket of live oaks, with each of the six fingers being tiny draws leading away from the thicket. The two Johns stood like sentinels on a flat spot of grama grass and scattered oaks in sight of the exits of the six draws. I slowly milled about the palm. Then a shot. I had seen or heard nothing, but the old buck had sneaked out ahead of me right into the Doyles. Young John

had gotten down on one knee like a soldier and placed an 85 grain 6mm bullet from his .243 Lynx just behind the shoulder of the deer.

The buck was non-typical of antler, a rarity for the Coues, whose rack is usually very typical and uniform. It won first place in the Tucson Rod and Gun deer contest for non-typical that year. Boone and Crockett initiated a non-typical category only a few years ago. At one time a B&C score of 90 points was bottom score for Coues records, but today a buck must score out at a minimum of 110 to gain entry. Non-typical minimum is 120.

Hunting northern Mexico, primary range of the fantail, is a gratifying experience, even though a slightly sticky tangle of red tape stands between hunter and license. A Mexican consul can render all of the details for obtaining both gun permit, which is necessary, and hunting license. Much of the country is open and untamed for miles on the larger spreads, and private ranches are the better spots. Mexican sportsmen will often trade hunts with U.S. nimrods. An American antelope hunt for a Mexican whitetail hunt is a common swap.

One fortunate season I ventured into the land of *mañana* for a ten-day trophy trek. Rain is a fickle lady in northern Sonora, and she had decided against us by dropping water for days steadily prior to departure date. Dry riverbeds were carrying unfamiliar torrents of muddy water. Roads were washed out. In places railroad tracks hung like spider webs where

Stacy Fadala with same deer.

of gasoline. We bedded in an adobe shelter and next day found us puffing up into ocotillo-covered hills. The rain had stopped. Sunshine had regained dominance and huge white clouds hung like washed cotton balls against a blue sky.

A few days later after much determined glassing, I located a really fine record-class buck as he fed on a narrow hogback, stuffing his nose down into the grass to tug at the low growths of false mesquite. He was so preoccupied that I was able to close the gap to about 350 yards, but I had been careless. In haste, I made no test for wind. Suddenly his head jerked up as if he had bitten into a skunk. He wheeled back off the ridge and into the canyon. I threw a shot which whizzed past his speeding body.

For two days I looked for that buck. Then I gave up and pursued new adventures higher into the mountain. There were plenty of deer, but after seeing the big fella, the smaller ones did not impress. I decided to give it one more try.

On the last day of our hunt I was back in the little canyons that the trophy buck claimed home. Later that afternoon I could not believe the image in my glass. There was that familiar thick whitish rack once again, bobbing back and forth as he chewed on a low bush. I tested the wind this time and tried to move in on him. But when I reached the hill he had been feeding on, there was no sign of the animal.

I spent the rest of the day slowly moving in and out of the little brush pockets which pockmarked the area. At last there

currents had undermined the earth. But in spite of impediments, luck was riding in our Jeep as my Mexican friend, Senor Victor Ruiz, wheeled and detoured for twelve hours from Nogales to a remote ranch south of Cananea.

We arrived in the middle of the night, but were still greeted by the foreman of the ranch, one Don Pancho, who offered us a ward against the chill in the form of a tea cup full of tequila. Ruiz drank his like weak tea. I sipped mine as I would a draft

Coues is the Name of a Deer

A Mexican vaquero comes in with a smallish, but not that small, fantail. He hunts with a .22 rifle, but admits that he seldom takes a decent buck, holding his shots to about twenty yards and aiming for a chest or head hit. This buck would weigh in at about eighty pounds dressed.

was a swish of grass and the buck shot from the ground like a soft brown rock from a Roman catapult. I swung on his shoulder blades and touched off. Using a 150 bullet in my .270, I had not counted on the hardness of that projectile. The slug ripped right through without registering a hit. But I always check after firing, and there was a broad blood trail on the path of the buck. I would find him just over the ridge, I knew.

But before I could get on the spoor, I was detracted by a volley of three shots fired rapidly, a distress signal to my ears. No buck could take precedence over an injured hunter, so I was off in the direction of the shots. Two hours later I found their source. My partner had gotten into a large herd of javelina, or peccary. He knew how much the Mexican ranchers loved to eat these little porkers, used for a chile-hot sausage called chorizo, so he bagged his limit of three, as did the cowboy who was with him.

With six pigs on the ground, help was needed, so Victor fired the shots, not realizing that three rapid firings constituted a danger signal to an American hunter. Now it was dusk and my buck lay back in the hills. We had to depart that night. I told the story to Don Pancho and the old man's eyes filled with tears. He promised he would look for the animal, try to save the meat for their own use, and the rack for me.

Six months later a package reached my house in Tucson. It contained the white rack of the buck I had gotten in Mexico.

The old vaquero had no way of getting the antlers to civilization until the priest who visits the out-of-the-way ranch country twice a year had passed through. He placed the antlers in the Father's care, telling him to give them to Victor Ruiz in Nogales, Sonora, which the holy man did. Victor mailed them to me. The heavy rack fell easily into the record class.

The most romantic way to claim a Coues trophy, I feel, is to obtain a top grade pack frame and filter into wildly remote whitetail country, such as the forsaken habitat of Sycamore Canyon in

My best Coues, 116.1 B&C points. This buck came out of the Tumacacori Mountains and was detected not more than a mile from the Nogales-Tucson highway. The spread is fifteen inches and the beam is nineteen on the longest side. Coues thrive well in semi-civilization.

Here is Ed Stockwell, Arizona big game guide specializing in Coues and desert sheep. Ed holds the world record Coues deer, and he is pictured with that magnificent animal here. The head scores at over 143 B&C points and was taken in 1953 in the Santa Rita mountains of southern Arizona. Ed got it with a .300 Savage as the buck got out behind a rock, trying to sneak from another hunter. It weighed in at about one hundred pounds dressed. No rack has come close to deposing this king.

northern Arizona, a place where I have found upwards of a half dozen lion kills in a single day. These were mainly bucks which are slower than the dainty flighty does, thus easier for the big cats to capture.

Prior to the advent of the Super Tent, a product of Frostline of Boulder, Colorado, a backpacker could bring with him only a moderate size home. But the Super Tent, though weighing a bit more than its diminutive counterparts, is worth every ounce of the packing, for it offers a bit of living space and precludes attacks of claustrophobia after days of campout. A person feels like staying a while after packing into remote country.

After the trophy is taken, the meat is cut from the bone entirely and the cape is removed. A taxidermist or guide can teach the process easily. A big buck earned this way will remain a source of wonderful hunting memory for life, especially if a favorite partner went along to share the adventure.

Aside from the thrill of taking a smart Coues buck in fair chase, another reward awaits the successful hunter. Arizona whitetail meat is some of the most palatable food in the world. Cutting the steaks thin, then soaking them briefly in salt water brine to which a dash of steak sauce has been added, then drying and pounding flour into the slabs of meat, prepares them for a smoking hot fry pan of clear grease. Memorable eating.

Managing the Coues herd is a process of boom and bust. Hunters have little to do with it. At times the wily animals offer the greatest threat to themselves by eating up their own food supply. Hunters won't believe this when they go into a territory and see so little sign. The rocky terrain holds few tracks, and droppings are lost in the wheat-colored grama grass. The animals are lying still, not standing out like cows on the hillside. Does are more skitterish and seen most often, thus a few hunters feel they have shot off the bucks. Actually, the mossbacks are there in the same locale, just doing nothing, except maybe thinking about how they are going to sneak off when the big-footed hunter comes by.

There is something almost magical about treading Apache country in the fall of the year when skies are usually clear, temperatures warm, and the land inviting. Crisp nights call for a fragrant fire of mesquite wood and the hunter has a tough time falling off to sleep because he is thinking of an encounter with a big Coues the next day, a dream deer, ten points to the side with a base wrist thick.

The little fantail will be around for a long time. He is able to cope with man on his own grounds. The largest head of the 1972 season was taken by Jim Russell of Tucson on a piece of property he owns in the Catalina Mountains scarcely out of the city limits of that sprawling metropolis. The huge buck had lived within earshot of a highway and had probably seen countless hikers and hunters in his day. But very few of them, no doubt, had ever seen him. That is his nature, and the way he earns the reputation of "our smartest game animal."

Bill Miller writes from his experience as a hunter, a wildlife manager with the North Dakota Game and Fish Department, and a veteran wildlife photographer with movie and still cameras. Commenting on his sources of knowledge, Bill says that the hunting experience must rank third—mainly because the hunter is in the field for such a limited time each year. As a field biologist, and later chief of game management, wildlife study was a year round job. Wildlife photography likewise has no closed season and no closed areas such as refuges and parks. And it takes more patience and skill to shoot a buck with a telephoto lens than it does with a .243. Certainly the photographer must use every trick he knows to locate and to approach his game.

The deer hunter does not learn everything from his own experience. Every observer of wildlife, the novice and the old timer, has something to contribute. Bill offers some observations from his many years of working with the deer, and I think many interesting pointers that will be useful in your next hunt for prairie deer.

16

PRAIRIE DEER

Wilford (Bill) Miller

DEER HUNTERS GENERALLY associate the number one big game animal in North America with forests and mountains. They may scoff at the idea of hunting deer on the barren prairie lands of North Dakota, South Dakota and eastern Montana. How could deer find adequate browse, safe places for rearing their young, and shelter from the winter blizzards in this bleak region?

Yet these states furnish excellent hunting year after year under carefully managed hunting seasons. As noteworthy as the decimation of the deer population in the early part of our country's history, is their comeback in recent years. Deer have not only repopulated most of their former range, but also have continued to increase in numbers in spite of intensive farming practices and land use changes.

The deer utilize small patches of waste land and the numerous shelterbelts that now dot the prairies. Better soil and water conservation practices also benefit the wildlife. North Dakota, once with almost no deer herd at all, now ranks among the top ten big game states in the country.

Deer are remarkably adapted to changing agriculture. Dietary changes have made corn, alfalfa and other crops a convenient source of food. The animals are accustomed to the sounds of tractors, automobiles and people. In the process of adjustment, whitetails and mule deer have learned a few survival tricks of their own to supplement their keen sense of smell, their sharp hearing and vision that is better than most humans think. Matching your skill with the behavior pattern of the prairie whitetail and muley offers a real challenge.

Perhaps there are as many ways to hunt

Prairie whitetails have adapted to the open country by utilizing shelterbelts, weed patches and farm crops.   WILFORD L. MILLER PHOTO

deer as there are hunters, and as many "right guns" as there are models. The novice may benefit from suggestions by the "old timers" who are successful hunters and everyone may get a pointer or two from experiences of others. The writer does not intend to tell you how to go out and bring back a prairie deer on every trip, but does offer observations that will be helpful.

Hunting in the flat open country can be quite different from hunting in the forests or in the mountains. Much of this land is level or gently rolling, but there is rugged terrain in the spectacular Bad Lands of both North and South Dakota. And there are timbered areas in eastern Montana, in the Black Hills of South Dakota and in the Turtle Mountains and Pembina Hills of North Dakota, as well as along most rivers and streams. The broad Missouri River valley was once excellent wooded

habitat for deer. Now all that remains is the sixty-mile stretch between Bismarck and Garrison. The Oahe and Garrison dams created two huge lakes in North and South Dakota. Thousands of deer were pushed back into the adjacent hills and out to the flat prairie farms and ranches.

Driving, stalking and trail-watching are the three basic styles of hunting deer. The individual has his preference and will have to select the appropriate terrain for his technique or modify his way of hunting. If he prefers to drive, he must seek out the wooded areas and secure permission from the landowner for his party. Driving can be very effective because areas suitable for driving in this region are usually small. Sections of the Turtle Mountains and the Black Hills are exceptions. Stalking is productive in open country. Trail-watching is good anywhere if hunters are moving the deer. Opening days and week-

WILFORD (BILL) MILLER

ends are the best times for parking yourself in a carefully selected spot and letting others chase the deer to you.

Driving is the most productive method of hunting in wooded areas. Usually drives are organized under the direction of local farmers and ranchers who are familiar with the terrain and who want control over the number of animals killed each year. They may permit the shooting of bucks only, regardless of state regulations that make any deer legal, or bucks and does may be shot but no fawns. Number one, you must get permission to hunt from the landowners. Number two, you must be willing to comply with his orders in every way.

In farm country, top deer habitat may be a thirty-acre patch of sweet clover or soil bank land in tall grass. Driving is best during mid-day when no other method is very productive. Drivers fan out in a wedge-shaped formation about a mile from the point where the standers are stationed. The drivers work downwind and usually keep in sight of one another. They try to drive the deer ahead of them to the shooters who are placed to take advantage of open areas or ridges in the path of the moving deer. Selected sites of the various stands are most important.

Some parties prefer to walk crosswind rather than downwind. Deer have an extremely keen sense of smell, and human scent will alert these animals long before drivers are in sight. Then the deer are likely to take off to the right or left, instead of continuing forward to the shooters.

I have watched and listened to drivers

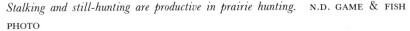

Stalking and still-hunting are productive in prairie hunting.   N.D. GAME & FISH PHOTO

in the Missouri River bottoms from a high ridge of hills nearly a mile away. On one single drive I saw more than a dozen deer slip out from the line of drive through the woods and sneak off through small creek bottoms and other escape routes leading away from the hunters. A buck and a doe hid in a nearby gravel pit. Some went into small patches of chokecherries and buffaloberries, while a few continued over the top of the ridge where I sat.

After watching this drive I knew how to get my deer—trail-watching on a ridge above a drive. If deer did not come past me, I would stalk those seen going into patches of cover on the hillside or in the creek bottoms.

Watching the deer escape emphasized another point to remember. The biggest bucks go into tiny, obvious hiding places that most hunters would never bother to check. One trophy buck hid in a patch of cattails in a pond, actually lying in the water. And he was still around after the season, back in his usual haunts.

Some hunters prefer the noisy drive, others the quiet. Noisemakers are not permitted in some states, so check regulations first. The drivers may yell, bay like dogs, ring bells and make other noises that are intended to send the deer dashing toward the shooters. Many deer are taken by this method, as they are frightened by unusual noises.

A few deer—and it's usually the smart old bucks—will take advantage of the noise to find the holes between the drivers.

Finding an opening, they will either sneak back through the lines or temporarily hide in a thicket until the noisy line has passed. Then they take off in the opposite direction. A couple of shooters placed some distance behind the drivers may intercept these smart ones.

Organized like the noisy drive, the silent drive moves at a much slower pace and with as little noise as possible. While the noisy drive sends the animals running past the shooters, the still drive results in shots at walking deer. Another advantage of the quiet drive is that the deer have difficulty locating the openings in the line and can't slip back between the drivers as easily.

First-hand information on the smart bucks that will crouch and almost crawl on their bellies back through a line of drivers has come from my experience in game management, rather than in hunting. In some hunting areas, a Piper Cub was used in making observations that cannot easily be made on the ground. This was opening day in the wooded Turtle Mountain region in North Dakota, and an organized drive was in progress. Drivers were no more than one hundred feet apart, yet several near-trophy bucks picked their openings and literally crawled back through the line of drivers.

Another experience in a field game-checking station in that area the same day should impress upon the novice hunter the importance of checking his downed animal to see if it is dead before beginning other field operations. A bewildered

Smart whitetails seek small patches of brush and often stay hidden as the hunter walks by. WILFORD L. MILLER PHOTO

hunter came to the station and stammered sheepishly, "I lost my gun." It turned out he had dropped a nice buck, then laid his rifle across the antlers. While taking out his knife for field dressing, he watched helplessly as the buck scrambled to his feet and took off through the woods, rifle and all! I never did find out whether he found his rifle—or his knife.

Stalking is a slow, careful type of hunting that requires great patience and a knowledge of deer behavior. If you feel that success in the hunt depends upon the number of miles covered, stalking is not for you. You should also have a sense of direction or know how to use a compass.

Experienced stalkers may cover only two or three hundred yards in a half hour. They quietly move forward a few feet, then stop, looking and listening for several minutes. They don't expect to see a deer. Rather they look for a line, a shape or a color that is not part of the natural landscape. It may be an ear, the tip of an antler, a patch of white or reflected sunlight from a bit of hair. When an animal is well concealed he may let the hunter pass by without making a move to take off. Short, frequent stops by the stalker will make most animals and birds nervous, and they'll leave the security of cover.

As the whitetail takes off in twenty-foot bounds at twenty-five to thirty miles per hour, it appears that he will go for miles before stopping. But he may go into another patch of cover only a few hundred yards off, preferring to remain in the familiar parts of a rather limited range.

Because you cover very little ground in a half day of stalking, you should choose an area that has a good deer population, and you should have a good idea of the habits of those deer so you know where they will most likely be when you are hunting. Most deer travel before 9 A.M. and after 3 P.M. as they return from feeding grounds in early morning and return to them before dark. They feed and bed down during the night. In early morning they move to a hillside or a thicket to wait for the evening feeding.

On a cold day, where ridges and hills are available, deer like to lie on the sunny, protected side of a slope where they can look down. Most animals look for danger from below, rather than from above. Approach likely bedding areas with the wind in your face, keeping in mind that currents of air move upward in a valley from about 9 A.M. until 3 P.M., then reverse and move downhill. A coming storm will cause a downward movement of air, clearing weather causes upward drafts. So stalk your deer from above during midday and in clearing weather, and from below on stormy days.

Again calling upon my experience as a field biologist, I know that you are not going to get many shots at deer if you just ramble through the woods—even in good deer country. During fall and winter months, the North Dakota Game and Fish Department conducted ruffed grouse counts by walking miles of transects on designated study areas. I have walked hundreds of miles in prime deer territory in the Turtle Mountains and the Pembina Hills, have seen hundreds of whitetail beds, and often heard cracking brush as the deer departed ahead of me. Not once did I see a deer that would have given me a fair shot had I been carrying a rifle. Of course, I paid no attention to wind direction, nor did I move slowly and quietly—two requisites of successful deer stalking.

In the flat prairie country deer must use fence rows, small patches of brush, dry potholes and other bits of obvious cover if no farm shelterbelts are present. Don't pass up the little plots of cover. They're excellent spots to look for your trophy buck. Hunters tend to seek out the trees, the larger clumps of shrubbery, and the heavily grassed slough bottoms. The buck lies undisturbed in the fence rows or the buckbrush that apparently couldn't hide anything larger than a jackrabbit.

In this flat prairie country, I like to hunt whitetails just as I do pheasants, working the likely patches of cover and flushing them out. I hunt alone and I do not need the patience of the stalker. Instead I take off cross country and make no attempt to conceal myself or to walk quietly. I approach a likely clump of brush or weeds indirectly and casually, as though I were bypassing it. If a deer is in hiding, I am sure he has been aware of my presence for some time, but chances are he will remain hidden as long as I keep moving. When as close to the cover as I wish, I stop, walk a short distance, and stop. If nothing moves, I may then walk into the cover. Usually the alternate walking and stopping will flush a deer just as it will a cock pheasant. I have used this technique with great success in my wildlife photography during all seasons.

This is a good time to expound briefly on the advantage of hunting with a camera. It can be done throughout the year, on refuges and in parks as well as on open land. It is far more difficult to get a deer within the range of a telephoto lens than it is to approach within the range of the .243. So you learn more about deer behavior, your trophy is permanently recorded on film, and you have 365 days a year to work at it.

In photography and wildlife management work, I have had many opportunities to verify or disprove various statements from deer hunters. During the few days the average hunter spends in the field each year, he has little time to make

244

A spooked whitetail takes off in twenty-foot jumps at speeds twenty-five to thirty miles per hour, but he may go only a few hundred yards before going into another familiar clump of cover. WILFORD L. MILLER PHOTO

Stalking flushes whitetails from all types of cover. N.D. GAME & FISH PHOTO

observations or to carry on any experiments that may not be productive. He is out to get his deer as quickly as possible, then get back into town.

When making a film on deer with the North Dakota Game and Fish Department, we saved time by using a small plane for locating animals. When a deer was spotted, the plane circled and dipped one wing toward the spot. On several occasions I had the plane circle more than once to convince me that a deer could be in such obvious, unlikely looking cover. One unusually big buck was lying flat in a patch of buckbrush no bigger than a living room—and I had to walk into the brush to flush him out.

Another was in a sparse clump of chokecherries. I walked around it two or three times before I saw a small part of the rump and one tine of the standing animal. In the meantime, the pilot again circled low and dipped one wing, but the buck did not move even though I was walking within twenty feet of him. Only when I stopped for a few minutes did he take off—otherwise I might have kept walking around him all afternoon.

With snow cover on the prairie, the stalker can easily spot deer trails at great distances. When these conditions exist the best plan is to stay parallel with the tracks rather than to follow them directly. Stop frequently to glass every bit of cover on either side of the trail. If a deer is spotted, I prefer to use the indirect approach described previously. Undoubtedly the deer is already aware of your presence, so a direct, steady approach may spook him faster than staying in full view and walking as though you were bypassing him.

In nice autumn weather, or if you are dressed for a cold wait, you may want to get your deer with the least possible effort. Then you trail watch. While some hunters like to tramp all day, others enjoy leaning against a rock or tree stump, waiting for the deer to come to them. This technique has little value on flat lands, but in the Bad Lands and other hilly regions it can be very productive. Other hunters should be afield to keep the deer moving, or you must know the trails and the feeding habits of the deer so you can intercept them as they go to and from their feeding grounds.

For morning shooting you should be at your station before sunrise, along a trail that is used in traveling from feeding sites to bedding places. After 3 P.M. you should be stationed at a likely interception station along a trail that takes the deer back to feed. During the day—unless you want to try stalking the bedded animals—you may as well go back to camp. Or you could go hunting coyotes, foxes, rabbits, or even gamebirds.

Mule Deer

Early sportsmen who came to the West considered the mule deer foolish compared with the whitetail of the East. In some respects the mule deer was an easy target, but that was before the hunters' guns taught them the tricks of survival. Today this species is surviving the hordes of hunters plus the depletion of habit, and they are actually increasing in numbers in many parts of their range. This is especially true in the prairie states of North Dakota, South Dakota and Montana.

Bailey states that the mule deer occupied all of North Dakota before the country was settled, but the Bad Lands was their favorite haunt. It was here that Theodore Roosevelt ranched and hunted. T.R. wrote, "I have perhaps shot more mule deer than all other big game species combined."

During the time of scarcity in the 1900's, the Bad Lands was the only place in the state where mule deer could be found. Bailey in 1926 wrote: "At the present time there may be a few mule deer in the most remote corners of the Bad Lands and an occasional wanderer from the Canadian side of the Turtle Mountains and Pembina Hills, but, if not already extinct, this finest of all native species of the smaller deer will soon have vanished from the state. Its disappearance, while greatly to be regretted, is as inevitable as that of the elk and the buffalo."

By 1950 there were an estimated 2500 mule deer in the Bad Lands. In 1972 more than 5000 permits were issued to mule deer hunters in North Dakota. In addition to increasing in the Bad Lands, the mule deer are reclaiming some of their former habitat and can be seen along such

Typical mule deer habitat in western North Dakota. N.D. GAME & FISH PHOTO

streams as the Heart and the Cannonball. Small herds are found in every county west of the Missouri.

In South Dakota mule deer are also plentiful, mainly west of the Missouri River. They prefer the Bad Lands and the hilly country, while the whitetails prefer the river bottoms and the timber. In the forested Black Hills, about 75 per cent of the deer are whitetails, the remainder, muleys.

Montana's whitetails likewise occupy the river bottoms and the forested places, while the mule deer stay in the rough, open country. Decide which deer you wish to hunt, then check the regulations for each state early enough to apply for permits in specified areas.

Before hunting the mule deer, it is well to remember the keen hearing that accompanies those large ears, from which he derives his name. As in other deer, the sense of smell is also very acute. Eyesight may not be as good as that of the pronghorn, but it is better than most people think. With binoculars I have watched them watch me—they are not nearsighted!

In the rough open country favored by the mule deer, you will have to change some of your hunting tactics. In driving, your party will be working canyons and

The last look before going over the ridge is a weakness in the mule deer's defense. WILFORD L. MILLER PHOTO

draws instead of wooded plots. One driver may be in the bottom, some on the sides, and shooters at the head. When flushed, the mule deer is more likely to take off over the side than to follow the canyon to the head.

Mule deer have one weakness in their defense—especially the does and young bucks. They will stop for one last look before going over the ridge. I have shot more mule deer with my camera at that instant than in any other way. However, don't depend on your trophy buck taking that last look. He is a trophy buck because he has not stopped in the past.

When censusing from a plane or hunting alone with a camera, I have found mule deer remaining motionless in a clump of juniper even when aware of my presence. As with some whitetails, the plane could not drive them from the cover. On the ground I had to alternately walk and stop, or actually go into the cover to flush them.

Some of my best shots of mule deer have resulted from stalking. An intensive glassing of rock ledges has often located a big buck lying in the sun or shade, depending on the temperature, about one-third the way down from the top of the ridge. That's the time to come down from the ridge top above him, moving quietly and keeping the wind in your favor. You may get within fifty feet of your prize, or you may see him bounding up the opposite slope three hundred yards away because of your own clumsiness or unfavorable wind.

Young bucks and does can nearly always be counted on to run down the ridge on which you have jumped them and go up the opposite side. Then comes the last look which offers the gunners a good long shot.

The older bucks with the massive antlers will also disappear over the ridge, but instead of going directly up the opposite side, may circle around ledges or other cover and get behind you. Again, that is why they are trophy bucks.

In mule deer country, lone hunting can be productive. Even during mid-day the hunter can work the heads of draws and canyons or come over the ridges to likely looking cover below. Warm air rises, letting the deer smell anything coming up the canyon. Most big game animals do not look for danger from above, so an

WILFORD (BILL) MILLER

approach from the top is all in the hunter's favor.

Hunting small patches of cover for muleys is similar to hunting for whitetail. Younger animals have a tendency to bounce off as soon as they are aware of the hunter's presence. The wiser bucks may choose to lie tight as long as they think they are not seen.

I definitely choose mornings and evenings for photographing mule deer. They are most active during the twilight hours, and I have hundreds of silhouette shots to prove it. Most of them are stopping for that last look before going over the ridge. If you use the gun, be on the ridge well before sunrise. In the morning the animals invariably move to higher ground to bed down for the day, and if you have stationed yourself overlooking their return trail, your chances of intercepting them are excellent. Learning to locate and recognize such trails takes time and experience. Several trails may lead from the bedding area to the feeding grounds. They include well-used ones for most trips, less prominent trails for escape routes, and meandering paths that can be used to approach the bedding areas when the winds change. Ideally, the hunter should locate on one knoll that overlooks the junction of two or more trails.

In the evenings the deer again may be intercepted on their return to the lower feeding grounds, or it may be possible to stalk them on their feeding grounds. The rough terrain used by the mule deer in this prairie region offers many op-

A trophy mule deer buck watches from sparse cover. N.D. GAME & FISH PHOTO

portunities for stalking as well as for trail-watching. You can utilize every hour of the day for hunting this fascinating land of the "bouncing deer."

Regulations in Montana, North Dakota and South Dakota vary from year to year, so the prospective hunter should write for regulations which are usually available in the spring or early summer. Respective departments are located in Helena, Bismarck, and Pierre. The following information from recent years will indicate approximate seasons and restrictions in various areas into which the states are divided for the best management of deer herds.

In eastern Montana, whitetails are found in the river bottoms, in the Custer Forest and in other areas of pine and juniper. Mule deer favor the rough, bro-

A trophy buck in mule deer country—more of a challenge to a photographer than to a hunter. SUSAN STEELE PHOTO

ken land and the region along the Continental Divide.

Some districts permit taking only whitetails, some mule deer. In other areas the hunter may have to take antlerless deer only, to cut down the populations, in southeastern Montana especially. The numbers of permits for the districts will be limited, and you may have to hunt only in the district for which you applied. A non-resident deer license is $35. The general big game license for $150 permits the taking of an elk and two deer in most areas. The gun season usually runs from October 21 to November 25 statewide. Statewide bow season is from September 8 to October 13.

South Dakota has three main divisions of the state for deer hunting: the Black Hills, the West River, and the East River.

In the Black Hills, the population runs about 75 per cent whitetails, the rest muleys, mostly along the edge of the woods. Some years, hunters can take any deer, other years, bucks only. The season runs throughout November.

In the West River Prairie division, the season starts the second Saturday in November and runs for nine days. Only mule deer bucks can be taken in some counties, any deer in others. Regulations are made to fit the deer populations. Whitetails damage the haystacks of ranchers more than mule deer, so emphasis must be put on reducing the whitetail populations when damage complaints are high.

The season in the East River District also runs for nine days, starting the fourth Saturday in November. Any deer may be taken, and although mule deer are found in every county, 97 per cent of the harvest is whitetails. Non-residents cannot hunt in the East River area. (Remember, all season dates mentioned are subject to change.)

In the West River Prairie, 4 per cent of the licenses allotted for each county can go to non-residents. A limit of four thousand non-residents is placed on the Black Hills district. But the total allotment was taken only once—the first year Minnesota had a closed season. In 1972, three thousand non-residents hunted in the Black Hills, five hundred in the West Prairie counties.

WILFORD (BILL) MILLER

Stalking in open country demands the utmost skill.   WILFORD L. MILLER PHOTO

Overall license sales totaled 40,000 in 1972, of which 3500 went to archers. Prospective hunters will be interested in the success ratio. In the Black Hills, in buck only seasons, the success ratio is 30 to 35 per cent; during any deer seasons, 45 to 60 per cent. West River Prairie boasts a 75 per cent hunter success, while the East River jumps to 85 to 90 per cent. It is evident that seasons must be carefully determined to manage the deer herds properly.

In the 1972 big game season in North Dakota, 56,694 deer hunters took thirty thousand deer. That's a good success ratio anywhere, and it's hunting away from the crowds during a ten-day season in November. Only 571 were non-resident licenses.

The state is divided into several units, each with it's own restrictions, so check the regulations carefully. Mule deer are found west of the Missouri River where

special permits must be used. Slightly over five thousand mule deer permits were issued in 1972. Whitetails are found mainly in the river bottoms of the mule deer country in the Bad Lands and may be hunted without the special permit for mule deer.

If you enjoy the delightful autumn weather of the prairies, you can start hunting with bow and arrow the latter part of August and hunt any deer statewide until gun season opens. After gun season, the bow season again opens and continues through December.

You should check regulations on other game species available this time of the year. You may want to go after foxes and coyotes or waterfowl, pheasants and sharptailed grouse. It's a great time to do your hunting, your photography and your camping. The prairie country invites you. Come and enjoy this "big sky country."

Russell Tinsley killed his first deer at the age of nine, and during the thirty-one years since, he has hunted deer, both whitetails and mule deer, throughout most of the United States. He began writing about hunting while a student at the University of Texas at Austin when a professor advised him "to write about something you know." The story, about his first deer hunt, was sold to a national publication. Since then more than eight hundred of his magazine articles have been published, along with four books on outdoor recreation, including the best-selling, *Hunting the Whitetail Deer.* He also authored the booklet entitled "Deer Hunting" in the Garcia Corporation's hunting series. His home is Austin, Texas, where he is an outdoor columnist for the *Austin American-Statesman.* Tinsley hunts deer with firearms, bow and arrow, and camera, and some of his color photographs have been featured on calendars and magazine covers. He is hunting editor of *Archery World* Magazine and an advisor for the Deer Sportsmen of America.

17

TEXAS DEER HUNTING

Russell Tinsley

I HAVE SOME good news and some bad news concerning deer hunting in Texas.

First the good:

Texas' deer herd is estimated at 3.2 million, more deer than in any other state. The kill in 1972 exceeded 350,000 (about 12,000 mule deer) and wildlife biologists say twice that many could be harvested with no significant threat to the total. The hunter bag limit is liberal with four tags on a license, one exclusively for mule deer, the other three for whitetails, with no more than two bucks allowed. Since antlerless deer hunting was initiated in 1953, almost one million females (810,000 through 1971) had been taken. More than 85,000 antlerless deer were killed last season, and the number creeps up with each successive year.

The fact is, Texas has too many deer, rather than too few. The "bonus" mule deer tag was added to the license because an expanding white-tailed deer population was threatening the mule deer's range in West Texas and the northern Panhandle. The extra tag for an antlerless deer only was aimed at reducing the overpopulation. Too many deer is a particularly acute problem in the so-called hill country of central Texas. In one county of this region (Llano) more than twelve thousand deer are taken annually, exceeding the total kill of many states.

The overpopulation crisis even has begun to reach into the thorny brush country of southern Texas, a locale where many Boone and Crockett Club record bucks have been taken. The concern is that deer in this area eventually will start regressing in size, as they have done in

Whitetail buck photographed near Pearsall in southern Texas.

central Texas where overcrowded conditions have resulted in a stunted whitetail deer, the average field-dressed buck weighing no more than eighty pounds, usually even less. The Texas Parks and Wildlife Department keeps liberalizing the means and methods of taking deer, trying to encourage the harvesting of even more animals, with the regular season running almost two full months from mid-November into January. Yet nature continues to replace the deer faster than man can take them.

Now temper this with the bad:

If you hunt deer in Texas you probably will pay for the privilege. The state has only minimal public lands, the bulk of it being scattered patches of national forests in the pine-and-hardwoods country of eastern Texas. When the Republic of Texas entered the Union, it retained own-

ership of all public lands, and most of these subsequently were disposed of. The best deer hunting, by far, is on privately owned land. And in Texas the landowner charges to hunt. It has become a big and lucrative business.

Most ranches are leased for a season. A group of hunters, the number depending on the size of the respective ranch, pays a specified fee per gun for the privilege of exclusive hunting rights on this acreage. The price ranges from one hundred to five hundred dollars, the lower range being for the Edwards Plateau (hill country) region of central Texas (Mason, Llano, Gillespie, Kerr, Blanco, Burnet, Travis, and other counties of the area), and the higher price is for hunting in deep South Texas near the Mexico border, where the record-sized bucks are killed. (The charge for a lease also covers wild turkey, javelina and quail hunting, where they are available.)

Then there are day-long leases. You pay a fixed price, usually between ten and twenty dollars, to hunt for one day. Hunting on such a lease is done primarily from designated stands, for safety purposes. The kill percentage on a typical day-lease probably is between 10 and 15 per cent (my guess), with a majority of the deer taken the first two weeks of the season, before the animals get wild and spooky. Most of the day-leases are centered in the hill country west of Austin.

And for the hunter whose time is limited, there are commercial operations for "guaranteed" hunting, such as the YO Ranch in Kerr County (near Kerrville)

Russell Tinsley

and the Dolan Creek Ranch in Val Verde County (near Del Rio). On the YO Ranch, for example, a price of two hundred dollars guarantees a buck with eight or more points. White-tailed deer are plentiful on this huge ranch (about 75,000 acres) and usually a person gets his deer in a day or less of hunting. Guides drive hunters about in vehicles until shootable bucks are sighted. (In Texas it is legal to hunt from a vehicle on private land.)

The statewide archery season commences on October 1, and runs the entire month. With a few exceptions, most of the 254 counties have this October 1–31 sea-

A "legal" eight-pointer killed on YO Ranch, where hunter is guaranteed a deer.

son. One deer of either sex can be taken with bow and arrow during this time. In eight central Texas counties—Travis, Burnet, Blanco, Llano, Gillespie, Mason, San Saba and McCulloch—the bowhunting season starts thirty days immediately preceding the regular season.

In late summer the Texas Parks and Wildlife Department issues its free *Texas Hunting and Fishing Guide* with details on the various seasons. A copy can be obtained wherever licenses are sold, or ordered directly from the Texas Parks and Wildlife Department, John H. Reagan Building, Austin, Texas 78701.

The regular firearms season opens on the Saturday nearest November 15 and runs through the first weekend of January, again with a few exceptions. In McMullen County of South Texas, for one, the season is November 1–December 15, and in a few other counties the season is November 16–December 31.

The mule deer season (whitetails also are legal) for the Trans-Pecos region of far West Texas (Hudspeth, Culberson, Reeves, Jeff Davis, El Paso, Pecos, Presidio, Brewester and Terrell counties) runs usually the last week in November through approximately December 10th, and in the northern Panhandle the season is about the last two weeks of November through the first weekend of December. Mule deer are fairly abundant in the Trans-Pecos, but they are limited in the Panhandle, this primarily being cultivated farm country.

One reason Texas' deer hunting is expensive is supply and demand. While the state's population continues to grow, hunting lands remain static or, in fact, actually shrink. Choice hunting leases are difficult to find; most are contracted for many years.

But one thing favorable to the landowners can be said; once they discovered deer as a profitable cash crop, they began giving the critters mother-loving care, and as a result the deer herd has thrived and multiplied and actually expanded its range. Each year deer show in areas where hitherto they were unknown to exist. Back in my salad years I used to spend much of my time between the communities of Mason and Brady in the heart of Texas. At that time just the sight of a deer track would have been major news. Now the number of deer in the area is astronomical, so much that overpopulation is the rule rather than the exception.

This expanding deer population has almost made hunting sure-fire for the person who locates a prime lease, even for the rank beginner.

Consider the case of my friend Wilbur Callaway. He took up deer hunting only three years ago. The first season he went to places where he could wrangle permission to hunt gratis. Most landowners who allow people to hunt free usually have few or no deer, a fact of life that Wilbur quickly learned. The second year he tried the same approach, but he was more selective, concentrating only on those places with at least a few deer. He did kill

a nice eight-point buck. Then last year, his third season, he joined a group of hunters on a season-lease in Kimble County. He got this three-deer limit, two bucks and a doe, and he actually spent *less* time hunting than he did either of the previous two seasons.

In the twilight of the season last year, during the Christmas holidays, I took my teenage son hunting on the ranch of a friend in southern Mason County. By noon we had sighted eleven legal bucks —in all counties under regulatory authority of the State Parks and Wildlife Department, and this includes most of the prime deer counties, a legal buck is one with a hardened antler protruding through the skin—and my son Reed had killed a respectable eight-pointer.

Meanwhile, I still had all my license tags. I'd been looking for a trophy-sized buck with no success. So with the season fast slipping away, I decided to do some "meat hunting" to get venison for the deep freeze. That afternoon my son shot a doe and I collected two others. All told, in less than a day of hunting, we'd taken four deer. And we had been selective, shooting only does that were in good physical shape.

Now this ranch isn't typical. Thanks to its owner, Seth Martin, management practices have maintained a high deer population with an abnormal ratio of bucks to does. But on most ranches in better deer country, it simply is a matter of picking the buck you want, assuming

RUSSELL TINSLEY

you will spend several days hunting, rather than merely shooting the first animal with antlers you see.

And if you aren't particular, doe hunting is a bargain. Many ranches have hunting for antlerless deer and you pay only for what you kill. The average price is about twenty dollars per doe.

I've resided in Texas for most of my forty years. Yet, as a professional outdoor writer, I have hunted deer throughout the United States. With very few exceptions, I've never found better or more enjoyable hunting than right here at home.

The fact is, I was raised in the farm-and-ranch community of Mason in the hill country of central Texas, one of the very best counties for deer in the entire state. I started after deer while in elementary school and have been an avid hunter ever since. I've long since lost count of how many deer I have killed. But while my enthusiasm for hunting hasn't waned, the idea of killing a deer simply for the sake of shooting one doesn't appeal to me anymore. I've begun hunting antlers, big deer. And I love the challenge.

Last season I had the opportunity to shoot several bucks. Some of them were much better than average, but I never did find that one impressive specimen which I coveted. So I didn't use a license tag on a buck, for which I do not apologize. It only makes me more determined to get a trophy this coming season.

I now spend most of my hunting time in what is called the brush country of South Texas because this is where the bigger bucks roam. Scan the Boone and Crockett Club record lists, both typical and nontypical whitetails, and you'll see this region represented by many deer. Personally, I never can recall sighting a buck during the open season, try as I might, that would qualify for the Boone and Crockett Club list, but I've seen some out of season that were almost too big to be true.

There is one picture that is vividly etched in my memory. I was walking along a brushy wash in Webb County, near Laredo on the Texas-Mexico border.

A real trophy for the Edwards Plateau region of central Texas.

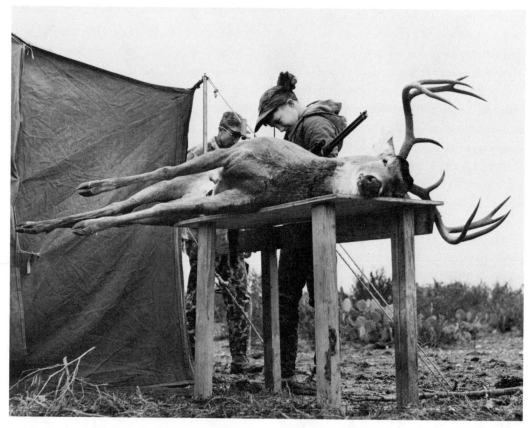

This trophy mule deer was bagged in Webb County near Laredo in deep South Texas.

It was February, as I recall, and some friends and I were searching for Indian artifacts. We often look along the earthen washes where rain runoff exposes arrow-heads.

As I slowly strolled along, my eyes riveted to the ground, a sudden noise in the brush ahead startled me. I glanced up just as a buck with massive antlers leaped into the open. He scrambled from the wash and, not fifty yards away, paused on the rim and glanced back, his antlers skylined

magnificently. They were high and wide and extremely heavy. If my experience is any judge of deer, that buck with its twelve long points would have made the record list easily. And all I could do was watch him turn and trot nonchalantly off.

For the next two seasons I searched grudgingly for that buck, trying every trick I knew. But I never saw him again nor heard of anyone killing him. Perhaps he died of old age.

The largest Texas whitetail I've shot

258

had only seven points, but his rack was heavy and high with a twenty-inch spread. That one, field-dressed, weighed 156 pounds, which is a nice deer for this part of southern Texas but nothing extraordinary. The really big ones will go from about 170 on up to almost 200 pounds. This buck was killed on the same ranch in Webb County where I sighted the deer of my dreams. He came to what is known as "horn rattling," one of the most fascinating of all deer-hunting methods.

This technique of striking a pair of antlers together to simulate two bucks fighting, in order to dupe other bucks within gunshot range, is widely used by South Texas hunters. It is effective only during the rut which usually comes in December, depending on the weather. It takes cold, preferably with some moisture, to start bucks chasing females, and not many fronts stab this deep into the United States.

Deer everywhere fight while they are mating. One buck is trailing a doe in heat and another bigger buck comes along and, charged with passion, challenges for her affection. While the two bucks are busy in combat, another buck, hearing the skirmish, slips in and drives the doe away.

So that's the idea of "rattling," to make a buck believe that two others are battling over a doe. He comes a-looking for the female that rates a fight and instead is suckered into an ambush.

Gosh knows how many times I've banged antlers together, yet I can almost

Author looks at buck he "rattled up" in southern Texas.

This big South Texas buck came to the sound of rattled antlers.

count on the fingers of both hands the number of respectable bucks that showed. It is, at best, a hit-or-miss proposition, but that is what makes it interesting. There is nothing that quite describes the drama and sensation of suddenly seeing a belligerent buck—his ears cupped forward, nostrils flared, the hair along his back bristling—appear on the scene. No hunting thrill quite compares to it.

Timing is the key to successful rattling, being at the right place at the right time. A crisp, calm morning is preferable. The deer must be mating, or at least getting in the mood, and a buck of course must be within hearing range of the antlers. And the hunter must be concealed properly where the crafty buck won't get suspicious before he blunders into rifle range.

The largest buck I ever rattled, in La-Salle County, came running at the first bang of the antlers, stopped about 150 yards away at the fringe of a clearing, looked for a split-second, then wheeled and disappeared twice as fast as he appeared. There was no chance for a shot.

If you are interested in learning more about this hunting method, I'd suggest that you write the Burnham Brothers (P.O. Box 100, Marble Falls, Texas 78654) for their free catalog of hunting equipment. From them you can obtain either an instruction tape (cassette or spool type) or phonograph record which explains all about horn-rattling.

One reason horn-rattling is popular with South Texas hunters is the terrain. Mostly it is flat and covered with head-

Horn-rattling is a fascinating method for duping a wily buck.

RUSSELL TINSLEY

high thorny brush and cacti. Trees are few and far between and most of them are just overblown bushes, primarily mesquite. At ground level it is difficult to see any distance, and about the only way of outwitting sly old trophy buck from the brush is to stay put and let him wander into range. Even then, unless he is chasing a doe or coming to horn-rattling, he isn't often going to expose himself in the open. Stalk hunting is just about out of the question, unless you're walking merely for exercise.

Visitors unfamiliar with this part of Texas are fascinated by the many windmill-like towers, ten to twenty feet high, with either swivel seats or box-like structures atop them. Due to an absence of trees, these man-made stands are the only practical means of getting above the brush and looking down into the scattered small patches of clearing. An elaborate stand might have a roof and be completely enclosed except for portholes through which to shoot. Inside, the hunter is hidden from the sonar-like eyesight of a wily buck, and he's protected against the elements. One reason I've enjoyed no better success while pursuing bragging-sized bucks of South Texas, is because I am nervously impatient. I am not willing to pay the price of many hours, sitting and diligently looking.

A few years ago I was hunting on a ranch in Dimmit County of southern Texas and the landowner directed me to a stand where, he said, there was considerable deer travel. I watched for two hours

Tripod-like stands are widely used in brush country of South Texas.

that morning, that afternoon returned for two more hours, then tried it for two more hours the following morning. I didn't see a deer. The landowner reluctantly honored my request to be put in another stand. He said I was making a mistake and, as it turned out, he was right. Another hunter occupied the stand that same afternoon and bagged one hell'va big ten-point buck.

But while quality belongs to South Texas, the hill country of central Texas is where you find quantity. Deer literally are everywhere. It isn't unusual to drive ranch pasture roads and see forty or more in just an hour or two. The average range in this region is diminutive when compared to others across the state. Acreage will average from one hundred to three thousand acres, with the typical ranch encompassing about fifteen hundred acres. Despite the deer kill in this region being abnormally high, the deer herd hasn't suffered. To the contrary. Overpopulation still is an acute problem in most areas.

This is fairly open country, rolling rocky hills covered with oaks and cedar and various brush, and not many bucks of any size are taken, mainly because not many live long enough to get the necessary maturity to grow large antlers. A majority of the bucks killed in the hill country are three-and-one-half years old or younger. Lots of forkhorns and spikes are taken. And of course the overpopulation retards antler development.

More than half the deer found in the entire state are jammed into the Edwards Plateau Regulatory District of the Texas Parks and Wildlife Department. This includes the counties of Bandera, Blanco, Burnet, Comal, Crockett, Edwards, Gillespie, Hays, Kendall, Kerr, Kimble, Lampasas, Llano, Mason, McCulloch, Menard, Real, San Saba, Schleicher, Sutton, Travis and Val Verde.

Taking deer in this area involves many means and methods, some not very sporting. Like, for instance, driving about in a vehicle or hunting over "bait." Both are legal in Texas. A hunter puts out shelled corn and gets deer attracted to the feed. Come opening morning of the season an unsuspecting buck wanders in for his breakfast and is greeted with a bullet.

Stand hunting also is popular. In this terrain a hunter can sit along a draw or valley and command a pretty good view of the surrounding countryside. Because of the many trails utilized by both deer and livestock, cattle and goats and sheep, it is difficult to ascertain exactly where there is any concentrated deer travel. But the landowner, familiar with the ranch, can direct you. You are his customer and he wants you to be happy.

Me, I'd rather walk and hunt. I like to catfoot along a wooded header, watching ahead for any furtive buck that might try to sneak away. It is a fascinating game of hide-and-seek.

Along the western fringe of this region, the country is rugged and wild. I like to hunt the Devil's River locale not far from the town of Sonora. Here brushy headers

RUSSELL TINSLEY

These are typical bucks found in hill country of central Texas.

come off the deep canyons like giant fingers. Bucks which are hiding in the brush are reluctant to leave. We often toss rocks into the headers and watch for spooked bucks to come scrambling hell-bent out the opposite side. As a friend once remarked, trying to hit a running buck zig-zagging through the brush and trees is like shooting at a bouncing rubber ball. Some hunters even employ sling-shots to lob pebbles into the more inaccessible areas where sly old bucks likely hide out.

Actually, deer hunting in Texas is a composite. In South Texas there is the flat, brushy semi-arid terrain. Central Texas is mostly rolling hills cut by spring-fed streams. East Texas more resembles the typical terrain of the Deep South, with moss-draped oaks and lush green forests. There is some public na-

tional forest land in eastern Texas, but the forests are a patchwork, broken here and there by chunks of privately owned land, most under the ownership of timber companies. It is difficult to determine where you can and cannot hunt. Boundary lines are not very well defined.

More and more deer are showing in East Texas with each passing year, particularly in the post oak country west of the pine forests. There are some areas where hunting is excellent. And some of the bucks brought out of eastern Texas will rival those of South Texas both for antler size and physical weight.

Short-range, quick-handling weapons, such as shotguns loaded with slugs or an open-sight .30-30 carbine, are popular with East Texas hunters. Because of the dense timber, any shot is apt to be at close range, often at a moving target. But the majority of Texans prefer long-range, flat-shooting rifles equipped with scope sights. Among the more popular calibers are the .243 Winchester, the 6mm Remington, the .30-06 and the .270.

A scope sight, I believe, is almost indispensable for most Texas deer hunting. Another valuable piece of equipment is binoculars. Optics give a definite advantage, particularly early and late in the day, in dim light, when deer are most active.

Personally, if I had to pick one rifle for all my Texas deer-hunting needs, I would choose either a .243 Winchester or a 6mm Remington (both are almost identical ballistically) with about a 2½X-7X variable scope sight. Nothing more powerful is needed. A rifle of this type is a joy to shoot, is lightweight, and deadly on any Texas deer. Even the desert variety of mule deer, found in the Trans-Pecos region of West Texas and the Panhandle, doesn't grow very large. Anything bigger than 175 pounds is a trophy.

The Trans-Pecos region, the prime mule deer range, is in sharp contrast to eastern Texas. It is difficult sometimes to imagine that both are in the same state.

East Texas which is flat with pine and hardwood timber, sluggish streams and bayous, and big man-made lakes, contrasts with the Trans-Pecos wild and forlorn rocky country, studded with stark mountains and just about every species of cactus imaginable—lechuguilla, ocotillo, prickly pear, sotol, huisache and haujillo, and semi-arid plants like sagebrush, juniper and piñon. Even the more familiar landmarks have distinctive names: Paisano Peak, Cathedral Mountain, Rustler Hills, the Christmas Mountains. Someone once said that when the Good Lord created the earth, he made the rest of the world and what was left over he pitched into West Texas. It looks it.

This is frontier-like country with people and towns scattered far apart. One county (Brewster) alone is larger than Rhode Island and Connecticut combined. It isn't uncommon for a kid to ride a bus more than fifty miles to school, and when a man talks about "his" ranch, he usually is speaking of 25,000-plus-acres. In the rimrocks along the mountains, on the high plateaus, you will find the mule deer of Texas, locally called the blacktail. Because of the wide-open country, shots are apt to be way out yonder and you select a rifle accordingly.

While there are deer throughout the entire region, the counties of Presidio, Terrell, Brewster and Jeff Davis have the better deer populations, with the Davis Mountains of Jeff Davis having the highest density per square mile.

The hubs of hunter activity originate from the towns of Marfa, Alpine, Van Horn, Sanderson and Presidio. When there was an official weather station there, Presidio, on the Mexican border, had some claim to fame in that it regularly led the nation in the highest daily temperature recorded—a dubious distinction at best, but it does give some inkling as to the type of hunting country you can expect.

264

Typical hunting country in Trans-Pecos region of West Texas.

Mule deer buck killed near town of Marfa in Trans-Pecos region.

In some parts of the Trans-Pecos it is even possible to kill three different species of deer: mule deer, whitetail, and the Coues deer, a miniature version of the whitetail that is locally called a fantail. The Coues' primary range is the Sonora Mountains of northern Mexico and southern Arizona.

But actually, deer roam the length and width of Texas. Some prime hunting that has gone largely unnoticed is found around the towns of Sweetwater and Colorado City in northcentral Texas. Colorado county (Columbus is the county seat) just northwest of Houston has a high population of deer, as does the country west of Fort Worth, in the vicinity of Possum Kingdom Lake and the town of Mineral Wells. The opportunity certainly is there, but finding a place to hunt, rather than finding a deer is the rudimentary problem.

There are several solutions. For one, you can try the public lands of East Texas and take your chances, minimal as they might be. There are the national forests, plus lands owned by timber companies which are open to public hunting. A couple of these companies even provide free hunting guides, showing tracts which are available. For copies write: Hunting Guide, Southland Paper Company, P.O. Box 147, Lufkin, Texas 75901; and Hunting Guide, Temple Industries, Diboll, Texas 75941. Both these companies have lands scattered throughout East Texas.

Each year the Texas Parks and Wildlife Department offers public hunting on its various wildlife management areas throughout the state. Anyone seventeen years old or older can apply. Only about 2,500 hunting permits are selected by public drawing, from more than twenty thousand applicants, but you have everything to gain and nothing to lose. Applications are available from the Texas Parks and Wildlife Department, John H. Reagan Building, Austin 78701, usually around October 1. You must apply for a specific area. The better ones include the Black Gap Wildlife Management Area (Brewster County) and Sierra Diablo Area (Hudspeth and Culberson counties) in West Texas; Kerr Wildlife Management Area (Kerr County) in central Texas; Chaparral Area (Dimmit and LaSalle) in South Texas; the Gene Howe Area (Hemphill), along the north bank of the Canadian River in the Panhandle; and the Gus Engeling Wildlife Management Area (Anderson) of East Texas.

Public hunts for bowhunters only are also held on the Aransas National Wildlife Refuge on the Gulf of Mexico coast near Austwell (this is the winter home of the famous whooping crane) and Laguna Atascosa National Wildlife Refuge in the Rio Grande Valley, some twenty miles east of Harlingen. Both areas have abundant deer populations and neither restricts the number of hunters. Usually weekend hunts are held in September and early October. But if you plan on making either of these hunts, bring plenty of mosquito repellent. The pests are big and hungry.

Then, naturally, you can lease a place from the landowner. This is the most sure-fire of all. One approach is to advertise for a lease in the classified section of any large-city newspaper, in Houston or Dallas or San Antonio or Austin. Most of the chambers of commerce in the county seats of the various counties mentioned have compiled lists of available season- and day-leases. For Llano County, as an example, you'd write the Llano Chamber of Commerce, or the Fredericksburg Chamber of Commerce for Gillespie County. But the time to inquire is early in the year. By late summer most of the leases are filled.

My friend John Jefferson authors the *Hunters' Guide to Texas,* which has a section on available deer leases in different parts of the state. The volume is updated each year and is available for $3.95 postpaid from Jenkins Publishing Company, 6925 S. Interregional Highway, Austin, Texas.

Really, if you've ever hunted deer you won't have any problems in Texas. The critter has the same distinctive look and the same innate habits as its cousins, both mule deer and whitetails, found in other parts of the country. Texas deer perhaps are smaller than those taken in most other states, but wildlife biologists have been warning both landowners and hunters that they can't have quantity and quality. Unfortunately, a majority has shown a preference for quantity, which means, quite simply, that the deer have gotten the upper hand and have overpopulated their habitat and the State Parks and Wildlife Department is urging that even more be shot.

Now that is a plea that any dedicated deer hunter can appreciate!

I suppose that even those living the life of Riley would be a bit envious of Francis E. Sell's setup in the wilderness of southwestern Oregon. Sell and his wife, Ethel, live in a huge old log house set in an apple orchard where the Columbia blacktail deer help to harvest the fruit each autumn. Sell has been a full-time writer for the past thirty years and has published innumerable articles and ten books, with editions in Spanish and Japanese. People came from all over the world to visit and study wildlife under his supervision.

Each autumn when the hills are turning gold and crimson, and the first frost bejewels the black huckleberry and salal brush, it is a yearly ritual for Sell to take a trophy blacktail buck. Not just any buck, but one sporting a regal set of antlers, one grown wise in the way of hunters and a worthy opponent of the most skilled woodsman.

Sell does his hunting in the forests, much of which he owns. Here, where a wise old buck has everything in his favor, Sell fills his deer tag—usually still-hunting, sometimes trail-watching—under conditions that always favor the game. Sell wouldn't have it otherwise.

18

HUNTING THE COLUMBIA BLACKTAIL DEER

Francis E. Sell

MY PARTNER AND I made a Siwash Indian camp for the night under a huge, bushy hemlock, well sheltered from the coastal Oregon rain. A Siwash Indian camp indicates that we were traveling light—no sleeping bags, no rain clothes. We expected to get wet to the skin. Matter of fact, we were wet when we made our camp. We had a coffee pot, a frying pan, one plate each, a spoon each, and two cups.

The rain fell on the West Coast rain forest with a snare-drum rattle. The low growl of the Chinook storm wind had us thinking about the day ahead, which we planned to spend hunting Columbia blacktail. We opened our hunting packs, got out an oily rag and wiped off our rifles—a 30/30 Marlin Carbine and a 6.5 x55mm 20-inch-barrel Mannlicher-stocked bolt-action rifle. After attending to our rifles we hung them from small limbs close to the trunk of the sheltering hemlock.

A fire, made from the dry twigs under the hemlock and brought to drying and cooking size by the use of dry fir bark from under the huge windfall, was carefully placed and handled so that our sheltering tree would not be damaged. In addition to cooking our supper, the blaze would dry our outside clothes, while our underwear dried as we wore it.

This sort of camp is quite often required in hunting blacktail. There is no possibility of getting a four-wheel drive within a mile or so of the best hunting, because of the press of weekend hunters.

Looking out across the logging slash, we watched the curtain of rain trail long silver streamers across the hills, as we dried our outerwear by standing close to the fire. It was typical blacktail territory. It was also typical West Coast weather for the later part of the blacktail season in northern California, western Oregon, Washington, and British Columbia.

Columbia blacktail deer have an extensive West Coast range—from central California to Alaska. Along the eastern edge of this range they come in contact with their cousins, the mule deer. In a few spots along the West Coast they are also in contact with the whitetail deer. Indeed, some of the big blacktails entered in the record books unquestionably carried the blood of this cross.

I have taken blacktails with perfect whitetail antlers—main beam with the tines subordinate, instead of the Y's forked as is normal for blacktails and mule deer. Although they may have infusions of foreign blood from the mule deer and whitetail, the Columbian blacktail is still very much of an individualist.

The adverage Columbian blacktail isn't as large as the average mule deer or the biggest whitetails. The largest blacktail I ever killed field dressed 205 pounds.

Sometimes the Columbia Blacktail has about the same type antlers as his cousin the Whitetail Deer. Here is a very good example.

FRANCIS E. SELL

I know of one monstrous Columbia blacktail that field dressed 263 pounds. they average about 125 pounds, ready for the packout. The antlers on a mature buck may be anything from a forked horn to as many as eight or ten points (western count, in which only one side of the antlers is counted.)

There is a positive belief by many old-time blacktail hunters in so-called bench-leg blacktail, who carries nothing but a set of forked horns. These "bench legs" usually have a wide spread of antlers and are shorter in the legs, seemingly, than the average blacktail. Game biologists maintain that the "bench leg" is a mature blacktail that has summered in very lush territory. Next season he may be a four-pointer, a six-pointer, or wear the same wide-spreading forked antlers he has this season.

While there may be some good-natured controversy about the "bench leg" forked horn, there is none about the blacktail's ability to survive the inroads of civilization, changes in his environment, and increased hunting pressure. The Columbia blacktail takes these things in stride. Pressed hard by hunters, he just becomes a bit more nocturnal in his comings and goings, a bit more secretive and prone to hold to heavy cover when hunted.

Sometimes, in the higher reaches of these West Coast mountains, Columbia blacktails migrate. Most times, however, they are in residence in a given territory the year around. During the past several years, when unusually heavy snowfalls on the West Coast took a heavy toll of mule deer, the Columbia blacktail came through without great loss.

At my wilderness cabin we had 24 inches of snow that lay on the ground for weeks. I was at particular pains to see how the blacktail populations made out. Their solution to the snow problem was simplicity itself. They moved into the heavy, lush growth where the snow pushed the high-growing huckleberry, vine maple, and hardhack salal brush much lower to the ground, putting their browse well within reach of even the smallest deer. Indeed, they had more winter forage available than they would have had otherwise. The herds came through without more than normal loss.

Blacktails are conditioned to the heavy winter rains, but they do not like cold sleet storms. They shelter at once, breaking off a feeding period and moving under the cedars and hemlocks, where it is always dry. One doe and her two fawns solved their problem of shelter from sleet-laden rains by bedding under my log house!

Considering all this ability to cope with their environment, you would expect the Columbia blacktail to be a worthy quarry, succumbing to nothing less than the best hunting techniques. Indeed, he takes such advantage of the heavy, tropic-like West Coast forest growth that many hunters feel that it is an exercise in futility to try to bring him to bag. To the many hunters who do not grasp the fundamentals of a blacktail hunt, this is about right.

Blacktails can be hunted quite successfully, however, if the hunter plays the game according to the blacktails' rules. Just remember, their comings and goings are tied in with the weather, so the hunt must be also tied in with the weather if you expect to get it out of the luck category.

We have blacktail fundamentals in mind at our camp under the hemlock at the edge of the logging slash. The slash was lush with a new growth of wild vetch, black huckleberry, salal wild rose, and elk clover, and was sprinkled with islands of small fir around the seed trees left for the reforesting. It would be hunted as the morning weather directed. We had everything going for us.

If the storm continued unabated, the deer would feed heavily, then move into adjoining heavy cover until there was a letup in the rain. If the storm slacked off during the late evening, ten chances to one they would stay in the logging slash, feeding intermittently during the night. Shortly after good morning shooting light they would retire to the heavy security cover for the day, coming again to the slash during the late evening. If this occurred, we planned on hunting the logging slash, trying for a trophy buck before the deer retired to their day bedding.

The storm didn't slack off during the night. Shortly after shooting light, we were examining trails leading out of the logging slash. These freshly used trails would be the tipoff as to where our quarry would shelter for the day, with a good buck in prospect for one of us, if we handled the hunt properly.

Handling the hunt properly takes in plenty of territory. With the slacking of the Chinook wind over the cover, and with the heavy rain continuing, we had to take the downdraft of thermal wind drift into consideration. This would hold all day unless there was a drastic change in the weather. Those deer would move out of the feeding area nose to wind until they came to a dense growth of sheltering hemlock, fir, and spruce. Here they would move downslope a bit, so they could have the thermal wind drift off their backtrail, as well as off the game trails coming into this section from the higher ridges.

This is almost a perfect security setup for the bedding blacktails. If hunters are not completely aware of the tie-in of trail and weather, they'll tip off their intentions long before they can come to terms with their quarry.

When we came to a complex of trails trending toward the heavy growth along the logging slash, Al Lyman and I separated. Al took a secondary trail well down the slope to the right of the ridge that carried the well-used main game trail. I took a trail downslope to the left of the ridge. Our selections were predicated on the fresh tracks, well rain washed, that were all about on the ridge.

I had traveled only a short distance before I found very fresh tracks on the trail I followed. Except where the trail occasionally passed under a shelter tree, the Chinook storm had washed out their sharp impressions. These tracks spelled out a good piece of hunting information. The smaller tracks were partly canceled out by a huge, blunt-toed set, which showed that a big deer had been the last to use the trail.

This traveling order, with the larger tracks following, spelled out one thing—a buck, and a plenty big one, judging from the tracks. This order of trail travel is brought about by the protective cooperation of the herd. Predators move in on deer by following and overtaking the herd, seldom by lying in wait along the trail. The thermal wind drift, coming from the direction toward which the deer travel, cancels out a predator's chances of pulling a deer down by trail watching. The buck or bucks at the rear of the herd have the most dangerous place. This is good information for a hunter after mule deer or whitetail. It is absolutely essential if he is prowling the West Coast jungle for Columbia blacktail.

I catfooted along the secondary trails, moving slowly, cautiously. I stopped often to examine the shadowed cover ahead. I made some noise, but this didn't worry me. I knew that proper noise was just as essential as sticking to those trails. Here, again, most deer hunters go wrong, believing in the "silent Indian" school of deer stalking. No deer moves in dense cover without making some noise, and the denser the cover, the more noise he makes.

Here is a buck spooking in toward the feeding area—the last one in line, and canny as they come.

This noise, to be reassuring to other deer, must have certain characteristics. First, it must be made at a time of day when deer expect noise on the trails. Second, it must move in the direction that deer expect movement at this particular time of day. Third, it must be of a type made by the slow, normal movement of unalarmed deer.

Let's examine those requirements from the standpoint of blacktail-deer hunting. Blacktails move out of their feeding grounds shortly after morning shooting light. They see and hear other deer moving at this time. Some individuals feed a bit longer than others. The deer that move out early and enter the heavy security cover hear other deer on the trails.

Here is a nice forked-horn, feeding in early morning. Shortly, he will be in the heavy security cover, snugged in for the day.

It's expected. The late-feeding deer, like all others, move very slowly, pausing occasionally to test the wind for the reassuring odor of the other deer as they approach their bedding area.

All this forms a pattern that a Columbia blacktail-deer hunter cannot ignore and be successful. A hunter pauses frequently to examine the cover as it unfolds, not moving until he has exhausted all the possibilities of the cover within view. It's the pace of unalarmed deer, from start to finish.

I think I had spent the better part of an hour on the trail and had moved about two hundred yards into the heavy security cover when I got my chance. Coming around a sharp turn in the turn, I had a four pointer (western count) under my gun at about 45 feet. The rest was routine. I clipped him behind the ear, and that was that.

As agreed before the hunt, the first shooting was to cancel out the hunt at once. We wanted only one deer to carry out to the old logging road where I had parked my four-wheel drive. Whoever fired first ended the hunt—a very wise arrangement, we agreed by the time we had my buck and our few items of camping equipment out of my Ford pickup.

Al Lyman showed up while I was dressing out my buck, and we admired it before getting down to the task of moving it out of the hunting territory.

This type of hunting is probably one of the most successful a woodsman can use for taking Columbia blacktail. It is a specialized still hunting that has enabled me to take some beautiful bucks. Still hunting alone touches upon the same facets of woodcraft, though it differs in certain respects from cooperating still hunting, such as Al Lyman and I did this morning, starting on the huge logging slash.

A hunter has about two hours in which to still hunt towards the deers' bedding ground. During this time, noise on the trails is normal and not disturbing. Stick to those trails under all circumstances, moving slowly, duplicating the gait of the deer. You travel nose to wind, too. The

274

essential thing for a still hunter to remember is that there is a network of trails laid down by the deer. These give good wind coverage, storm or shine.

Knowledge of thermal wind behavior during stable weather conditions is a must for proper still hunting, driving, or trail watching Columbia blacktails. Let's consider a twenty-four-hour thermal wind as it affects the movement of deer under stable weather conditions. During the night, starting very late in the evening, the air currents are down slope, down valley and draw, flowing from the

Author putting his tag on a four pointer (western count). This Columbia Blacktail buck actually has four points on one side, five on the other for a total of nine points, eastern count.

higher to the lower ground. This particular thermal wind drag holds all during the night and well into the early morning hours.

Deer, having fed, use this down-flowing thermal wind to keep their sensitive black nose on conditions up slope, up valley and draw, as they move out of the feeding area toward their bedding ground.

After the sun has warmed the cover slightly, there is a thermal reversal with the wind drag up slope, valley, and draw, from the lower to the higher ground. This particular drag of wind holds all during the day until very late evening. Deer moving out of the security cover toward the more-open feeding areas take advantage of this up-slope thermal wind drag to come to their feeding areas nose to wind. Coming or going, these blacktails move nose to wind, taking full advantage of these thermals to keep them posted above any danger on their bedding or feeding grounds.

After they've bedded for the day in the heavy security cover, the updraft of thermal wind drag keeps them posted about their back trail. Nothing can follow them after the thermal wind reversal from down-slope draft to up-slope air current, without those sensitive black noses getting the message.

When the weather changes, especially when a storm is growling across the cover, other trails are used to bring the feeding and bedding areas under examination before these blacktails commit themselves

Four deer moving out of the heavy security cover in late evening. They are inspecting and testing the wind before moving into the feeding area.

to either bedding or feeding. Deer move cross wind, angle back and forth, swing around to take full advantage of the prevailing wind. All this is indicated by a network of trails seldom used except when a storm is pushing across the territory.

Still hunting in the traditional manner, you cannot ignore the problem of wind coverage. It is not enough to hunt into a prevailing wind. You must duplicate the deer traffic on those trails. A good still-hunting rule of thumb, whether you have a cooperative still hunt going, such as Al Lyman and I used, or are hunting alone, is that you must be out early enough in the morning to take full advantage of the

wind, whether it is a thermal or storm wind.

Under stable weather conditions, you cannot follow these blacktail deer into the heavy security cover beyond the period when the thermal wind drift is down slope. Once the reversal occurs from down to up slope, your presence is detected at once. I once had a very interesting hunt with three very experienced woodsmen—Rogue River Indians, to be more specific. We moved directly to the higher ground, taking a round-about direction on an old pack trail that led to a long-abandoned gold prospect. Here we fiddled around, using a .22 to gather in a

276

few grey squirrel for a noonday stew. Then, breaking up, we followed individual ridges down toward the acorn flats where the deer fed. Each hunter was on his own, still hunting, but all agreeing to meet at the foot of the hills during the evening.

It was a beautiful hunt. The thermal wind drift up slope was strong enough to tick off a few golden and flame-colored leaves, sending them down through the forest canopy. I remember jumping three blue grouse but didn't dare shoot for fear of canceling out the deer hunt before it was started. I followed a series of blacktail trails that angled back and forth across the ridge, but found no fresh sign. This, however, didn't discourage me. I expected to find deer bedded very close to the down-slope oaks carrying a crops of corns. It worked out that way, too. At about three o'clock I got my shot at a bedded forked-horn, snuggled down under a squawbush. Range was about 35 yards. He was bedded as I expected him to be, back to the thermal updraft, watching up the ridge toward the higher ground.

Having dressed him out, I moved by easy stages down the ridge, and just before getting to the acorn groves, I heard a shot well up slope on a ridge paralleling the one I traveled. By dark we were camped on the Rogue River with a three-pointer and my forked horn, skinned, quartered, and hung up to cool out—less two sides of fat ribs roasting at our small cooking fire.

The entire hunt was tied in with a beautiful thermal, strong enough to be perceptible but not strong enough to cancel out the need for hunter caution.

Driving Columbian blacktail is also a very profitable way of hunting them. Forget about those loud tub-thumping drives so closely associated with eastern whitetail hunting. Remember the effects of those thermal and storm winds on blacktail movement. Actually, you must combine trail and area watching with still hunting to come up with a driving method that satisfies all blacktail requirements.

When blacktails bed down, there are always escape trails leading out of the bedding area toward other security cover. You'll not push them across an opening, because it affords a good clear chance for a shot. This must be remembered when you plan a blacktail drive. Standers should move into position beyond a known bedding ground. They cannot be noisy about this above the level of expected movement of unalarmed deer. They must not move directly across country to their selected stands. More to the point, those stands must be between the selected bedding area and the next available security cover.

In taking a stand it must always be remembered that the thermal wind drift will condition the movement of the bedded deer, once the drivers put them up. Under stable weather conditions, except a thermal updraft during the better part of the day, the escape trails will be those giving the best coverage to the moving

A posted hunter, trail watching, area watching, or on the receiving end of a drive, should have his stand far enough from the trails to allow the lesser deer to pass without being alarmed. If this yearling doe were turned back on the trail, it would cancel out the stand for all other deer that might immediately use it.

deer. They'll go out nose to wind, so to speak, taking the trail or trails having a cross current of wind drift between them and the next security cover, toward which they will always move when the drivers put them out of their day bedding grounds.

Hunters on stand have an obligation not to smoke, move around, cough, or break a twig underfoot. It is standing with a vengeance. Above all, the stander must position himself so that hunter scent isn't carried to the trails along which the deer will be moving. This means the stand must be well to the side of the escape trails—down slope from the escape trails if the thermal wind drift is in that direction. He should be far enough from the trails to enable any lesser deer to pass without being alarmed. Meet these conditions, and a Columbia blacktail drive is usually very productive.

One last method of hunting blacktails must be touched upon—trail and area watching. This method has produced several trophy blacktail bucks for me. It has delivered many more to hunters to whom I have taught woodcraft and deer hunting. Area watching is perhaps the more rewarding method, if it can be separated from trail watching, which is doubtful. At a complex of trails not more than a half mile from where I write this, I know of at least fifteen trophy buck being taken. Usually, the best time for watching here is during the first hours of good morning shooting light, when deer are moving out of the more-open feeding area.

Even watching here produces fewer deer, because these Columbia blacktails, coming out nose to wind, when the thermal is uphill and up draw and valley, can easily separate into smaller groups, some intent on reaching one of two old orchards, others electing to spend the feeding period on the browse and clover on the overgrown range adjacent to the dense bedding cover. In the morning, however, the larger share of the herd takes a main trail back toward the bedding ground.

Wherever you find an orchard in blacktail territory, you have an excellent place for either trail or area watching. If there is no moon in the sky, you can watch the orchard and the trails leading into it. If there *is* a moon in the sky, the blacktail is very apt to come into the orchard after good shooting light is gone. Explore the setup. Ten chances to one you'll find those trails leading out through cover capable of being watched *before* dark, when the blacktail is on his feet and traveling cautiously, timing his arrival to coincide with darkness in the orchard area.

This trail watching can be exceptionally profitable when there is a moon in the sky. One such setup has delivered several blacktails for me, and my trail watching is a good three-quarters of a mile from the orchard that is the primary attraction. It's a matter of tying the hunt in with the weather all along the line. Do this, and regardless of your experience, trail and area watching will produce beautifully.

Most blacktail shooting is short range,

Deer feeding in an old orchard on fallen apples. Note that the ears of the buck and fawn are turned back, funneling the sound of other deer approaching on the trail leading into this feeding area. These deer are feeding with their noses attuned to the thermal winddrift. My position is about 50 yards away.

with a few long range shots sometimes obtained on the huge West Coast logging slashes. Mostly, though, it is a brush show. And you want a bullet that isn't subject to blowup, or brush deflection. Regardless of caliber, this means a bullet of fair weight—140 to 200 grains, pushed at a muzzle velocity of not more than 2500 feet per second. Obviously, the caliber may be anything from a 6.5 MM to a .35 caliber. I base this observation on extensive bullet tests to see what effect velocity

has on brush bullets. Above 2500 feet a second I got plenty of bullet blowup and deflection.

Sights must meet a very strict requirement, too. A scope should be mounted with a quick-detachable mount. There will be days, with a West Coast rainstorm on the make, when the best possible place for a scope is in your hunting rucksack. Indeed, in the brush, with ranges reduced to about 50 yards, there is no great reason for a scope. A gold-bead front sight and a

280

wide-aperture receiver sight is faster and much less sensitive to the damp, water-laden forests.

Here is my setup for blacktail hunting. A 6.5 X 55 rifle (bolt action), a 150-grain bullet at 2500 feet a second velocity, a Tradewinds 1½-4 X adjustable scope, and a Williams quick-detachable mount and ace-in-the-hole aperture.

The iron sights are sighted in to hit point of aim at 100 yards. The scope is zeroed in to hit point of aim at 200 yards. The aperture, after being sighted in, may be removed and returned to zero without trouble. The same can be said of the scope with this Williams mount. During a hunt, if the rain and fog rolls in from the Pacific, as it often does, I take off the scope and replace it with the aperture rear sight. I also do this by perference when hunting the heavy cover. For the burns and logging slashes I find this scope just the ticket. Set at 1½ X power, it is also good for trail watching. It's especially good for very late evening shooting when the trails are growing dim with the approach of night.

All in all, the hunting of Columbia blacktail brings out the best a hunter has in woodcraft savvy. But once a hunter has spent a season with these deer, he is very apt to become a partisan of this Pacific Coast member of the deer family. Quite often he may feel frustrated, almost provoked beyond endurance, but he'll always enjoy the variety of methods by which the blacktail may be hunted, and the unique, sporting challenge he provides.

ABOUT THE EDITOR

Nick Sisley is a full time free lance outdoor journalist, and has a lifelong interest in hunting and fishing. He is a widely traveled individual, having fished across the United States, Canada, South America and Africa. He has hunted big game, upland birds and waterfowl in New Brunswick, Ontario, Colombia and Ecuador, Ireland, Angola, Mozambique, Iran, and virtually all over the eastern United States.

His outdoor column in the Vandergrift, Pa., *News-Citizen* has been appearing since 1966. His syndicated "Where to Go" in the outdoors column started in 1972 and appears in prominent newspapers of Pennsylvania, Ohio, and surrounding states.

In addition to contributing articles to most of the major outdoor magazines, Nick does the color and black-and-white photography to illustrate his stories, and is the author of the well-received book, *Hunting the Ruffed Grouse.*

He resides in Apollo, Pennsylvania, with his wife and two children.